THE
TRESEANELL

REAL CORNWALL - MY LIFE AND TIMES

Compass Publishing

KEVIN PETER BENNETTS

Foreword by Tim Saunders

The Tresean Eel
Copyright © Kevin Peter Bennetts 2021

First Edition published in Great Britain by:
Compass Publishing:
Registered Office: Number 11,
5 Vectis Way, Cosham,
Portsmouth, Hants PO6 3BW
https://www.compass-publishing.com/

ISBN 9781913713348

Edited, designed and typeset by
PED (Paul Eustice Design) Cornwall
Tel: 01209 716151 https://www.pauleusticedesign.com
e: paul.eustice@pauleusticedesign.com
Typeset in 11/15pt Bembo NT Roman

The CIP catalogue record for this book is available from the British Library.

The author would like to thank all those who have kindly agreed to contribute photographic images for this publication.

Printed and bound by
Booths Print
The Praze, Penryn, Cornwall TR10 8AA
http://boothsprint.co.uk/

Compass Publishing

For my parents...

who, like so many others of their generation did the best
they could with the little they had

The author at home

Before we start...
Kevin Peter Bennetts

All opinions expressed are my own. I have no wish to impose them on others or to intentionally offend anyone. However, if they happen to entertain, inform or enlighten you, that is all I can ask.

If you are offended by anything that is said then that is your prerogative. You will not offend me by being offended by what I say because I freely accept that individual opinions invariably differ, after all if you put two Cornish people in a room and three arguments will soon develop.

The events described in this book are true. Nothing has been added and nothing has been taken away. Events are as far as possible as they occurred but not necessarily in date order.

Anything I deem inappropriate has not been included. In almost every instance, I was there or thereabouts bearing witness to events through my own eyes (which may of course see them differently to others).

If for any reason you disagree, then that again is your prerogative... in which case we must agree to disagree.

There are some expletives and they are in the context of what was actually said at the time in question. They are not intended to be gratuitous in any way and you are of course free to form your own conclusions.

I sincerely hope you enjoy this collection of anecdotes as much as I have enjoyed assembling them into some form of order from my memory before I get too old.

I have never kept a diary or previously written anything relating to this down so this really is a 'straight from the horse's mouth' account of Cornish life as it came to mind over the summer of 2020 and, after being interviewed by Matt Blewett who was a PHD student on the Cornish Studies Course at Tremough Campus, 17th September 2019.

Foreword

Tim Saunders

Kevin Bennetts has done me the honour of inviting me to write a few words about his recollections. This I do with relish.

We've all met talentless nonentities slotted into well-paid jobs through family connections. The poor creatures genuinely think they're pocketing thousands because they themselves are 'very wonderful'. Kevin is the exact opposite. Here is a man who's achieved extraordinary things, but insists that he's just an ordinary man.

And we've all read reminiscences of life in Cornwall as it was. Life was bleak and getting through took resilience and ingenuity. Far too often, getting by, let alone getting on, meant getting out. Things are different now… up to a point. But Kevin goes far beyond the stock phrases we read in 'How It Did Belong To Be: Recollections Of A Ratcatcher Downalong In Old Porthfrantick.' He looks at the context of all of Cornwall, of Britain, of Europe and of the world. He tries to figure out how things got to be the way they were. And he also tries to figure out how they could be better. In conversation with veteran Cornish activist Matt Blewett, he gives us a picture of an active life in a community that matters to him more than anything.

I'm not saying I agree with Kevin on every point. In fact, Kevin doesn't expect anybody to agree with him. He tells us of his experiences in education, fishing, mining, fuel distribution, contentious legal proceedings and life in Cornwall generally. At every turn, he analyses and evaluates. What happened? How did it come about? What did it mean? How could we do it better? He's got ideas about how to run things more efficiently, more fairly.

In particular, he's concerned about Cornwall, its experience, and its future as a people. He doesn't take it for granted, a picturesque backdrop for one man's adventures. Cornwall, for Kevin, is the place where we take decisions and act on them. Cornwall is where we live and work, where we fight and make up, win and lose, fail and start up again. Kevin tells us of people we've all heard of (but sometimes wish we hadn't), and of people known only to family and friends but who deserve respect for their courage and diligence. He tells us more about Cornish society and its workings than most sociologists and economists know. As he paints this picture of his life in his homeland, he also gives us a sketch of Cornwall's possible future. He believes in self-government and wants us to take responsibility for our own affairs.

It's been too easy to complain of Cornwall's dire state and let somebody else take the blame. Kevin has no time for people whose patriotism is limited to wearing a rugby shirt and singing 'Trelawny.'

There's a big paradox at work here. Kevin says he hates politics. But that word comes from the Greek 'polis,' meaning 'the community of which we are citizens, and where our duty lies.' Kevin is passionately devoted to his community and his work as a Harbour Commissioner is a sign of that. What Kevin means, I think, is that he hates the three big Cs of Cornish public life – 'Cowardice', 'Corruption', and 'Catastrophic' incompetence. He's had his brushes with all three, and often come out on top. This is encouraging for us all. We should be encouraged.

But this is no plodding party diatribe. Kevin gives us a good read, with a brave turn of phrase. His Irish great granny had a tongue like a buggy whip, and an unsuccessful litigant carries on like … well, you read the story for yourself. Sea to land, underground to mid-air, yard to boardroom, we're treated to a bumpy and noisy ride. Sometimes, it's like passages from HMS Ulysses, while other episodes take in the atmosphere of Casualty, or Rumpole of the Bailey. Reading this book will entertain – and also prompt a lot of historians to look at their evidence again and go back to the sources. (Newlyn Archives might be a good place to start looking.)

Clearly, Kevin and I disagree on a number things. For example, I don't believe in the existence of political correctness (or the piskeys, spriggans, flying saucers, or the yeti). But this is in the nature of things. We all have different views and believe other people are wrong where their views differ. It's when we can't imagine another view is possible, that's when we're in real trouble. Kevin has been thinking out loud, painting the landscape of his life in his community and his vision of its future. If you disagree, tell him. He wants us to take responsibility for our own fate and to find better ways of running our life as a community. No sensible, decent person can disagree with that.

This is stuff that historians and sociologists will drool over, effectively history from the inside.

Tim Saunders originally studied Law at the University of Middlesex, is a Cornish Bard, writer and poet. His poetry books include: 'The High Tide,' 'Virgil's Fountain - A Seafarer's Tale' and 'Benyn Bennrudh (Red-Haired Woman) (Cornish Language Society).' He has also worked for BBC Wales as script editor on 'Pobol y Cwm'.

Chapter I
The Interview Transcript

Let's begin with the transcript from an initial interview in 2019 which wound me up like a clockwork mouse, incentivising me to get cracking on what turned out to be something of a saga. It did however, help me join up the dots and tell my story. A story of Cornish life from the inside, in a hopefully meaningful manner.

17th September 2019 Interview
Social movement

Interviewer: "I'm going to be asking you some set questions, but I'll also want to hear what you want to put on record about heritage, identity and democracy anyway, but I will start off with the Polson Bridge protest; could you give me your take on this please?"

KB: "Well the fine weather seemed to help draw out a better crowd than you would normally expect. It was a rare example of the various Cornish factions actually coming together with a sense of purpose and goodwill. There was none of the usual wrangling and rancour that you get. The other thing that struck me was that we were actually being a confounded nuisance on the bridge by inadvertently interfering with traffic. Encouragingly, the vast majority of those affected exhibited great goodwill. Even though they were being mildly inconvenienced, the whole thing was good humoured, friendly and fair.

Interviewer: "Assume our listeners don't know what it was about, could you say what it was all about and what happened?"

KB: "Yes, as a Cornishman I am not actually a huge Cornish nationalist as such. I don't speak the language and never will but I treasure the dialect. I love Cornwall, which undoubtedly is a separate entity to England as an ancient country and Duchy with the border set by an English king at the east bank of the Tamar. To me, that present boundary must remain inviolable, yet there was this ridiculous proposal to have a parliamentary constituency that is half in Cornwall and half in Devon, which would compromise that ancient border. Cornwall needs all the representation it can get from its own MPs who are not renowned for doing a particularly good job. That was what it was for me."

Interviewer: "And what convinced you to go?"

KB: "Frustration, because there's not enough positivity out there. The garbage that endlessly spews out of government departments, our own council and the media in general, tends to be negative, which makes my blood boil and everyone's lives more difficult instead of easier or better. The concept of a cross border constituency to me as an individual was an anathema and I didn't want to see it. I was extremely angry with those who came up with such a ridiculous idea."

Interviewer: "And were you representing any particular group while you were there?"

KB: "Well yes, I suppose it was 'Cornish Solidarity,' which is my particular passion. You are probably aware that it is an informal, non-political pressure group, which is not afraid to be controversial if necessary."

Interviewer: "What other groups do you recall being there?"

KB: "I can't recall the exact details now, but the encouraging thing for me was that there were several new faces with no particular axe to grind apart from universal outrage at what was being proposed. Polson Bridge seems such a fitting place to hold protests of this nature."

Interviewer: "And what makes Polson Bridge such a fitting place?"

KB: "It was formerly the main road to London and the border with England. That's the significance to me. I remember in my teens when I sometimes used to catch a ride up to London on the broccoli trucks going to Covent Garden and Polson Bridge was a significant place because you were leaving home."

Heritage

Interviewer: "So, changing the subject slightly." (Shows a picture of the Cornish Army crossing Polson Bridge).

KB: "I love that picture."

Interviewer: "What can you tell me about it?"

KB: "That is a beautiful depiction of 'An Goff' and 'Flamank' on the long march to London, which to me is a very emotional picture. My problem is that the Cornish were generally on the losing side. I like winners not losers. It truly was an heroic failure, but at least they tried and they paid the ultimate price and that should never ever be forgotten."

Identity

Interviewer: "And how do you think Cornish identity relates to the protest?"

KB: "There's more to being Cornish than wearing a black and gold rugby shirt, munching on a pasty or singing 'Trelawny'. Personally, I have some very interesting genes mixed up with my Cornish ones. Half of me is a bit of Irish, with a bit of German and a bit of English thrown in. But the Bennetts family originated in Madron where my great grandfather farmed a place called Boswarvah. They got evicted from there and ended up in Redruth working for the brewery. Grandfather worked as a farm manager at North Country

Protest at Polson Bridge with my sister 'Marie Gill'

and later Cubert where he ended up buying the Cubert farm from the brewery sometime in the 1930s."

Interviewer: "So what do you think makes someone proper Cornish?"

KB: "I don't know. Character basically. My father was a rebel and very unconventional. He got very badly hurt in the war when the minesweeper he was on struck a mine off Falmouth. We never realised until near the end of his life how badly he was suffering from post-traumatic stress and the guilt he felt because he survived and most of his shipmates didn't. But he would never talk about it, he would just lash out.

At school in Penwartha we had a teacher called 'Willy Tanblyn.' A fierce old bugger, but kind and passionate, he taught us proper Cornish history, At the time, archaeologists were excavating a Bronze age tumulus up at Polgase on top of Liskey Hill and we got ringside seats one summer afternoon to watch them work. None of it meant a lot at the time but the seed was planted in fertile ground and took root as he drummed into us that we were privileged to be Cornish and how we must look after our land as custodians of it.

Perran is one of the most Cornish parishes and the legend of St Piran is a smashing story. My theory is that St Piran came over in a curragh* which would be very capable of the 140-

mile voyage from the Cork or Waterford region in reasonable weather. There is little doubt that someone fetched up on the beach in a boat from Ireland, with definitely not a millstone but probably a prayer wheel or some such thing."

Interviewer: "Portable altar so I've heard."

KB: "Yes and he might have had that around his neck to make sure it didn't get lost if the boat capsized in the surf. I don't know, but as a kid I played on those dunes and walked them with Father. You always felt something spiritual there. I am not a churchgoer but I have strong beliefs and absolute faith that when your time comes there is something there. I was baptised a Catholic because that was my mother's Irish background but I never ever bought into it. It is meaningless to me. It is Cornwall that has got into my very soul."

Interviewer: "How do you think being Cornish relates to England?"

KB: "I identify as Cornish-British, not English. The minute I cross the Tamar I feel different. Coming back home my pulse quickens on first sight of the homebound trees, that distinctive circle of mature beech trees approaching Lifton Down. If I am ever going to be done for speeding it'll be there because subconsciously I always put my toe down to shorten the distance."

Interviewer: "What do you think are the best aspects of Cornish identity?"

KB: "Despite the fact that the Cornish have lost so many battles, it's the complexity and diversity of the place and the tenacity of the native inhabitants who've clung to the edge in spite of everything thrown at them - like barnacles on a storm lashed rock. They innovated and progressed, spearheading the first wave of the Industrial Revolution. It's a world in miniature, every few miles the scenery changes but the one thing that has always been constant has been the tenacity of the people.

How the hell did such a small race of men with candles on their heads for light manage to dig such bleddy great holes in solid rock in the pitch black so far underground? I worked at Mount Wellington for a short while and the size of the old stopes took my breath away - you could get Truro Cathedral in them. You know modern mining is hard enough, but you take a walk to Taylors Shaft at Consols and ponder what fabulous wealth came up from that one hole alone. Penpol, Devoran, Portreath, Hayle and Newquay were turned, by need, into significant industrial ports. A network of mineral tramways was built to serve what was the richest square mile on earth at that time. I marvel at the sheer ingenuity, the ability to solve insurmountable difficulties. We were literally the back of beyond away from the centre of things, yet there was all that industry and technology that grew out of sheer necessity. Most

---

A currach (curragh) is a type of Irish boat with a wooden frame, over which animal skins or hides were once stretched, though now canvas is more usual. It is sometimes anglicised as "curragh". The construction and design of the currach are unique to the west coasts of Ireland.

valleys with a stream had a foundry or explosive works. For example, look no further than St. Day which had six pubs, a brickworks, a scientific instrument maker and a survey instrument maker. By contrast, sadly look at what is left there today."

Interviewer: "You mentioned the tenacity of local people. How has that changed today?"

KB: "Yes, there was a network of relationships and roots, the kids, the community, the worthy Methodist Liberal tradition which saw poor people through brutally hard times, that is all but lost in an age of greed and consumerism. So often now, we are increasingly seeing the resigned servile civility and absolute apathy there is among a majority of Cornish people who basically have lost their birthright, and have been defeated and beaten into submission."

Interviewer: "Do you think some expressions of Cornish identities have changed over your lifetime?"

KB: "Yes, most certainly. I used to look up to and learn from older people who worked hard for often scant reward but made the best of a bad job to feed the children. Now we have a problem, a clash of cultures. I have a way of life that involves a respect of tradition and roots and continuity, while still fostering a desire to progress. I grew up on a small farm, became a fisherman, was a miner for one winter and then started a successful business and I got there by my own efforts and a burning desire to better myself. The modern breed seems to have a lifestyle based on consumerism greed and short-termism. They are often rootless and seem to lack any coherent culture other than instant gratification as they stare endlessly at their phones rather than engage in proper, face-to-face talking. I get together with my mates in the pub less frequently than I used to, but when we do it is never long before someone strikes up a song. We reminisce, we converse and often tear each other to pieces."

Interviewer: "What did you do first – farming or fishing?

KB: "We had a 23-acre farm and milked ten cows. My father's farm was at Threemilestone where the industrial estate is now. The whole valley and land south of the A390 was all small farms – 15 or 20 of them between Dangerous Crossing and Calenick.

One of my most enduring memories are the milk churns left on a stand at the end of the lane for collection. These 10 gallon, upright, cylindrical containers, made latterly of aluminium were collected by the Milk Marketing Board lorry each morning. The sound of churn lids being beaten off with a wooden mallet is another enduring memory, just like the cows calling to each other coming or going from being milked. Families were reared on those little places and within a few years they were all gone, condemned as uneconomic by a change in government policy."

Interviewer: "Is that right? What are they now then?"

KB: "Most of the land in question is an agricultural wasteland, with much of it basically untended, especially the Tregothnan land."

Interviewer: "Mind you, is it just Tregothnan land, because there is a narrative that the whole industry post-war has changed?"

KB: "No doubt about that. The section of Tregothnan Estate we are talking about is all small farms. The estate is mainly interested in how much rent they get for the houses. The Tregothnan land in question is now unviable to actually farm, so tenants keep horses or hobby farm as a lifestyle choice.

Interviewer: "Why did you swap farming for fishing?"

KB: "I was very impressionable as a child. When I was nine, we went on a mystery tour one Friday evening and ended up in Mevagissey. I'd never been there before and they were there landing fish and it just came to me; I want to be a fisherman when I leave school.

I could have done a lot better in school but didn't want to. I was more interested in being home on the farm or things like that. We had the Youth Employment Officer come around. The spiel was, "Hello sonny, and what do you want to be when you grow up?" So, I said, "I want to be a fisherman." And he said, "Don't be ridiculous, boys from your background don't go fishing. How about being a plumber?", because they must have been short of plumbers that year. So, we reached a compromise and I went to what was then called 'Camborne Tech,' on the agricultural course – a City and Guilds course in farm management. I did the Stage One and part of Stage Two. In the interim, I became friends with a boy from the Scillies who was on the same course. He didn't want to go home and work. He wanted to work over here on the big farms. His father had around a 20-acre place that employed two people. I went over there to work for the summer, on the flower farm, and made a lifelong friendship out of it. It was fascinating and I went back again in the winter when I was fishing a couple of times to help out.

Then the chance came to go fishing. My cousin was skipper in a crabber for Harvey's in Newlyn and he needed crewman urgently and he rang up… "You want to go fishing? Be ready in an hour's time!" Well I was out in the field ploughing. Old man hated tractors, he preferred wheel barrows and horses. I left the tractor with the plough in the ground and just went. There was hell up. Father said "you will starve like a rat in a trap, you'll never make no money fishing." The first day I nearly died – I wasn't sick but I felt sick. And the second day I was fine and loved it. For three days work I got nine quid. This was in 1968. Then farming wages was a fiver a week and your keep. So, I had almost two week's wages for three day's work. And I thought "this is alright getting paid to do what you enjoy."

And it went on through the summer. We were earning a lot of money by local Cornish standards.

A few years later, I went on a trawler for a very short time, this was with Stevensons in

Newlyn. Then I graduated to beam trawling which was just kicking off in Newlyn and I got put aboard one of the beam trawlers as the cook. There were only three beamers there at the time. The world then opened up to us. We were pioneering a new fishery with new techniques, which was an amazing experience."

KB: "You hear people say how dangerous fishing is. Yes, it's potentially dangerous and there are casualties. Luckily there are fewer casualties now than there used to be because the boats have got better. And the crews have a lot more emphasis on health and safety as well, which is no bad thing. But we weren't made to go fishing. We went fishing because we wanted to. Basically, fishing and mining is what Cornish boys did. We earned good money even though we got fired regularly. I think the record was five times in one morning."

Interviewer: "Really?"

KB: "Yeah, it was crazy. In between it all, we worked hard and played harder and achieved great results. You know between the rapidly growing fleet we opened up a vast area of fishing ground where Cornish boats really hadn't been working a lot before.

I still kept a farming interest. We had cattle and my first wife used to look after them when I was away. I had a tractor and I wanted a drop of diesel so one day I went into Opie Oils in Redruth. I knew the chap who ran it and he overcharged me and I complained. Well I didn't really complain, I commented. And his response was, "if you don't effing well like it, start your own oil company."

I was out on the boat one night, winter time in the Trevose season up on the north coast and the fishing was crap. The gear was constantly smashed up. The weather was crap. And it was one of those days when you had a bitter cold north-easterly wind. In the middle of the night that isn't very pleasant. I was lying in my bunk. I had a lovely bunk up in the wheelhouse of the boat, because by this time I had got my Skipper's ticket. That was probably the proudest moment of my life because I'd actually achieved something academically. Um, the more I thought about it, the more feasible the idea about the oil job seemed to be. That's how my company, 'Consols Oils' started.

I think I demonstrate the adaptability of the Cornish. I had a marvellous life because I've had a series of adventures. I don't believe in committing financial suicide, but I will push it to the wire if I think I'm onto something. If not, I'll retreat as safely as I can."

Democracy

Interviewer: "Have you heard of the Letts Scheme?"

KB: "What's that?"

Interviewer: "There's one in Redruth where you barter your skills."

KB: "Yes, yes I have. I didn't realise what it was called."

Interviewer: "Yeah, so people put in hours and they get…"

KB: "It's a good concept but the model I would like to see would be like the Channel Islands or the Isle of Man; a degree of autonomy to decide your own fate, keeping the taxation that's sucked out of Cornwall within Cornwall. Social capitalism expands into a circular economy. If you can keep the profits of an albeit fairly low-key system circulating where they originate, you're there! People don't need to be fantastically rich, but they do need a degree of security, and slightly more income than expenditure. I don't buy into the fact that people need three holidays abroad a year. I always joke, I don't mean it really, but I always say abroad is full of foreigners. I don't want to go abroad, I love it here too much."

Interviewer: "But then how is that different to Cornish nationalism?"

KB: "Cornish nationalism, from my point of view, tends to attract a malcontent often bitter and churlish element. The ne'er do wells who are bitter about everything. If you want to make it go, you can't be bitter. You've got to be magnanimous and see other people's points of view, then argue your corner from there. Give them hell, kick against it, but at least look at their points of view. You want small government, not bigger government, small government that doesn't micromanage; that surely creates the right conditions for a country to function and prosper."

Post interview conversation

Interviewer: "Well, thank you very much."

KB: "You're welcome."

Interviewer: "Is there anything you want to add to Cornish heritage, identity and democracy that we haven't mentioned already?"

KB: "I could add quite a bit but it would take too long, I think I've said enough, I just wish… there's still a lot of good Cornish people out there, brilliant Cornish people. I just wish they'd gain a little bit more courage and speak up for themselves. Because there are people who are destroying everything we treasure and they need stopping. They must be stopped legally, via the ballot box."

Interviewer: "What I think is good is the protests recently have been arranged by people totally new, and totally ordinary and not affiliated to any particular group."

KB: "Do you know, the saddest thing to me? Some of the best people in Cornwall aren't actually Cornish. They are adopted Cornish who come here. They brought something to the table and they contributed and fell in love with the place and the people."

Transcribed by https://otter.ai

Chapter 2

The Early Years *(Ross Poldark meets Forest Gump)*

The roots of the Bennetts family can be traced back for centuries in Madron Parish Records where the family appear to have originated.

By physical make up and complexion it is entirely likely that some Spanish blood was introduced around or since the time of the Spanish Armada when the area around Penzance was, for a few days, pillaged and raped by Spaniards.

My father's side of the family were 'Downs Farmers', good horsemen who seem to have also operated as carters, transporting goods around the area for others as well as farming. I get the impression that the youngsters were hellers.

The rich side of the family became the J H Bennetts conglomerate operating as ship agents and ship owners who later branched out as coal and oil merchants on a considerable scale before a serious decline set in from the 1970s onwards.

There does not appear to have been much, if any, contact or interaction between the rich and poor branches of the extensive family.

Great Grandfather, Harry Bennetts, being a tenant of the Bolithos of Trengwainton, farmed Boswarvah Farm, Madron and liked to hunt. He used to breed classy hunters to sell.

One day out hunting, being keen to impress Squire Bolitho and with an eye to selling him his current mount, he jumped a gate ahead of the master. Great umbrage was taken and it ended badly when, as a consequence, the Bennetts family were evicted from Boswarvah at short notice.

In those days if the local landowner or squire frowned upon you, you would never prosper within their sphere of influence. That probably explains the Bennetts family's arrival in the Redruth area working for the brewery before World War One, eventually ending up in Cubert Parish where this story begins around 1930.

For the purposes of my part in this story, it all started in Redruth Miners' and Womens' Hospital at 11:20 am on third of May 1949. My mother was an East End Cockney of Irish-Jewish extraction who Father had met as a Land Girl in the latter stages of World War Two.

17

The old man in his Navy uniform

My mother in her Land Army days

The London connection

My maternal great grandmother was an Irish catholic born in Skibereen in 1860. She became a sailmaker in London's East End who married a German-Jewish sea captain called 'Stein'; an odd match to say the least. They had one daughter called 'Rose' and changed their name to 'Stone' at the outbreak of WW1.

By the time Great Granny Stone died at the age of 99 in 1959 she had been a widow for 40 years. My limited memories of her were of a wizened old lady in black widow's weeds with a still discernible Cork accent, eyes that sparkled like fire and a tongue like a buggy whip, who, well into her late nineties, still liked her tot of grog.

Rose Stone married Charles Culverhouse, a Billingsgate fish porter who had been badly gassed in WW1, meaning that he never enjoyed the best of health. They lived in Cable Street, Stepney moving south of the river to Surrey Docks in Bermondsey in around 1940 when they were bombed out of the East End.

They had seven children, five girls and two boys, my mother, born in 1919, being the eldest.

Before the outbreak of war, Mother had worked at the Strand Palace Hotel as a chamber-maid. When war broke out she went to work on the railway at the Bishopsgate marshalling yard. For many months her gang was engaged on permanent night work unloading wagon loads of coffins for the thousands of victims of the Blitz.

To Cornwall

When the call went out for Land Girls she volunteered and got sent to, of all places, Trengwainton for training. In another coincidence, her four youngest siblings became evacuees who ended up with the Cargeeg family at beautiful Botallack Manor, which became the mythical 'Nampara' in the first Poldark TV series. They always spoke of how kindly and well they were treated by the Cargeeg Family.

Mother fell in love with Cornwall and never returned to London unless to visit her family. When the war ended she worked as a domestic at the Holywell Bay Hotel with Father's youngest sister Sheila.

Mother ended up billeted with the Bennetts family at Plemens Farm, Tresean, Cubert where she learned to bake pasties under the eagle-eye of Granny Bennetts (née Prowse), a fiery redhead with a fearsome reputation for taking neither nonsense nor prisoners. There must be some truth in that for my father to be afraid of her.

Plemens Farm, Tresean in Cubert Parish

Grandfather Bennetts had been employed as a farm manager by the Wicketts who, at that time, owned Redruth Brewery. They also owned Plemens and various other farms pre the

19

Mother (right) with Grandmother 'Ada Bennetts' in Newquay circa 1947

1930s, where hay for the brewery horses and malting barley for the brewing process was grown. Part of Grandfather's wages as a brewery employee was a gallon of beer a day.

Father always used to say that the north coast strip from Gwithian to Padstow was the best barley ground anywhere, and Padstow barley was the variety best suited to the sea air. Padstow barley is no more. These days, much of the land now grows broccoli in vast acreages, which is just one example of how things have changed in my lifetime.

In the 1930s the brewery horses were replaced by trucks and Grandfather took the chance to buy Plemens when the Wicketts put it on the market in very depressed times. I think the price was £10 an acre for the 25 acres of surprisingly fertile, light blown sand land that made up the holding.

Having bought Plemens, Grandfather's beer ration ceased, so he had to walk to Crantock for a pint of a Saturday night. Once, while slaking a whole week's thirst, he drank far too much St Austell beer which gave him an almighty hangover. The story goes that he never

Me and mother at Plemens circa 1949   *The old barn at Plemens circa 1951*

drank again… he claimed he was more used to the Devenish brew.

Buying Plemens must have been a big deal even though it seems so cheap in hindsight. But grandfather was always regarded as exceptionally hard-working and a good farmer as the fertility of Plemens testified.

This was due to the manure liberally applied over many years from the pigs that were reared on home-grown barley meal and skim milk from the cream and butter that Granny used to make from the Shorthorn and North Devon cows.

Farming, West Cornwall-style, in those days was effectively a closed loop. The mixture of stock and crops complemented each other and the produce was mostly sold locally in the form of eggs, milk, cream and butter.

The barley, straw and skim milk went to the pigs that helped to feed the big family, with the surplus sold to the local village butcher. The pig dung went into the hungry land and surplus calves were reared and fattened on Cubert Common over which Plemens Farm had grazing rights and again, sold to Ronnie Eastlake, the village butcher.

Preston Thomas's baler at Perran Church circa 1953

The old man with me and Jack (the lurcher) at Kirkdale circa 1953

Days of poverty

The Bennetts family in the seriously economically depressed 1930s may have been large and dirt poor, wearing hand-me-down clothes. They may have lived rough, but the grandparents ensured through their never-ending hard work and thrift that the children were never hungry.

The poverty stricken 1930s may have been made harder with the thirteen Bennetts children to feed and clothe but after WW2 with the children working and the farm paid off, things got a little easier.

Like most farmers the war years were good to grandfather after the poverty of the previous decade. Then, tragically at the age of 62 in 1947, just as the fruits of all that labour came good, they were threshing when Grandfather, who was cutting the binds atop the machine, dropped where he stood and was gone before he hit the ground from a massive heart attack.

I often try to imagine the sombre scene as six Bennetts brothers bore their father (known to all as 'Cap'n') on their shoulders from Tresean up to Cubert Church about a mile distant.

He was laid to rest in a grave looking out over Ellenglaze where my father first worked for Sam Phillips for a short while as a 14 year old boy on leaving Cubert School.

Cubert's influence on my boyhood

Cubert Church is ancient and lichen-covered, testifying to the purity of the bracing sea breezes it is constantly buffeted by. It is somewhat of a rarity in Cornwall, in having a proper spire instead of the more usual tower. To a child viewing it from afar it looked like a rocket awaiting launch. I still see it that way today.

Standing by grandfather's grave in later years gazing over and beyond Ellenglaze across the broad expanse of Gear Sands towards St Agnes Beacon makes one realise how high and exposed Cubert village and the agricultural parish around it actually is. But it makes it possible to fully appreciate the glorious vista of my beloved north coast in front of my eyes.

Stretching away south west beyond the brooding hump of St Agnes Beacon and the Cow and Calf in the middle distance, the indent tucked out of sight behind the Beacon known as 'Bassets Bay' ends at Navax, with Godrevy and St Ives Bay with the high Galvas of Zennor, which terminates at Pendeen Watch in the far distance.

To the north and east beyond the wind-pruned, low scrub of Penhale and the towering cleft of the Madrips or Carters Rocks, is that queen of beaches, Holywell, with its little sister Polly Joke hiding coyly beneath the wind-blasted inner and outer Kelseys tucked away in behind the Chick.

Towards the High Galva's of Zennor and Pendeen Watch in the far distance

Further on around the corner of the totally exposed, swell-pounded West Pentire Point lies Crantock and tucked in the far NE corner of Crantock Bay, the mouth of the Gannel opens up with its shallow tidal waters reaching inland as far as Trevemper.

Even the ragged eyesore of the Newquay skyline cannot subdue the beauty of the rounded hump of Trevose in the distance, with the Quies standing offshore in the tide of Ramsey Alley low and menacing like battleships frozen in time, defying the very worst an Atlantic storm can throw at them.

To the east, the high granite mass of Hensbarrow and the looming man-made outlines of the massive Clay Country burrows dominate the landscape, which forms a dramatic backdrop for the rich farmland between.

Everything within that vista became my country, with the grave of my paternal grandfather who I wish I had, but never knew, as its epicentre.

From earliest childhood I have always felt a sense of belonging, an unbreakable bond that has always reinforced a desire never to leave it. My childhood roots in this land became deep and strong as I grew up to be a true north coaster and Perraner in that hard, unforgiving but beautiful land and seascape blessed by the legacy of St Piran that truly nurtured me as a child.

The loss of Plemens created a deep rift

With Granny Bennetts now a widow it fell to the youngest Bennetts, 'Brother Jack' to run Plemens. After Granny passed on, sad to say, he didn't make a very good job of it, being too fond of drinking and womanising. He was a lovely, kind-hearted man who personified the laid-back concept of 'easy come - easy go.'

Jack got involved with a glamorous, high-maintenance, married woman. Subsequent developments were scandalous by 1950's Cubert standards. There was friction in the family because he eventually lost the farm and had to migrate to Australia with his now wife, under a very dark cloud as far as Father was concerned.

I remember being about seven going to Plemens with Father on the eve of Jack's departure for Australia. In the mowhay, the embers of a bonfire of Granny's furniture were smouldering away.

Frowning deeply, Father bent down and retrieved the charred remains of the big, brass- bound family bible from the ashes. That book had recorded in copper plate handwriting, the details of family births, marriages and deaths going back generations. All that historic record now just charred to ashes.

This wanton destruction resulted in a sharp angry exchange as to why the bible, such a significant family archive, had not been saved. There was no proper goodbye from Father to his departing, disgraced, younger brother as we got back in his truck and drove home to

Uncle Jack and Eliesabeth ne Vulling, his second wife

Scott and Laura Kneebone both have strong connections with Cornwall on the other side of the world

Kirkdale in an angry silence.

The Cap'n must have been turning in his grave as his lifetime of graft turned to dust.

The twins

My father was the younger half of twins. He and his older twin, Glenlee, were very close and both were gutted by the loss of Plemens, knowing that they would have made a much better job of things had they only been given the chance.

Father was born several hours after his twin and was not expected to survive the night so he was left wrapped in a towel at the foot of the bed by the midwife. However, in the morning he was still hanging in there and fortunately made it to relative old age, outliving his slightly older sibling and best mate Glenlee by ten years or more.

Both twins had joined the Navy together along with so many others from the Newquay area in 1939. Father ended up on the minesweepers until he got invalided out after the trawler 'Welbeck', which he was serving on at the time, got blown up by a mine during sweeping operations somewhere off Falmouth in 1942.

His injuries were grievous. Only his physical strength and determination pulled him through. After 4 months in Stonehouse Naval Hospital he was discharged as unfit for further service due to burst eardrums which made him very deaf. It was made even worse by never-ending tinnitus.

He was not allowed to resume his former job as a rabbit trapper but he was put in charge of a gang of Land Girls working on rat control, where he first met my mother. This was probably akin to putting a fox to watch a chicken coop.

Glenlee served on the salvage tugs that accompanied the Atlantic convoys. He also had a very tough time of it. Unbeknown to either of them at the time they had, at one point, both survived the same Arctic convoy to Murmansk.

Thankfully, all the Bennetts boys who went to war and, in one case, down a coal mine in Wales, returned home to tell the tale alive, if not in some cases, entirely unscathed.

Plemens today AKA 'Kiddleywink Cottage'

Ponies now graze on what was formerly very fertile Plemens land which has been neglected and allowed to become a mess of outgrown, unkempt hedges and ragwort-infested pasture. A couple of modern houses stand squeezed in the mowhay and, as everywhere, there are fewer Cornish voices to be heard in Trevail or Tresean these days.

Beyond the still thankfully unspoiled Commons and toward Holywell, the flat airy expanse of the inner and outer Kelseys still stretches, also unspoiled, out to the cliffs between Holywell and Polly Joke. It is now, largely for the better, owned by the National Trust and grazed by a local farmer.

Father always banged on about how, in 1946, he could have bought the entire Kelseys for £400, but as a penniless, partially disabled, ex-serviceman, no one would lend him the money needed. It was not until 1963 that he was eventually able to purchase his own small farm.

To Perranzabuloe

Our little family moved out of Plemens while Granny was still alive. Father had found a big house called 'Kirkdale' at Perranchurch, which was owned by an old man called 'William J Hodge' who was the miller at Bolingey.

The deal was that Mother and Father could occupy the majority of the large house in return for caring for Mr Hodge's basic needs. The arrangement worked well until Mr Hodge's demise.

Mr Hodge had never married. Apparently in 1914 he had fallen in love with the family servant girl but permission to marry beneath his station was refused and the servant girl was banished. He remained a confirmed bachelor for the rest of his days while running the

Bolingey Mill for a living.

Mr Hodge had always corresponded with Miss Watson who lived in Rugby. On his passing, Kirkdale was left to the former servant who had remained a spinster her entire life. However, being very old, she did not want it, so it was sold to my parents for £600 in 1956. I was too young to recall the move to Kirkdale but can vaguely remember Granny calling one sunny day dressed in a bright flowery dress and a straw hat with cherries on the brim, all noise and bustle like a summer squall. That was the only time I actually remember her and she had a heart attack and passed away in Jack's arms not long after that around 1953 when I was about four.

My earliest real memory was the Queen's Coronation in June 1952 and being presented with a commemorative porcelain mug by some posh lady wearing gloves after queuing for what seemed like an eternity on the village green next to the beach at Perranporth. My sister, ever the collector of family memorabilia, still has the mug in her china cabinet.

More specifically, I can remember being in great pain after a wheelbarrow load of sand I was playing with fell on me and hurt my hip. That night, father took us to Trenance boating lake at Newquay to see the commemorative firework display but the hip was agony and I was crying so mother made him bring us back early. I never saw the firework display.

The trapper

Father had a pre-war, bull-nose, Morris commercial truck with gun carriage wheels and a temperature gauge on the bonnet. He would use the truck when trapping. There was a photo of me in the back of the truck with the 180 brace of rabbits caught that day – all gutted and ready to be packed in crates to be sent away by rail to his salesman in Nottingham.

The rabbit crates were very strongly made in the typical shape of a doll's house, with no roof but gable ends with a ridge pole from apex to apex, which the braces of rabbits were hung over. The crates had to withstand being repeatedly handled. They would hold six brace of rabbits. There was no refrigeration so trapping was effectively a job for the colder winter months from October to March.

If I had been good, I was sometimes allowed to go with father down to the station in the Porth on Friday nights to put the rabbits on the 20:30 train. It was a ritual sure enough. Arriving in plenty of time in the station goods yard, the crates were taken on iron-wheeled, flat trolleys over the track at the Bolingey end of the platform by the signal box and up onto the Chacewater-bound platform.

That done, Father would adjourn to the signal box where Glen Pedlar the signalman, would have the tea brewed and standing ready in pint-sized, enamel mugs. They would light their pipes and keep a weather eye out for the approaching train, chewing the fat with each other while slurping down their tea. Imagine that happening today?

Perranporth Railway Station in its hey day

I can remember once being lifted up by Glen Pedlar and held with my hands on the big signal levers as he pulled them to set the signals and points. You could actually see the signal outside the window move as the appropriate lever was pulled.

Perranporth had a passing loop in the form of a second platform for the Newquay-bound train, so points needed to be correctly set with signals in the correct sequence. The trains would exchange tokens, which authorised them to run on the specific track length. You could see the lights of the Chacewater-bound train a fair way back toward Bolingey on a clear night from the signal box windows. It would draw up on the platform with a squeal of brakes in a cloud of steam.

Mr Morgan, the station master would appear from nowhere resplendent in his uniform, complete with watch and chain to oversee the proceedings, while the two porters would quickly load the crates of rabbits and any other goods into the guards van. Mr Morgan would check his watch, the guard would blow his whistle and off they would go.

The rail freight logistics in the 1950s, long before computers ran things, were amazing. Rabbits despatched from Perranporth Station in the late evening would, via Chacewater mainline junction, be with Jesse Robinson the salesman in Nottingham the following day. Unlike other trappers in the area, Father never sent his rabbits to London because he considered that demand and prices were never as good as they were in Nottingham, which, he maintained, was a very good place to sell rabbits due to the big demand from the numerous coal mining villages in Nottinghamshire and Derbyshire.

The station goods yard back then was a busy place handling animal feed and fertiliser as well as most of the coal used locally. The coal man called 'John Rose,' was also a farmer from Mithian so the coal often got done in the evenings. They would weigh and bag the coal out of the rail wagons under the light of a flickering hurricane lamp and deliver in the dark far into the winter nights.

A body blow

In 1955, just after my sister Marie was born, Father's world came crashing down as myxomatosis wiped out the rabbits. From relative prosperity, he was without work with next season's 200 brand new gin traps bought and paid for being nothing but scrap.

To add to his despair his ferrets, several with litters of kits, got distemper and I remember him choking back tears as he dug a pit to bury them and his former life with it.

People who didn't know dismissed this disaster as irrelevant, one or two sneering that ''Happy would have to get a proper job now" but, in reality, a piece of the surprisingly complex jigsaw that was the local economy was vaporised.

Trappers paid good rents to farmers for their rabbits. Father had two men working for him in the winter and the loss of freight from the demise of the several local trappers on the Chacewater branch alone was yet another nail in its coffin.

Gin traps were barbaric. There were plenty of three legged cats around in those days and the by-catch of foxes and badgers got short shrift via a hard blow from a trapping spade. But the rabbits had to be controlled and trapping was very effective in the right circumstances, with ferreting and lamping taking up the slack.

The men involved were not bad or even in most cases unduly cruel. They had generally been hardened and desensitised by all-out war and the plain fact of the matter was that this was the way things were in order for them to earn a living in those different times.

The plague of cabbage whites

Strangely, the following year with the broccoli plant growing well without the rabbit menace, there came a plague of cabbage white butterflies that decimated the crop. There were so many caterpillars on the move that they were getting squashed on the roads and stank. With less feed, the buzzards virtually disappeared and foxes turned on the chicken coops.

Every action has a reaction, none more so than when nature rebalances in the face of sudden forced change.

Lessons in life's harsh realities

'Jack,' his favourite lurcher, used to go everywhere with Father in the truck. On Fridays, he would deliver rabbits to his butcher customers in Redruth, 'Pooleys' at Broadlane, Illogan and 'Leslie Dunstone' at Rounding Walls.

Pooleys had their own slaughterhouse at the rear of the combined shop and house, where Father used to go to scrounge some raw tripe for the dogs. The stuff used to stink but the dogs thrived on it.

I used to get left with Mrs Pooley in the large conservatory out the back where there were beautiful coloured begonias. The table was covered with a lino cloth which used to be piled with stacks of counted coins from the shop. Mrs Pooley was kind and would give me a chocolate biscuit or a bluebird toffee. She often used to give me a threepenny bit to get some more sweets.

In yet another amazing twist, a younger member of the Pooley family would re-enter my life 40 years later as the plot thickened.

Just once I was taken in to the slaughterhouse where they were in the process of killing a bullock. As we came in, it was brutal and scary. The harsh crack of the humane killer made me jump but the poor bullock never realised what hit it. The slaughterman was brutally and ruthlessly efficient for sure.

Father knew exactly what he was doing by letting me see that bullock being knocked down. In his own inimitable way, he was showing me, without a word being said, that not everything necessary in life was always pretty.

As we were going, the slaughterman cut a piece of steak off another bullock that was hanging there and gave it to Father. Afterwards he went to Matt Turrill's chip shop opposite Dunstone's butcher shop at Rounding Walls to get the steak fried and had it with chips which I shared.

Auntie Clarice

When we had finished, Jack the lurcher was missing from the truck. He used to jump out of the always open window, probably off after a local bitch on heat. Father drove off without him as he often did, calling in to see his oldest sister Clarice Baker at Shallow Adit by Mount Ambrose.

Her husband, Ted Baker, worked for A H Dingle who were, at that time, significant Redruth-based, civil engineering contractors. He had driven the first Caterpillar bulldozer to come to Cornwall before the Second World War. I've seen a picture of him working at Treamble Mine with a scraper box in tow.

The mine was on the Great Perran iron lode that ran inland from Gravel Hill where its outcrop can be seen in the cliff. During the war it was worked for iron ore and Fullers earth, a form of decomposed kaolin. A mineral branch line had been constructed from Shepherds Station to ship the ore out but then the project was abandoned, although most of the original track bed still exists to this day.

Sacked

Ted Baker had got Father a job before the war when jobs were hard to come by. Dingles were building concrete roads in Newquay. There was no ready mixed concrete back then and cement came in 2cwt sacks. Father was working with Roy St Clair Gregory, a well-known Redruth wrestler, wheeling the bags of cement to the mixer on wooden wheelbarrows.

Being young, silly and far too strong for their own good, they had a competition to see who could push the most bags. Father pushed four bags and Roy St Clair was pushing five bags when the handles broke just as bowler-hatted Mr Dingle turned up in his Packard car. Seeing the broken barrow, he fired them both, a very serious matter when there was little or no work elsewhere.

Having had a cup of tea and a yarn with his sister as was his way and given her the brace of rabbits he had saved for her, we headed back home. When we eventually got back to Kirkdale, Jack, the cunning lurcher, was sitting outside the front gate waiting for us with his tongue hanging out panting. He'd come the nine miles home quicker than us.

Out of cow's teats

As a child, I always clearly understood that milk did not just come out of bottles, it actually came out of cow's teats as on William Rowlings' Lambourne Castle Farm across the road from Kirkdale where I used to spend so much time.

Likewise, I learned in a practical way that food, such as bacon, chicken and steak did not magically materialise into cellophane wrapped trays as so many children think today. At the point of production, blood and gore was, and still is, inevitably involved.

Actually, being exposed to the processes involved would be frowned upon now but as a child they were part of my informal education and I was never unduly traumatised. It actually taught me that everything has a cost and where food animals are concerned, the cost is their lives. This should be respected by never, ever wasting food or, heaven forbid, even worse, taking it for granted.

The trappers' week

Trappers, like father, worked from Sunday to Friday tending traps in the morning, leaving them all tripped on Friday before resetting them again on Sunday morning ready for Monday. They would often go ferreting in the afternoons when cold and dry and lamping at night when conditions were right. Ideally, it needed to be wet and windy when lamping with a powerful battery-powered spotlight and he would work a pair of lurchers with his men following on, picking up the rabbits in sacks. It really was a physically hard life.

The lurchers were proper working dogs who were treated well. There were usually four who lived indoors with their own settee in the kitchen. As long as they performed to father's exacting standards, they had to catch and retrieve rabbits alive into his hands with no bites allowed. Hard-mouthed lurchers would soon be moved on.

I have clear recollections of him asleep in his chair by the range in the kitchen dressed in his old American Army surplus padded jacket and trousers with the cut off tops of Wellington boots as leggings over his hob nail boots, smelling of damp and rabbits, catching forty winks after lamping far into the small hours.

He used to tell a tale about another trapper-cum-pig-farmer called 'Jimmy Powell' from Wheal Frances who had a large family. He was a bit of a lash up not known for his appearance but doing the best he could. During the war, being too old to fight, he was drafted into the local Home Guard under Parson Harvey who bollocked him for his poor turnout.

Jimmy Powell unexpectedly rounded on the Parson saying "it's like this Passon Boy, I am a rabbit trapper, the more I look like a bunny rabbit and the more I smell like a bunny rabbit the more bunny rabbits I catch and there's hungry people out there who need rabbits to eat." The Parson had no answer to that one.

There was also another much older trapper called 'Jethro Greet,' who father suspected of deliberately poisoning one of his lurchers with a piece of meat laced with strychnine, a deadly poison used to control moles. The enmity was mutual and beyond resolution. Fortunately, they avoided each other like the plague lest they murder each other.

Weekends were easier, the gin traps would be tripped (made safe) for the weekend. If he was moving farms it would usually be done on a Saturday and home mid-morning for a shave and a bath in the tin tub in front of the range.

Kirkdale

Kirkdale, being a gentleman's residence, had a back stairs and an outside flush toilet but the water had to be pumped up by hand from a deep well in the back yard. Hot water in quantity was got from the copper boiler in the wash house linhay mainly used for boiling clothes on washday. The hot water was carried into the kitchen in a white, enamel bucket for baths.

The wash house had a hand-cranked paddle system in a wooden tub which was a primitive Victorian washing machine. There was also a huge mangle which my sister once wound her fingers into and a genuine washboard of the type which skiffle groups later played as an instrument.

Coal for the copper boiler and the huge brass-adorned Cornish range in the kitchen was tipped through a trapdoor from the road outside. Our coalman, another of life's absolute gentlemen, was Bonzo Johns, the celebrated Cornish rugby player who worked for 'Reynolds' who shipped their coal from Wales into Portreath in small coasters.

The hole in the wall

Portreath Harbour was a miracle of construction, literally a hole in the wall along the otherwise unbroken line of the so called North Cliffs. The harbour was built by the Bassets of Tehidy House to serve the mines via a couple of ingenious tramway systems; one reaching inland as far as Poldice, the other via a massive incline worked by gravity linking to the Carn Brea mines and Hayle Railway at Illogan Highway.

The development of Cornish mines was ruthlessly driven forward by necessity, which truly was the 'mother of invention'. Problems arose and solutions were devised in what was, at that time, a literal powerhouse of industry at the cutting edge of the Industrial Revolution that Cornwall was in the vanguard of.

This natural culture of aptitude and enterprise has tragically been eroded over time. Were the current *'powers that be'* as innovative as our forebears rather than the defeatists they seem to be, Cornwall might be a very different place today.

33

The rations and a haircut gone wrong

Saturday's ablutions completed it was then down to the Porth for the groceries referred to as 'rations'. Mother would write her list and Father would take it to Ferguson Bown, the grocer at the foot of St Georges Hill. Strangely, apart from writing the list, Mother never actually went shopping.

While the rations were being sorted, it was over to Reynolds the butchers for the meat and once a month to Ted Langdon's at the bottom of Liskey Hill for a haircut.

Poor old Ted the barber was a hunchback with a club foot. Once at Father's behest, 'to take a bit more off' he made a mess of my haircut much to Mother's horror. She burst into tears and flew at Father yelling "what have you done to my little boy? He looks like a bloody Jap!"

Mother hardly ever swore, but on Monday morning she was on the 09:30 bus down the Porth to give the hapless barber a very rare piece of her mind.

From then on, she uncharacteristically took charge of my haircuts watching old Ted like a hawk. As he snipped away at my hair all the while he would be shaking like a dog trying to shit a worm. She was not a fan of crew cuts and my ridiculous parting had to be exactly right, glued down with that awful Brylcream stuff. Haircuts seemed to bring out another side of her normally benign personality.

Father's response was "gesson with 'ee woman you'm carrying on like a hen with one chick" but to her I was her pride and joy and no one was going to compromise that.

The final Saturday afternoon job was to call at Trewarthas for his week's supply of brown roll twist tobacco and given that sweets were now off ration, a quarter of coconut mushrooms for himself, a big slab of Cadbury's fruit and nut and a week's supply of Woodbines for Mother with a tube of Smarties or a Turkish Delight for me.

Father was very possessive of his coconut mushrooms. He would count them and woe betide us if temptation got the better of us and one got pinched. Ask and you would receive but there would be hell to pop if the numbers didn't tally up on a recount.

'Overtaker' and the purple heart

On the theme of Smarties, an hilarious incident occurred. Father used to race greyhounds at the Cornish Stadium track at Par Moor near St Austell. At the time, purple hearts (amphetamine tablets) were all the rage with doctors who handed them out as the instant fix for everything. Two of Mother's sisters even worked in the factory in London where they were produced, so they were easily available.

One of Father's greyhounds was called 'Overtaker' although she was anything but that, almost always coming in last. One night he had a brainwave and gave her a purple heart and she romped home to win the race by a good length. Father, as usual, backed her and cleaned up, but there was a problem when another dog owner twigged that something was up.

He approached Father who admitted that he was in possession of a magic pill but they were very expensive. It was agreed that he would sell ten pills to the other dog owner for seven pounds (a good week's wages at that time).

But Father didn't want to reveal his secret weapon. He was racking his brains for a solution. The cogs in his brain were turning over and on the way back from the Porth as I was eating my Smarties, you could almost hear the click of his 'Eureka' moment.

He grabbed my Smarties as soon as we got home and took five green ones and five red ones out of the tube and put them in a brown envelope and sealed it carefully.

The next race meeting he handed over the envelope explaining that the green ones made a dog go faster and the red ones were to slow it up. The money changed hands. Needless to say, they didn't work and naturally enough there was hell up, but Father had a broad back and just brazened it out.

Despite being doped if only just the once, Overtaker lived to the ripe old doggy age of eighteen.

In deep doo doos

Once after Sunday school in the autumn I was in my best turnout when several of us went scrumping apples in an overgrown orchard down at the bottom of Cocks Hill. The owner never bothered with the lovely apples but wouldn't let anyone have them either and they simply rotted where they fell.

He caught us scrumping and we ran off to escape through a hole in the hedge in the far corner. Suddenly, a couple of us sank up to our knees in something that smelt revolting. It was where he buried the lavatory bucket in the days before flush toilets. The old man went off laughing, obviously that was punishment enough to be explaining how we got in the state we were in.

Summary… justice indeed!

The Porth was a proper community

The Porth has never been an architectural gem, having evolved out of a rough mining camp and seining station, with the seine boats tucked away in the scant shelter afforded by Chapel Rock.

Unlike many other much more picturesque Cornish settlements, nature had compensated by blessing it with a truly magnificent surf-pounded, three-mile sandy strand.

In the 1950s it was a proper 'warts and all', rock-solid Cornish community. A hotch potch jumble of substantial Victorian houses and hideous, jerry-built, pre-war, mundic block bungalows, where everyone knew each other and generally looked out for each other. Father's

Saturday shopping sorties were always filled with conversation and good-natured banter.

Father's Christian name was 'Howard' but hardly anyone actually knew that. He was universally known as 'Happy,' which was a bit strange really when he was often such a grumpy old bugger!

In those days, most adults had been touched to some degree by war. There were still a lot of WW1 veterans around; the limbless, the blind and the insane, each wrestling with the demons that haunted them and generally with precious little help or understanding outside of their immediate circle in the tightly-knit community.

It actually took decades to discover and understand how this applied to my father and mother who never mentioned the horrors they had both witnessed during WW2.

The mantra was typically 'pull yourself together' and so they did and just got on with a hard life the best they could. In my parent's case, this involved remarkable stoicism and fortitude aided by lots of roll tobacco and Woodbines.

One remarkable example of the inherent kindness involved manifested itself when Mother decided to start doing bed and breakfast but was struggling to afford all the bedding needed. Mr Sam Pally who was, I think, a former Polish or Hungarian-Jewish refugee had ended up in the Porth.

He had opened a haberdashery store known as 'Porth Stores.' No one knew who tipped him off but he had gotten wind of the situation, which to him represented a business opportunity. He stopped Father in the street one Saturday afternoon and told him to send Mother down to see him on Monday morning. Nervously, Mother got the 09:30 bus down to the Porth as instructed.

She went into Mr Pally's shop and, as usual, true to form, she was nervous. ''Mrs Bennetts,'' boomed Mr Pally in his, to me strange accent, "they tell me you need bedding, then why did you not come to see me?"

Mother was lost for words as he put his deal to her. She could have whatever she needed and he would not expect any payment till the end of the season in September. That got her off the ground with her bed and breakfast and suddenly we were sharing our home with strangers paying 12s 6d per night.

Come September the debt was settled and Mr Pally said something significant, that I will never forget, "this country accepted me and my family as refugees when I had nothing. It is a pleasure to be able to pay something back by helping you." That is the way that amazing little community was in those days of shared austerity.

Proof as if any were ever needed that a 'little practical help, not outright charity, but a genuine helping hand,' is worth infinitely more than a whole lot of theoretical sympathy. What a dramatic contrast to the corporate, money-grabbing, so-called 'charities' today that appear to be more geared to the welfare of overpaid executive fundraisers!

The 'Tresean eel' itself

Some Sundays we would go back to Tresean to visit Father's twin brother Glenlee and his wife Florrie (née Sugar), who was another former Land Girl from Tottenham, North London. Other Sundays they would visit us and I always eagerly looked forward to playing with their two boys, my cousins, Steven and John.

We kids would often get sent down to the old well on Tresean Moor, which everyone used to draw their water from in the days before the mains arrived, to fetch some water back in enamel pails. The well itself was a sort of stone hut with grass on the roof and a rickety wooden door, all set in the middle of what can best described as a bog, with stepping stones from the road to the door.

If the door was opened carefully you could often see a huge eel in the deep pool of the well, which must have been living there for years, but it would quickly disappear into the stonework when disturbed. It had obviously not got as big as it was without a very secure bolt hole safe from predatory children over the years.

Subsequently, I have often speculated about the fate of that particular eel. Hopefully, when its instinct dictated, one stormy, wet, autumn night it slipped away down that brook that rounds about under the Commons to meet the Atlantic head on at Polly Joke, to then face the epic swim to the Sargasso Sea to fulfil its destiny and reproduce.

Did it make it? Did one of its offspring ever make it back to that well on Tresean Moor to continue the amazing epic circle of life and death that is the life cycle of Anguilla anguilla, the common European Eel, a truly amazing species that these days is sadly, critically endangered by human activity?

I will never know, but one cannot help but wonder when such an enigma occupies one's thought's over time, having had such an unconscious subliminal influence on subsequent life events.

To me, the fascinating, uncatchable Tresean eel triggered, at five years old, in the most unlikely location, my lifelong interest in fish and fishing, which was to have such an impact on my life in years to come.

The small trout that darted in the streams at Callestick and Ventongimps became a challenge to catch especially when occasionally you caught one big enough to actually eat.

That interest was later cemented when one summer evening we went on a mystery trip on Bobby Mitchell's bus which eventually ended up in Mevagissey. There, as a nine-year old, I saw three boats called 'Ibis,' 'Snowdrop' and 'Little Pearl' landing their fish. I was hooked! I knew in an instant what I wanted to be when I grew up.

A birth that rocked my world

The arrival of my baby sister was a shock. I knew nothing other than Mother had disappeared and I was suddenly being looked after by my grandparents from London, which, while no hardship, seemed strange. Ten days later mother reappeared with a noisy baby, announcing that I now had a sister called 'Marie.'

Marie was at first a sickly baby who turned out to be allergic to cow's milk. Father always having an answer, went out and bought a goat. The first time Marie had goat's milk she convulsed. Not to be outdone, father decreed that the milk was a bit rich, so mother watered it down and gradually got her acclimatised to it, whereafter she really began to thrive.

I was never told anything about the pregnancy beforehand and precious little afterwards. From Mother's perspective, she would much rather that the bit of body between the shoulders and kneecaps didn't exist.

Whatever will people think?

Mother's worst nightmare was that you must always have clean underwear "in case you have an accident," as she used to say, "Heaven knows, what would everyone think if your pants were dirty?"

My dear mother really was her own worst enemy. Her biggest fault was that she always spent far too much time worrying what others might think and far too little time standing up for herself, unless it involved haircuts!

Her worst fears were realised when Annie Rowling, the farmer's wife from Lambourne Castle Farm across the road, who had the only phone in the hamlet at that time, came rushing over to announce to Mother that she had just had a call saying that Father had had rather a nasty accident and had been rushed unconscious by ambulance to Truro Infirmary.

The trapping season was over but father had been obliging Jack Rowe (a farmer over at Mithian) by trapping some rabbits that were ravaging his corn. Any rabbits caught were fed to the ferrets and lurchers. Sometimes, Father would go out on his pushbike instead of using his truck in order to save petrol. It transpired that he had a few brace of rabbits slung on the handlebars and the cross bar of the bike and, while descending the newly tarred and chipped hill down into Golla Water by Lambriggan Mine, a rabbit's head had caught in the front wheel throwing him over the handlebars. He had landed on his nose on the freshly chipped road.

No one was sure how long he had been out for the count before he was fortunately found by the district nurse out on her rounds. But to Mother's absolute horror, as a result of this accident, his underwear was anything but clean. He was a real mess with a badly broken nose, severe concussion and a very nasty gravel rash from his forehead to his chin.

Father's world implodes

This episode was just before the myxomatosis outbreak that was to destroy his livelihood, which had been providing his little family with a decent living and, with a mortgage to pay, he had to find a job. Father happened to know a mining engineer called 'John Jeffers' who lived in Crantock, who he had done a bit of Cornish hedging for in the past. Mr Jeffers gave him a job at Hydraulic Tin in Bissoe where he was the manager.

The job went well for around eighteen months. Although the wages were low, the plant was busy working the floor of the Bissoe Valley along the route of the Carnon River for alluvial tin washed down from the nearby Gwennap Mines. However, there was friction with a new shift boss who took charge, which culminated in the shift boss getting thumped and Father getting fired.

He was summonsed for assault and fined heavily but he fell on his feet when he got a job on the construction of the new Queen Elizabeth dry dock in Falmouth. At the time, it was the biggest dry dock in the world, built specifically to cater for the new breed of supertankers being built during the mid 1950s.

The wages were exceptionally good here but the work was hard and dangerous, with very long hours. He was with a good gang and stayed to see the job out, getting back on his feet financially in the process. Although no Royalist, he got to meet the Duke of Edinburgh who, on its completion, formally opened the new dock.

Mr Willy Tamblyn, our teacher at Penwartha School, shaped my future

I had started school at Penwartha tucked away at the top of the Coombe of that name that runs back to the west from Bolingey. It was a happy place where one particular teacher, still teaching well past retirement age, inspired me with his tales of Cornish history - particularly the mines and the skills that they fostered.

Willy Tamblyn was a staunch Methodist and a local preacher who kept firm discipline. But to this particular seven-year old Cornish boy, he was a hero.

He was friends with the legendary Donald Healey of Austin Healey fame who was a celebrated Perraner who had actually won the Monte Carlo rally in one of his work's cars in 1931.

He was also an acquaintance of Winston Graham of Poldark fame, but clever as it was, the Poldark saga was romanticised fiction, while we grew up in the real world of mine dumps and engine houses that he brought vividly to life for us in our lessons.

Winston Graham used to write his books in the famous green-painted, wooden hut overlooking Flat Rocks where a commemorative seat now stands. I have often wondered if it was actually Willy Tamblyn who provided the background mining knowledge for him when writing Poldark.

39

Penwartha School (illustration courtesy Perranporth Women's Institute

'Legh Carrygy' originally owned by Harry Tremewan was rented by author Winston Graham and is where he was inspired to write some of the famous Poldark novels

Class from Penwartha School with teacher Willy Tamblyn - an inspiring figure in my life. I am front row and cross-legged, second from the right

We were taught the history of the local area, the significance of the local mines, particularly Wheal Leisure (of Poldark fame) and, the potentially mighty Perran St George before the litigation involving a boundary dispute between them bankrupted both mines.

He described how the seine net boats once huddled together on their moorings in the scant shelter between the natural arch and Chapel Rock. Even today some of the mooring rings can be seen near where the stepping stones cross the river.

We became junior experts on the drama of and chemistry involved in the manufacture of explosives in the Nobel works up at Cligga, as well as having a vivid mental picture of the schooners coming and going from the harbour at Trevaunance and how it was destroyed by a savage storm in 1917.

Much of this had been witnessed first-hand by Willy Tamblyn as a younger man. So to me, as an impressionable seven year old boy, he was my living link with a local past that totally absorbed me.

But above all at every opportunity he hammered into us all what a privilege it was to be born Cornish and how we were all heirs to and custodians of a mighty heritage.
The history of England was barely touched upon during this most impressionable phase of my childhood.

He also made sure in the process that we became both literate and numerate. Whenever possible, he fostered a hunger for knowledge and, in my case, an innate curiosity about the world around me that has remained to this day.

To his great credit, I am sure that my peer group benefitted as much as I did from Willy Tamblyn's unique, albeit by today's standards, unconventional but nonetheless highly effective style of teaching at that most impressionable stage of our lives.

Almost without exception we all went on to make something worthwhile of our lives and careers.

Bobby Mitchell's bus, school dinners and the dentist

Bobby Mitchell's rickety old bus used to pick us up by the war memorial at Perranchurch. The Williams and Bilkey tribes from Ventongimps and the Watkins from Callestick were all big families who walked there to catch the bus while I was lucky enough to live just across the road.

The Williams were cousins and one of Father's sisters, Joyce, had married a Welshman, Bungay Williams, who turned out to be a bigamist. He made headlines in the 'News of the World' when found out and was jailed.

Despite the scandal and the shockwave it provoked, everyone got over it and moved on. The marriage was strong and the family was large and happy, albeit poor. Father used to drop rabbits off to them and we were very close until he moved them all back to Wales.

We all used to have school dinners which were delivered from Mount Hawke School, where the central canteen for the area was located. The meals came in insulated, aluminium boxes delivered by a distinctive black Austin van in Cornwall County Council livery driven by Mr Cripps who used to help the dinner lady with the serving before taking the boxes back to Mount Hawke.

Then there was Nurse Shanklin, the district nurse in her pale blue Morris Minor car. She was affectionately known as 'Nitty Nora', the head explorer, but to the best of my knowledge, despite a lot of rummaging, she never found any, which apparently is more than can be said today.

The worst nightmare was the annual visit of the dreaded school dentist. A cream caravan that was the mobile surgery would be parked in the lane running up the side of the school and we would be summoned out one by one to sit in the chair and open wide. If anything was found, an appointment was made to have a filling drilled by the dreaded 'string drill' without anaesthetic!

Thank goodness dentistry has moved on these days!

I successfully weather my first storm on the water

In summer, there were rowing boats on the boating lake in Boscawen Park. Six old pence for half an hour. Mother hated me going out in them. One day there was a terrific thunder storm and while I was out in the middle of the lake, torrents of rain and dramatic flashes of lightning came and I lost a paddle. This caused the usual panic with Mother who hitched up her dress and jumped in to save me. Luckily, the water was only knee-deep because she couldn't swim. I would have been fine if she sat in the shelter till I drifted into shore. That was the first experience of many future storms in various boats safely and successfully weathered.

Brian Mitchell and tragedy

Bobby Mitchell was an archetypal, old-school Perraner. He ran an ancient bus and a taxi and to us kids was even more ancient than his bus. Quietly spoken, he had dark eyes, a rotund body that seemed to hang off the sides of the driver's seat and he had masses of hair sprouting from his ears. I always remember the taxi slogan, *'if you are in a fix phone 2126.'*

When we moved up to secondary school his son, Brian Mitchell, had taken over the reins and bought better buses. Kids who messed with Brian were making a big mistake.

Me aged 11

He caught me messing about one day on the way home from Penwethers. Stopping the bus out at Pendown Cross he dragged me to the front giving me a clear ultimatum, "walk home from here or I stop outside your house and tell your father what a little bugger you have been." The choice was clear. I walked home because father would have probably killed me.

The Mitchells were a tragic family. Brian died of cancer far too young while his son was later killed in a terrible house fire in his house at the bottom of Liskey Hill while attempting to save his baby son who also perished. Dear old harmless Bobby lived to see it all which was so sad.

Failure

I failed my 11+ exam even though I was promised a new bike if I passed. I did not want to catch the train to Newquay Grammar School with all the rich kids, which was a complete misnomer because the rich kids actually got sent to the C of E Truro Cathedral School or Methodist Truro School. In reality, the clever ones went to Newquay.

The Boarder

My older cousin, Roger Snell's mother 'Freda,' was one of Father's older sisters. The Snells farmed Lambourne Farm at Penhallow just up the road from Perranchurch. She had worked very hard doing bed and breakfast and decided to send Roger to Truro Cathedral School as a boarder. Roger looked very dapper in his light blue uniform and cap on parade at the church fête.

Up came the Reverend Harvey to chat with Aunt Freda. Some of the Bennetts' sisters could be inclined to put on the airs and graces given the opportunity, and the church fête presented an ideal one to this hard-working farmer's wife who had bettered herself as a result. Having finished his small talk with Aunt Freda, he turned his attention to Roger, enquiring what he wanted to be when he grew up. Expecting to hear, "solicitor, doctor, maybe bank manager," Roger's reply that he wanted to be 'an ice cream man' did not go down at all well with his fuming mother.

Aunt Freda lost her cool exclaiming "I have not spent all this money on you to be an ice cream man," before dragging him off in disgrace.

Roger went from school to work as a proof reader at the West Briton newspaper. At that time, the paper was a highly respected, eagerly anticipated weekly event, unlike the rag it has been allowed to degenerate into today. He later left the West Briton to become a very successful local builder and heating engineer, building his own house in the Porth. We are still close but latterly his health has slowed him down.

Uncle William and Auntie Annie

I used to spend a lot of my time over on the Rowlings Lambourne Castle Farm which was quite large for the area at about 120 acres. The yard was a magnificent but somewhat neglected courtyard of stone barns and linhays, with cow housing beneath the barn section on three sides, with the dung being piled in the middle in a bit of a depression.

The buildings are now known as the 'White House Court' and are very smart holiday lets. When the Rowlings retired to a small terraced house in Redruth, the farm was sold off by Coulter Hancock (a Truro solicitor) who was the landlord. In lots, the land south of the main road and Perranchurch Woods was integrated into the Holman's Chyverton Estate.

The farmyard buildings were bought by a builder for conversion and the rest, including the big farmhouse, mowhay and block of land north of the road, retained its integrity as a smaller farm in its own right.

This was the time when barn conversions started to become a big business, which saved so many farms from financial ruin, irrevocably changing the very nature of our countryside in the process as prosperous, non-farming occupiers grew in numbers.

The Rowlings were a strange couple. I knew them as 'auntie' and 'uncle.' Even though they were not related to us, our family were very close to them and they were good neighbours. They had moved to Lambourne Castle Farm from the Constantine area just before WW2.

Auntie Annie was a very big lady with a braveeish old rump on her who always looked a bit top-heavy. She was chaotic, untidy and chain smoked 'Players.' Mother used to be appalled to watch her baking and letting the fag ash fall into the mix, carrying on as if nothing had happened, Auntie Annie's take on it being "what doesn't fatten will fill", she carried on regardless. Whatever else, she was always kind to me.

Uncle William was the polar opposite, being small and tidy, with round glasses. He looked as if his ruddy complexion had just been polished with Mr Sheen. They were the personification of the Jack Sprat story. There were two sons, Donald and Robert who I never had much to do with, as they were much older than me and had nothing to do with the farm.

A black eye leads to deep depression cured by special medicine

Michaelmas (the 29th day of September) was the traditional time for tenant farms to change hands, so there would be a flurry of farm sales in the run up, which were great social occasions. Father had arranged to go to one with William who had left strict orders that he wanted his dinner ready early.

Annie had ordered a rabbit for dinner and Father had left a brace of youngish, tender ones hanging under the linhay by the wash house door for her.

True to form, she left it late enough to waddle over to fetch the rabbits in order to cook them on time. She ignored the smaller, more tender rabbits set aside for her and instead took a big tough old buck put there for the ferrets.

When dinner was served, the rabbit was predictably rank and tough as boot leather. The workmen left theirs and the normally placid William blew his top. They had a blazing row and he gave her a black eye before storming off to the sale without any dinner.

Afterwards, he was full of remorse which degenerated into deep depression and he took to his bed and stayed there for days going downhill rapidly. Father used to see him every night describing him to mother as being 'like a sick hen, going home to roost.'

William was a pillar of the community. A Methodist preacher, district councillor and strictly teetotal but Father decided to cure him. He got four bottles of strong barley wine and took them over that evening.

Being a strictly teetotal preacher, William did not want to drink the stuff but Father insisted that it was 'medicine.' He eventually took a couple of sips and licked his lips. He ended up drinking the four bottles of 'medicine' and fell asleep like a baby for the first time in many days.

He was awake at 'sparrow fart' the next morning and went straight off down the yard, chasing the men who had hardly seen him for days. They had been muddling along the best they could without direction. From then on, there were always a few bottles of medicine (barley wine) on the sideboard.

The question being, did Father corrupt him by leading him into temptation or did the ends justify the means?

The callous casting aside of Captain and Blossom

One day, the pair of horses that did most of the work on the place disappeared like so many at that time. They were coldly sent for meat as they were replaced by tractors and in Uncle William's case, a smart new Fordson Dexta as an addition to the little grey T20. That summer, hay was no longer moved to the rick by a horse sweep and put away by the hay pole worked by the other horse. No more riding one great Shire called 'Captain' leading 'Blossom' up to Penhallow to Reggie Harris, the blacksmith at Penhallow for a new set of shoes or, riding on the shaft of the cart to take corn out to the ewes in the fields overlooking Cocks or Perranwell.

Modernisation

Chyverton Estate had got a new Fordson Major, a blue monster with orange wheels alongside William's little grey diesel Fergie T20 that had complemented the horses previously, or even the shiny new Dexta in the same blue and orange livery.

The Fordson Major was paired with a new-fangled, 'Massey Harris' pick up baler driven by an Armstrong Sidley diesel engine so that year for the first time, the hay was baled in the field and the heavy job of carrying the bales became the new norm.

When the corn harvest came around, Chyverton again led the way. William's horse drawn Albion binder was left in the linhay to gather dust and rust quietly away as the rats chewed at the canvas belts, while Chyverton came over with a shiny Allis Chalmers Super Gleaner Combine that dispensed with the twice yearly visit by Preston Thomas's Field Marshall powered threshing set.

The threshing set

Threshing days were exciting times. The threshing set would usually turn up the evening before and set up ready for the next day.

If it was coming from the Perranwell end you could hear the bark of the Field Marshal labouring up Perranchurch Hill, with both the threshing machine and heavy stationary baler in tow way before it crested the brow of the long steep hill and into sight.

The actual machine had to be level with the big stationary baler on the rear and positioned to catch the straw. The grain would be run into 2 cwt 'West of England,' hired sacks, which men would stagger off up the barn steps with. It was all in a day's work back then but unthinkable today.

Preston Thomas in his scruffy grey suit, waistcoat and flat cap (think Fred Dibnah) was a cantankerous old bugger who took no nonsense from anyone. He would not hesitate to give boys like me a quick clip around the ear if we got in his way or on his nerves. William was very circumspect with him and would defer to him, then quietly retreat and just let him get on with it.

Crib time was a big deal. The food came in a large wicker basket lined with a red gingham tablecloth with a big urn of sweet tea. At dinner time when threshing, Preston Thomas and his men would eat in the farmhouse with the two regular farm workers.

At harvest time, William would bring the basket of food and tea urn out to the field. Typically, corned beef and tomato sandwiches with halves of pasties and yeast cake. The men got first pick, us kids got the knockings, but there was always plenty.

As the rick being threshed was getting lower, we boys would gather with our terriers and lurchers and pikes to catch the fleeing rats. We thought nothing of spearing the poor buggers on a pike prong and tossing them to the waiting dogs darting around like mad things. Evil it was, but rats were the enemy and no quarter was ever given.

The threshing machine used to talk. The steady thump thump of the single cylinder Field Marshal, the slap of the belt accompanied by the whining drone of the thresher rising and falling as the sheaves were fed into the drum and the crash of the baler ram travelling back and forth.

Then suddenly it was gone, replaced by the roar of the combine out in the field, one man doing what five or six did before. A farming revolution was gathering pace and I got to drive the T20 when my legs became long enough to reach the pedals.

To Penwethers and a shock

That autumn, along with the rest of the Penwartha failures, I ended up at the relatively new Penwethers Secondary School at Highertown on the outskirts of Truro with 480 other 'failures' from a large local catchment.

As a North Coast kid, it was my first encounter with the kids from Coombe, Kea, Feock and Devoran. They seemed a different breed. Generally, more cautious, quieter and to my mind indecisive. The Coombe kids were a breed apart for sure.

Later in life I learned to understand the Coombe Kaffirs (a local nickname for those who lived by Coombe Creek) a bit better and how they were perfectly adapted to their softer, more wooded environment of plum orchards and pittosporum and eucalyptus groves.

Most of the area was Tregothnan territory, with the huge Gothic Mansion an ever-brooding presence on the other side of the river.

Coombe Kaffirs were survivalists and, as tenants, always beholden to Tregothnan. They would harvest oak bark from the coppices along the river for tanning leather. In winter, they would harvest the stripped oak limbs for firewood, dredge for oysters and tend their orchards. Foliage in the form of pittosporum and eucalyptus was cut and sold to florists for decoration. Kea plums are a deep dark purple and full of tart flavour. They make the ultimate jam to pair with cream and splits (never those blasted scones). For some unaccountable reason, the unique type of plum trees cannot be persuaded to grow well anywhere far from the creeks around that part of the River Fal.

In my opinion, Rippons - the Perranporth bakers, made the best bread and splits ever with a dark, crispy crust and incredible texture and yeasty flavour. They used to deliver to Perranchurch twice a week.

Proper splits are not often seen these days and scones are no substitute. I get weary of the idiotic 'jam first' argument, it is my treat and I happen to like a thin layer of cream first then a generous dollop of Kea plum jam on top, then more cream. There can never be too much cream!

On the subject of cream, there were two sorts; 'separated cream' that was put through a centrifuge, and 'scalded cream' where the milk was left to stand in an enamel pan in a cool dairy for the cream to rise and set on the milk, which was then scalded over another pan of boiling water to cook the cream, which was then left to cool when the crust of cream was scooped off leaving the sweet nutty skim milk to drink.

The first assembly at Penwethers

All of this was a culture shock to say the least. During the first school assembly, the Headmaster, Mr Lavin, made it clear that owing to his reputation being at stake, failure was not an acceptable option. So, it was very clear that we all needed to adapt to change and buckle down.

It was a good school with some inspirational teachers – some of whom later became friends. The fact that I was a little unconventional made no difference, my interests were farming and fishing and they were not on the curriculum but they were savvy enough to work around that.

My favourite subjects were English, geography and rural science which I loved. I hated maths, never really getting to grips with it. In fact, it was not until 14 years after leaving school that the practical reason for maths and trigonometry became clear but that is another later part of this story.

The move to 'clay country'

Out of the blue, one of Father's bombshells dropped. He had heard of the high wages being paid in 'clay country', so Kirkdale was put on the market, while Mother and Father searched for a house in the St Austell area. They soon found one, Moorland House was in Trethurgy, high on the downsy granite land, east of St Austell which, in 1961, was a boom town because of the endlessly rising demand for 'White Gold' (china clay).

Kirkdale was sold to a gay male couple, which nonplussed my alpha male father a bit, but a sale was a sale and just for once, he bit his tongue and took the money. They soon renamed Kirkdale the 'White House' and turned it into a notorious private member's club, which certainly not the pudding club variety, pardon the pun.

The place is still the White House but as a full blown, full-on pub, greatly extended under different ownership. To me, it will forever be Kirkdale. A warm, safe place of happy innocent childhood memories.

The move was a mixed blessing in the manner of the proverbial curate's egg. I missed Penwethers but West Hill School was OK and I soon made a few friends but missed my old ones back home. My country and comfort zone was to the North and West of Hensbarrow.

The thief

One day we were in woodwork. I was hopeless at it and frustrated. I just could not grasp even the basics, so foolishly I decided to cheat. I pinched another boy's piece of work. He was good at woodwork so I assumed he would just make another piece. Not so. There was a big inquest and naturally I got caught red handed.

The woodwork master, John Storey shook me and sent me to the headmaster called

'Archie Smith' who was a Bomber Command war hero and county cricket player. A very imposing figure of a man.

I was dying of shame at what I had done, wishing the ground would open up and swallow me. Mr Smith listened to my story and explained that theft was not on and would never be tolerated, but I think he realised that my frank confession and abject shame and contrition was punishment enough.

I had to face Mr Storey in future lessons, which was not easy for me knowing that I had betrayed his trust. Strangely, not having heard anything about him for 55 years, his son Nicolas, a retired barrister, turned up on Facebook in 2018 when we both commented on the same post and we got talking.

I told him the story of my misdeed and wondered if his father recalled it. He did and I was able to tender a proper apology which was willingly accepted. I was hoping to meet Mr Storey but he passed away before the chance arose. I did however, attend his funeral to pay my respects in appreciation of the salutary lesson that crime does not pay.

But the real lesson indelibly stamped in my psyche is that if you are prepared to commit any act always be equally prepared to face up to and accept the almost inevitable consequences of what you have done. For better or worse, mistakes do get made, but are halfway to solution if they are recognised, admitted and the consequences accepted.

The angler

My developing interest in fishing found an outlet through angling. Many disused clay pits were teeming with fish but the pools could be deep and dangerous so one had to be careful. The real bonus was that I was within cycling distance of Mevagissey and its pier which was a mecca for 'worm drowners' like me.

'Duchy Canners' as the name implies, canned pilchards and the waste was tipped off the end of the pier which attracted a lot of fish and the place used to teem with anglers. One day, I caught a 6lb 2oz mullet, which dangling from my bike handlebars attracted a lot of attention from people on the way home, making me very proud.

White Gold boom times

At home, my bedroom window looked out over St Austell Bay to Gribbin Head and there were the anchored coasters awaiting their slot to load in Par or Charlestown. Par had 14 berths and the average coaster was around 500 tons. So, if things went smoothly they could, when necessary, load 7,000 tons every 12 hours.

Clay came from the pits down pipelines to the dockside driers. It also came from inland driers like Blackpool, which was the first super pit in vast tonnages night and day by truck and rail. I remember seeing Blackpool driers being built by a company called 'Condor.' The

The angler

place was massive.

Palletisation was still in its infancy, so much of the vast tonnage was manually handled, often more than once. Father got a job loading railway wagons, which involved humping 2 cwt bags of clay from the conveyor into the truck. Twenty tons a shift was the relentless norm and the pay in 1961 was the princely sum of 12.5 pence, or in old money half a crown an hour - £1 a day.

Two seemingly mundane low tech elements that came from the invention of fork lift trucks were about to converge and change the face of cargo handling and international freight logistics for ever. These came in the form of palletisation and containerisation which lessened the need for men like my father to break their backs humping 2cwt sacks.

The penny dropped. The big money demanded skills or the right connections. The clay works were nepotistic and hierarchical albeit booming in the face of the exploding demand for kaolin products. Mr Bennetts was not in the know and given that he was not related to anyone unlikely to ever be.

Then he saw an advert by St Austell Rabbit Clearance Society for a trapper, as rabbits were coming back in the area. He applied and was accepted. The pay was better and he got a van supplied. After a few months, the group was wound up because, as is often the case, the government never came up with the promised funding so a job on the building sites was the only immediate option.

ECLP, the clay company, was so successful it was diversifying and having acquired Selleck Nicholls and Williams, a local volume builder, houses were going up everywhere. It all went well with decent wages while the weather was fine, but we were all anxious to return home, so Moorland House was put on the market and sold easily at a profit.

The big freeze of 1963

Around the same time, a lovely 23-acre holding on the outskirts of Threemilestone came on the market and a deal was done. Father bought Woodbine Farm. It was a good move at the right time and, at last, he had the farm he had always craved.

On New Year's Eve 1962, we all went to Glenlee's new house in Crantock. They had recently moved from the rented house in Tresean to a big house called 'St Andrews' on Vosporth Road, Crantock which would be a guest house once renovated and converted.

The weather was fine and dry and not unduly cold on the way down. After midnight when we left to return home to Trethurgy it was freezing, like iron. All the way back the windscreen was continually frosting over and the van did not have a heater. We eventually got back and the snow started while it froze hard for the next three months, which put a stop to the building work.

For Father, it was life on the dole and free school meals for my sister and me. It amazes me today what a performance it is to load children into cars and the bags of stuff that seem so vital to that process. In the time being described, we were just thrown in the back and told to sit down and be quiet.

Vehicle excise duty rules dictated that if a van had a passenger seat it was a higher tax rate so most lacked a passenger seat. In our case, Mother sat on a sturdy wooden egg crate and simply held tight on the premise that third class riding was infinitely preferable to first class walking.

Don't get me wrong, the safety advancements we have seen are excellent. Back in the day, we worked with what we had and the vast majority survived, but I cannot help thinking that the safer cars have become the faster they are driven so that when they crash, the outcome can be just as devastating.

In the meantime, my London grandfather died during February which was no real surprise, given the parlous state of his health and a lifetime's prodigious puffing of roll ups. It was a miracle that the old warrior had lasted so long. Mother managed to get up for the funeral despite the travel difficulties caused by the relentless deep snow. When she got home she had pleurisy and became very ill for a time.

Endless cold

As the days opened up, the cold remained relentless, the old adage, 'as the days get longer the cold gets stronger' was never more true. In late April, it was time to move home as a very slow thaw finally set in. Woodbine Farm had an orchard in full sunlight but on 1st of May that year the daffodils which had come up through snow were still surrounded by thawing splats of thick clear ice.

I clearly recall being in the metalwork period at West Hill at the time of the funeral. It was cold and grey and even inside the classroom it was freezing. I was thinking of Mother and the rest of the family united in grief in the biting cold, enduring the endless rites of a Catholic funeral.

A scary encounter with a priest

Over the years having attended many funerals I am convinced that a short, respectful, Methodist-style funeral is the answer for me. Even though I was baptised a Catholic, from an early age, something has told me that it is not for me. This stemmed from an unpleasant encounter with a nasty Catholic priest at my grandparent's London home when I was seven. My maternal grandparents lived at 5 Maynard Road, Lower Road, Bermondsey, London SE16, within a 100 yards of Surrey Docks, which mainly handled cargoes of timber with the scent of pine always in the air.

Lower Road, basically ran from Greenwich through Deptford to the Rotherhithe Tunnel and Tower Bridge, so was always very busy with trucks going to and from the docks.

They occupied a lovely yellow brick, Victorian, terraced house in a row, with a useful back garden that had survived the saturation bombing of the docks, although about ten doors down the terrace ended in a recently cleared bombsite.

Mother used to try to see her parents every year and they, and her brothers and sisters, would often spend their holidays with us, but on this occasion, we travelled up to Paddington on the iconic Cornish Riviera. Mother took a taxi from Paddington to Surrey Docks which had her worrying about the cost. Having arrived, her younger brother Peter, paid for the cab.

When we got inside the house the Parish priest was present collecting his tribute in brown envelopes and remonstrating with Mother's younger brother Mick for not contributing enough. He then enquired who Mother was and she bit her lip in terror of this cadaverous, austere monster as Granny explained, almost apologetically, that it was her eldest daughter up from Cornwall with her children.

Then the monster turned his attention toward me and squinting through rimless glasses he said, "and what of the boy, is he of the faith?" Mother said "yes Father." "I see," the monster replied, "and does he attend a Catholic school?" "No Father," mother replied on the verge of tears, (the monster was obviously incapable of deducing that Catholic schools were a bit thin on the ground in the Duchy). "I see," he retorted, obviously used to having the last word. "Baptised a Catholic and reared a pagan!"

By now Mother was in tears and her bottom lip was bleeding where she had bitten it in a mixture of terror and anger at this appalling treatment. I don't know where I found the courage because he terrified me but I just blurted out, "don't you dare talk to my mother like that!" and kicked the nasty old bastard hard in the shin because I would do anything to protect her as she would me.

Hot stuff

The situation was saved by descending into the farcical as a very loud, very piercing scream of extreme distress shattered the stunned silence. Everyone rushed from the sitting room into the kitchen which seemed to be the source of the commotion which if anything, was intensifying.

My baby sister's face was purple and she was dribbling what seemed to be yellow gunge. Panic set in because Grandfather's many tablets were stacked on the table.

But on further investigation, Marie was pointing at the mustard pot and her fingers were thick with the stuff. She soon got over it and has never touched mustard since.

Not of the faith for sure

The monster had seized the opportunity, as is the manner of all bullies, to escape in the face of superior odds.

I shudder to think how that awful priest treated his altar boys, and even more to think how the institution he represented turned a blind eye to priestly misdeeds for so long. In my humble opinion, any system of belief based on fear rather than love and respect can never be right. Give me my own simple, do–it–yourself, conscience-based form of belief any day.

Conscience is a strange abstract and I strongly suspect that it is intimately linked with karma, insofar as your deeds follow you around and either bless you or bite you. I am convinced that you manufacture your own luck by your own actions and equally your own despair and depression if you allow the malign maggot of a bad conscience to gnaw away at your thought processes.

In a similar respect, gut instinct seems to be linked to a sense of déjà vu, insofar as I often get a strong sense that I have been somewhere totally unfamiliar to me before. Some places seem to make the hair on the back of your neck prickle, while others such as Geor, where I am now so fortunate to live, exude an air of almost womb-like comfort and security.

I strongly believe in the concept of a guardian angel. Many times, particularly at sea when conscious of the danger, I have been aware of a presence, impossible to clearly articulate other than sensing an invisible, kindly hand on your shoulder willing you to do whatever necessary to prevail even though you might, in truth, actually be scared witless, the trick being never to show it.

If my schooling and parenting did nothing else it taught me the important distinction between right and wrong and life experience has dictated that those witnessing great wrong but who choose to remain silent for their own security are as guilty as the actual perpetrator of that wrong. To me they are beneath contempt, wilfully perjured individuals who are devoid of all moral worth.

That said, as I know from experiences where I did not choose to remain silent, you can place yourself in an incredibly lonely and dangerous place where vested interests are the mortal enemy and the shield of truth must be your impregnable, indeed only, defence if you are to ultimately prevail. On a more secular level, you need a bloody good lawyer and they are not cheap.

But those episodes occurred much later.

The quote 'there is a very thin line between confidence and arrogance, where confidence smiles, while arrogance smirks,' springs to mind when attempting to define wrongdoing. I would suggest that almost without exception, greed is the catalyst, with arrogance as its nasty outcome.

A little humility never goes amiss to tone things down by keeping everything within due bounds.

Authority is another matter entirely. The ability to quietly control and influence the best outcomes without undue fuss or drama is a gift in scarce supply. That is true leadership.

Chapter 3
Teenage rampage

The spotty phase

I often shudder to think how, as a teenager, I was so bolshy and aggressive yet struggling with extreme shyness and a lack of confidence. My father was always prone to tell me how useless I was, something that at the time I vowed I would never inflict on my own children.

However, in his own inimitable way he was incentivising me and, painful as it was to me at the time, it actually worked insofar as I developed the mindset that *'I will show you.'* He never said the two words I so desperately wanted to hear; to his dying day, he never said, "well done" to me.

An honest man gives me closure

At his funeral one of his mates came up to me as we walked away from the grave and said "do you realise how proud he was of you?" Then he handed me a small, heavy felt bag containing a round object. He went on, "he bought this from me months back but never came back to pick it up so you had better have it instead."

I opened the bag and it contained a beautiful, solid gold pocket watch which I still treasure to this day and at that moment a vision came to me of him puffing on his pipe saying with that characteristic twinkle in his eye, "you didn't do so bad after all boy, well done."

That simple bit of total honesty was profound. It would have been so easy for that man with the watch to say nothing and keep it, which on the weight of gold alone is worth a pretty penny. With no one being any the wiser, it actually gave me the closure I so badly needed on exactly the right day.

Back at Penwethers

Telling this story, I am beginning to realise how easy it is to digress, so onwards and upwards we must go.

The second period at Penwethers sped by. Coming back at 14 after a two-year absence involved re-establishing your place in the pecking order which was not straightforward.

My grandmother had died suddenly and unexpectedly from a massive aortic embolism and Mother was distraught. Again, she had to go up to London for the funeral. Due to 'slum clearance,' Granny had been moved out of her lovely little house with its back garden which she deeply missed and onto the 10th floor of the new tower block the council had dumped her in which was just around the corner. She never really got over it.

At school I was being bullied by a pair of little scrotes, the ringleader of whom was a scouser boy who for a time terrorised me because I was daft enough to let him. At home, Mother sensed what was going on and spoke to Father about it. Father being a staunch advocate of the 'eye for an eye/tooth for a tooth' philosophy, his entirely predictable response was "stand up for yourself."

A day or two later things came to a head when the two came up to me at morning break time in the corner of the yard. The scouser kid jabbed me in the ribs. I had my back to the wall so the only way out was to advance. I shoved him backwards hard with both hands on his shoulders which caught him completely off guard. One more hard shove and he was on his arse in the middle of the yard.

The red mist came down and I leapt on him straddling him and raining jabs at his face till it was a mess of blood and snot. His howling brought two teachers running over to pull me off while the crowd that gathered cheered.

One of my biggest failings has always been the inability to balance reactions, being either too hard or too soft. However, on that particular occasion, the hard option was the right option and devastatingly effective. The two nasty little bullies were a snivelling, and in one case, bloodied, busted flush who slunk away into playground oblivion.

I was sent to the headmaster's study to explain myself. He understood but obviously could not condone what I did so I ended up with a detention, which was well worth it because I never got bullied at school again. It turned out that the one I had pasted and his pathetic little sidekick had been terrorising several others. The bullying had stopped forthwith.

John Jefferies

There was one boy called 'John Jefferies' who was universally known as 'JJ.' He was dark-featured with jam-jar glasses and he became very ill. We were told in assembly that he had a rare form of cancer and was not going to survive however, survive he did and has lived with the disease ever since. A truly remarkable remission.

One day, we were in English and Mrs James set an essay. Pretending we were reporters, we had to write a newspaper report on a sporting event of our choice. JJ wasn't really interested and within a couple of minutes he put his pen down having finished.

This exasperated Mrs James who told him to bring his work to her. She looked at it and frowned. There were four words in total; the headline was, 'CRICKET' and the story read, 'RAIN STOPPED PLAY.' Mrs James was furious but had no answer to it. JJ had written what he was told to. It was clear, concise, complete, correct and, much to everyone's amusement, JJ got away with it.

Many years later at Trevithick Day several of us were chatting with JJ when the Mayor of

Camborne came along. JJ said, "watch this," then, going up to the Mayor he said, "good afternoon Sir, if I were to pull your chain would you flush?"

The Mayor was a good sport and saw the funny side of it, but when the irrepressible JJ is around you're never quite sure what the bugger will come out with next. He is honorary entertainments officer in our circle.

I learned some powerful lessons; firstly, all bullies are cowards who must be faced down, secondly, never to submit to threats or blackmail and thirdly, to always fight your own corner, alone if necessary, but, above all if you have no alternative but to fight, then fight to win with every fibre of your being.

A double execution

We used to go fishing off Dynamite Quay at Newham for schoolie bass and flounders. For a time, two blokes used to turn up on a motorbike and sidecar with really poor rods and they never caught anything. One used to chat to us a bit and it seems he was from St Keverne but lived at Kenwyn Hill caravan site. The other one seemed shifty and never said much, then they suddenly stopped coming.

There had been a vicious murder of an elderly reclusive bachelor farmer called 'William Rowe' at Nanjarrow Farm, Constantine during August 1964. He had apparently been in hiding since he deserted during WW1 and was reputed to have a hoard of money hidden away.

It transpired that the pair, who had not been seen anymore at Dynamite Quay, were Russell Pascoe and Dennis Whitty who had been arrested, charged and convicted of the capital murder of William Rowe. It emerged in court that Pascoe had once worked for William Rowe.

Both blamed each other but both were sentenced to death at Bodmin Assizes. Pascoe was executed at Bristol on the 17th December 1964 and Whitty, at Winchester the same time. The recollection of this still sends a shudder down my spine to this day.

The Youth Employment Officer

It was time to think about a career and I knew exactly what I wanted to do. My year was the first to take the new-fangled CSE exam. I took seven subjects getting five grade ones, one grade two and a predictable grade five in maths. I cannot honestly say that those exams ever did me much good though.

Careers matters involved being interviewed by Mr Gribbin, the Youth Employment Officer. Mother attended looking worried as usual while Mr Duggan sat in, picking at his fingernails with his thumb.

Pleasantries exchanged the first obvious question was, "what do you want to do?" I replied,

From l-r: Mike Morris (partly obscured), John Manley (Penwartha House), Jimmy Skewes (Manor Farm Penwartha), JJ and me (pulling a face). Pictured at a vintage tractor day at Lambriggan, Perranporth in 2019

"I want to be a fisherman" to which the exasperated reply was, "boys from your background don't do that, how about plumbing?" (they must have been short of plumbers that year).

By this time my attention had drifted to a tractor working in a field in the middle distance and my reputation as an awkward customer was obviously growing, confirmed by the frown from the headmaster directing his steely gaze at me. In the end, a compromise was agreed that I would go to the then, Camborne Technical College, on the City and Guilds Stage One Course in Farm Management.

Little did I know that several years hence Mr Gribbin would re-enter my life in a completely unforeseen, life-changing manner but once again more of that later.

Eric Duggan

By now there was a new headmaster called 'Eric Duggan.' He was a short, wiry, Welshman probably under five feet six tall with the most piercing blue eyes that burned right through you. He had been a Colonel in the Chindits in Malaya during the war and his health had suffered badly during his time as a prisoner of the Japanese.

At around six foot I was head and shoulders above him in height however, despite his stature, you did not mess with Mr Duggan. He used to silently stalk the school corridors in his grey suit, hands clasped behind his back, waiting to pounce on any miscreant he happened to chance upon.

Gangly, spotty, teenage hooligans were no match for Mr Duggan and he would grab them by the bottom of their tie and, hand over hand, yank them down to his diminutive level holding the tie in a vice-like grip while wagging his right finger in strict admonition at the hapless boy.

If the gravity of the situation warranted it he would, without a second thought, drag them to his study for six of the best, but it would almost certainly have been a more than fair cop.

He might have been fierce and an absolutely rigid disciplinarian but underneath all that fierceness he was a kind, passionate and dedicated teacher who I thank for kindling my passion for classical music. A man who even today in my memory I regard with great respect and affection.

One hilarious incident involved a boy who had raided the bathroom cabinet at home and taken his father's industrial-size box of Durex to school. He opened one up in class and the girls were tittering but the teacher never cottoned on. We were on the second floor and at break time he went into the boy's toilets at the top of the stairs and filled one with water before tying it like a balloon.

Then the idiot leaned over the stairwell and dropped it. Splat! It narrowly missed Mr Duggan who was passing on the ground floor on his way to the staff room. He came up the stairs at record speed, three steps at a time and homed in on the culprit for whom it did not end well. There were some other hilarious anecdotes that I recall too.

The Emmet family

I wanted a wristwatch but had no money. Robert Emmet, a classic Coombe Kaffir and a classmate had an older brother who went to sea on BP tankers. Whenever he got home on leave both his arms were always full of watches under his sleeves to get them past the Revenue men.

Tom Emmet was Robert's father, a part time trapper and fisherman who drove a black Austin Somerset car whose boot in summer was always loaded with lobster bait. It would be followed by a posse of flies. On Wednesdays it was often found parked outside the Market Inn on Truro's Lemon Quay complete with flies.

Robert's mother was Conway Bailey's sister. They lived at Trelease above Coombe on the road to Higher Trelease and the Tolverne foot ferry.

In the run up to D Day, Conway was 14 and carting dung with a horse and cart at Higher

Trelease when he came upon a parked American military jeep. One man was in a dark boiler suit and smoked a cigar whilst the other wore an American army officer's uniform. They were looking down at the river through binoculars. Young Conway thought they might be spies. But it turned out to be Winston Churchill and General Dwight D Eisenhower who were checking progress on D Day preparations around the area. They both shook Conway's hand thanking him for helping in the war effort on the farm. That was quite a claim to fame, (Conway Bailey figures again later in this story), small world is it not?

The ferret deal

Robert Emmet wanted a ferret and had even less money than me so, we had a deal on our hands. I took a lovely little white ferret to school in a drawstring canvas bag which was the way it was done... I soon became the proud owner of a watch and Robert had his ferret - a classic 'win, win' deal.

We were in physics when the bag under the bench began to move. This was spotted by Carol Mufford, the nosiest girl in the school who was sitting next to me at the time. I opened the bag to tease her and out popped a dear little pink nose. Carol shrieked loudly alerting Mr Herbert the physics teacher.

Mr Herbert used to keep order with a chair leg with which he slammed on his desk to obtain our attention. As the class was in uproar, he demanded to know what was going on. "Nothing sir" did not cut the mustard. He knew full well something was going on and he intended finding out what it was.

He demanded to see what I had back there. I went up to his desk with the bag containing the ferret which he grabbed from me as I tried to explain what was in there in case he got bitten, but too late, he had already opened it and stuck his hand inside. There was a roar of shock and pain as he pulled his hand out with the ferret firmly latched onto his finger.

Mr Herbert was not amused. I managed to catch the poor ferret and put it back in the bag before I was sent off to explain myself to Mr Duggan in full expectation of six of the best. While he tried hard not to look amused, the Head obviously saw the funny side of the situation.

I was highly relieved when he not unexpectedly pronounced that ferrets were banned forthwith, "now get back to your class and behave yourself Bennetts." That really was a close call, but I had got the watch that I wanted.

A near miss... literally

Another time as a prank, we stuffed a large spud that had been dropped by the canteen door up the exhaust pipe of Mrs James, our English teacher's, Singer Gazelle car. When the last bell went we were out waiting for the bus home as Mrs James tried to start her car which wasn't having any of it due to the blocked exhaust.

A flat battery was diagnosed by another teacher who organised volunteers to give Mrs James a push. The school drive was slightly downhill so the car rolled well. Third gear was engaged, Mrs James let the clutch out and the car stuttered. There was a loud pop, like a muffled explosion as the spud shot out like a cannonball narrowly missing Mr Duggan who, true to form, had sensed mischief.

He went ape but just for once was powerless. He didn't have a shred of evidence apart from a seriously mangled spud and no one knew anything which was just as well because I reckon blue murder would have been committed if he found out who did it.

The Prefecture

For the life of me and I can't think why but during the last year I was made a prefect. We were allowed to dish out a hundred lines as a sanction and were all guilty at times of abusing this authority. I had dished out a hundred to a Perran boy called 'Bobby Trevail' for 'lipping me.' Bobby was short and fiery. He didn't say a word, he just lamped me one right on the chin and nearly lifted me off the deck.

It actually served me right because I realise now that I was being a complete prick and I got exactly what I deserved. Bobby is still going strong, running a very smart fleet of tipper trucks and diggers. At seventy he still turns out occasionally to play a charity game of rugby for the Bolingey Barbarians. We always laugh about the incident when we meet. The lesson here being; *'you sometimes get exactly what you asked for and it is not always the size of the dog in the fight but rather the amount of fight in the dog that inevitably prevails.'*

I won a school prize for English and another for Geography which were presented by 'Sir Alan Dalton,' the managing director of clay giant, ECLP. Sir Alan was another inspirational character. A great egalitarian who valued the people who worked for the huge company which at that time was a beacon of Cornish industrial success.

The books I chose were 'Coasting Barge Master' by Bob Roberts and the 'Quest of the Schooner Argus' by Alan Villiers.

Sir Alan Dalton was another character destined to re-appear later in this story.

Out into the world

The last day at Penwethers was strangely emotional. The one advantage of being pigeon holed as a Catholic was that you did not have to go into assembly until the very end - just to hear the announcements. But that final day was different because we were leaving and some of us were never going to see each other again.

Mr Duggan in his gown was impressive. He made a short, impassioned speech that put a lump in many throats, mine included. He said "friends, you are leaving here today to continue your lives and I wish you every success in whatever you choose to do. I am not going to lecture you but let me try to define success for you… success is being where you want to be, doing whatever you choose to do at whatever level you choose to do it at. As long as you do the very best you can, no one can ask more of you, that truly is success. God bless you all, goodbye and good luck."

With those amazing words ringing in my ears I walked out of school into the wider world that awaited me.

An agricultural student and an enduring friendship

Life as an agricultural student was good. We were treated as adults and generally we responded accordingly. There were, dare I say, the first signs of adulthood as callow, spotty youths who a few months ago were at the caterpillar stage, began to pupate into proper adults. Heaven alone knew what might eventually emerge but for certain it would not be butterflies.

I had made friends with Bruce Christoper, a Scillonian from Tresco, where his parents grew flowers and new potatoes on 23 acres at Borough Farm. Bruce wanted to work on the mainland but his father needed a worker so I jumped at the offer of a summer job lifting bulbs.

Tresco

It was strange going across on the Scillonian. It was my first time properly away from home for real. When I got to Tresco Quay in bright warm sunshine my new boss, Frank Christopher was waiting with his Ford Dexta tractor and trailer. We shook hands and he loaded the box of meat and a couple of bags of poultry corn that had arrived on the same boat for him from St Mary's.

His youngest son, nine-year old Ritchie, was with him and spent the trip back to Borough looking me up and down in an unnerving manner as he quizzically sized me up. I must have passed muster as he turned out to be a great kid who I remain in touch with to this day. After an apprenticeship as an agricultural engineer with 'TF Hosking' he returned to Scilly to work for the Steamship Company.

The rest of his career was with the South Western Electricity Board and latterly with Western Power Distribution where he managed the power station on St Mary's.

Off we went toward Borough. The trip was interesting insofar as there was no actual road up over what I learned was Middle Downs which was a short cut. We rocked and rolled our way across the downs through giant Monterey pines planted as windbreaks over a century before.

Eventually we emerged behind a substantial granite farmhouse and just past that was Borough. A glorious vista opened up out over the Eastern Isles and St Martin's round to Tean,

Bruce Christopher R.I.P (left). Frank Christopher (top right), who was my first boss on Tresco. Frank's wife, Beatrice Christopher (lower image).

Round Island topped with its white lighthouse to St Helen's and Men a Vaur with the small Islands in the foreground.

It was Saturday and dinner was on the table. Meat pie and veg with rhubarb crumble and cream for afters. There was gorgeous cream on the table for every meal and food fit for a king. It was obvious that Mrs Beatrice Christopher was one hell of a cook.

I was shown my bedroom with its window looking out directly at Round Island. That night and every night, the red beam of the light traced its arc around the walls if the blind was left up. If a big ground sea was running you could hear the rumbling roar of the fearsome Kettle Shoals and Golden Ball Bar breaking.

They kept three Guernseys for milk. Good scopey sorts on the thinnish side as proper Guernseys often are. Just before tea Frank went out to milk. He just took a stool and a bucket, went up to the first cow, sat down and started milking away. I did the same to show willing. The cow just standing there chewing her cud. All went fine till I was nearly finished when she walked off putting her foot in the bucket on the way.

I was worried about what Frank would say but he just laughed and said, "that old bugger does that sometimes." He took the bucket from me and tipped the spoilt milk into the trough in the pig sty where a porker was being fattened.

Sunday was free apart from milking, separating the cream and feeding the pig and chickens. Come Monday, after milking, there was an early breakfast of cream-topped Cornflakes followed by bacon and eggs. Breakfast done, Frank got the tractor out and off we went down to the fields. Borough was like an amphitheatre all in a bowl overlooked by the house and buildings.

Work (if you could call it that)

There was never any rush or tear. Stress was an alien concept but we still got through a lot of mostly fascinating work.

The first job was to cut some maize grown for the cows and fed green. It was like rocket fuel making the milk golden and creamy. While I was doing this Frank fetched the cows down after putting a loop of chain around their horns. Each one was tethered on a chain held by an iron pin hammered into the ground.

Next, Frank fetched Prince, a great skewbald horse of uncertain breed but nearly 17 hands and hitched him into the single furrow plough left at the end of a row where work had finished on Friday. We were lifting Soleil Dors which are the definitive Scillonian-scented narcissi variety.

Sols were grown in rows and in beds on the flat, unlike other varieties grown in ridges and lifted regularly, sols were left in the ground for years unless showing signs of disease. The plough turned up one row at a time when we would start raking them out of the comb and pile them on the ground in windrows to dry out before being picked up into net bags to be taken to the steriliser.

It was a pantomime to see Frank and Prince performing. It did not take long to suss out that the horse was underworked and overfed and loved playing a game with Frank, who was obviously more fond of the nag than he would ever care to admit.

He would align the plough in the vore saying "steady boy steady there", with the horse prancing around before taking off at a cracking pace with Frank hanging onto the plough handles like grim death shouting "steady, steady you bloody thing whoa!" While the horse was all the time trying to speed up until the end of the row where he would stand quiet as a mouse before ambling back to the start again and standing there nibbling grass until we had done the row.

At 10.30 a jug of weakish tea and some cake or flapjacks would be brought down to us for crib by Mary Birch the cleaning lady. If it rained we would crouch behind one of the escalonia or pittosporum shelter hedges which doubled up as emergency fodder for the cows in dry times. Beatrice would spend most of her time gardening, or sewing if wet, when not cooking.

Borough Garden and burning the sols

The garden at Borough was incredible. Not that big but an absolute riot of colour and form amongst huge flat granite outcrops. It had the tallest Echiums I have ever seen, great mauve spikes dancing in the breeze buzzing with bees and other insects.

Clumps of agapanthus, mesembryanthemums and later on, nerines and naked ladies, (better known as 'bella donnas') to name but a few put in their appearance. As such, the eclectic garden was rarely without colour. Her vegetable patch in the field below was the same – chaotic but richly productive.

Beatrice was another former Land Girl who ended up in Tresco Abbey Gardens where she met Frank, the eldest of three brothers, when he returned home after six years away in the army. Beatrice was a convent school girl, the daughter of a wealthy Harrogate tailor's shop owner and she was gorgeously eccentric and was often seen smoking a corn cob pipe while riding her bike to the island shop.

So many Land Girls turned up from every corner of the country and many stayed on after the war marrying Cornish men which must have really enriched our gene pool giving lie to the slander that the Cornish are 'nothing but a bunch of inbred retards.' One hears all too often from ignorant incomers with serious chips on their shoulders.

Dinner times we would go up about 12:30 and after eating, Frank would usually have a snooze while we listened to the news at one. As he dozed off there would be a sort of click and Frank's false teeth would appear on his tongue. Beatrice would tut a couple of times and yell "oh Frank!" He would wake with a start, retract his teeth and that would be the signal to get going again.

The sol patches that were not being lifted were covered with dry bracken cut the previous autumn on the bank between the fields and Rushy Bay and stored in a rick over the winter. The spread bracken was lit and left to burn out, taking great care to avoid the fire spreading to the hedges.

This burn controlled weeds, enriched the soil with the potash from the ashes and encouraged the bulbs to flower earlier.

My hatred of Allen Scythes

The ferns used to burn the sol patches were cut by a fiendish contraption called an 'Allen Scythe,' consisting of a reciprocating cutter bar about three feet wide. It was self-propelled by a Villiers engine, driving two, big narrow wheels and steered by two handles at the rear.

It was a sturdy bit of kit but the Villiers two stroke engine was incredibly unreliable being difficult to start and near impossible to restart when hot. Starting involved winding a piece of rope with a knot in the end that went into a notch in a pulley wheel on the end of the crankshaft. After setting the choke and tickling the carburettor, a sharp pull on the rope might produce a pop.

Repeated pulls often resulted in a whack on the ear from the knot and further pops. Frayed tempers were guaranteed, but eventually the thing would burst into life, rattling and shaking. You then had to be very careful that it didn't jump into gear before you could grab the handles and take control.

Once in control you could start cutting – being very careful not to end up in a rabbit hole when the thing would rear up and start trying to cut you in half as it gyrated around. It was hard work and I hated the thing with a passion.

God alone knows why but they are now sought after, collector's items. For me, the only good Allen Scythe is a crushed one.

A very social life

The social life was amazing. Outside of the working day, Frank had a 20-foot fishing boat called the 'Naida' which was built by the Thomas Yard in St Ives in 1939. It cost £100 and was in typical Hake style. It was powered by the original legendary 7 Kelvin petrol paraffin engine. In the evenings we worked half a dozen pots off Gimble Point out across to Pipers Hole with varying degrees of success. Some nights we would do the pots then go after mackerel and Pollack using feathers or patent baits between Round Island and the Black Rock Ledges. Supper on those nights would be boiled mackerel with bread and butter instead of the usual cheese and crackers.

The pub was lively with island regulars and there were discos in the Reading Room at the top of Towns Hill. Occasionally, a boat would do a trip down to St Mary's for the pictures.

I got paid £5 a week and my keep and managed to save £1 a week. It's just as well that Frank didn't realise that I would have paid him £5 a week to work there in that lovely place.

Inexorable changes destroy an island community

In those days, Tresco was a thriving community with a large estate farm and a cracking herd of about 60 fine Guernseys as well as the flowers and early potatoes that provided a lot of employment. Around this time, growers on the mainland started to grow first early potatoes under polythene. This soon robbed Scilly of its early climate advantage while the Cornish economies of scale and the ever-rising freight charges to send the crop over to the mainland finally killed the early potato job on Scilly.

This was very interesting because in the Channel Islands, the Jersey Royal potato became a strong, high quality brand which saw its continuing popularity with consumers ensure its continuance unlike the unbranded Scilly potatoes.

There was also the upmarket exclusive Island Hotel that employed a lot of staff, but it was all beginning to change even then as the workers were going and the vacated tied cottages were being turned into mega-expensive, time shares.

I first fell in love on Tresco although the beautiful, slim, dark-haired maid in question didn't know it because I was too shy to say. She later turned up living at Mingoose near St Agnes after her widowed mother was required to quit the shop she had been running on Tresco - which became yet another holiday let.

We had a brief, lovely teenage affair before she left for teacher training college and thlast I heard was that she had married a trainee Tesco Manager. Hey ho... I learned that you cannot win them all and a faint heart never won a fair lady.

Frank and Beatrice retired early to Lelant where they transformed their large garden into a little piece of Tresco in Cornwall. They enjoyed many happy years there.

Bruce married Maggie Harris from Newlyn East and returned home to take over Borough where they converted the former flower packing sheds into lovely holiday lets and enjoyed forty wonderful years together. I was very proud to be their best man as Bruce was mine.

Bruce and Maggie took the plunge when they got an EU grant to put up a proper modern farm shed that freed up the old buildings for conversion in addition to the wooden chalet which was their first home before Frank and Beatrice retired. This gave them another string to Boroughs' bow.

Freight charges pile on the pressure

The flower trade was also being killed by the horrendous freight costs that were involved. The Julians, an enterprising family at Highertown Farm on St Martin's, had the simple but brilliant idea of sending individual gift boxes of flowers by post. Bypassing the middle men, Borough became a main supplier.

This involved picking and bunching the flowers as usual but all that had to be done next was to ship them across to St Martin's for a very fair, fixed price and a major cut in crippling overheads for boxes, freight and sales commission.

Time and time again it has been the innovative but simple business concepts that emerge from a bit of lateral thinking that prove to be the winners. Necessity truly is the mother of invention and that almost invariably involves the courage to dare to think outside of the box and be different.

The loss of a friend and the end of an era

One awful summer day in July 2013, I was at work when I had a phone call. Unusually for Bruce it was in the afternoon. He was very emotional and calling from Treliske Hospital where, out of the blue, he had just been diagnosed with terminal pancreatic cancer and given just six months to live.

That evening we went for a walk around the hospital grounds and had a very difficult conversation. I have had considerable experience of loss and tragedy over the years but what the hell do you say to a dear friend in that awful situation? I didn't know, so we just talked and talked about everything including death.

Over the next six months I watched him pass through disbelief, optimism, anger, fear, despair and finally resignation as we said our last goodbye when nothing more could be done.

He returned home to die on Scilly as a broken husk of his former self almost six months to the day from diagnosis.

Bruce passed away in the little hospital on St Mary's. His two brothers and his two sons rowed him in his coffin home to Tresco in the bow of a gig named 'Czar' which he had rowed in his prime.

It was a very emotional picture but the job was done properly according to time-honoured Scillonian tradition when the gigs were proper working boats crewed by hard men in blue jerseys rather than the performance-obsessed, competitive fanatics in garish lycra and gloves that seem to have hijacked them today… but that's progress for you!

Newquay's 'Old School' gig rowers sum it up perfectly in their song that that goes like this; 'Newquay Boys get drunk you see, beer for breakfast, dinner and tea, blisters on yer hands and blisters on yer arse, don't go catch another crab,' it goes on but that bit gives a flavour of the real gritty, original gig culture that can still be found in the NRC Clubhouse of a Sunday afternoon.

I have often pondered the question, 'why do the good get taken too soon?' My only comfort is the certainty that everything happens for a reason even if we cannot comprehend it at the time.

The funeral on Tresco

The funeral was difficult. I flew over from Newquay Airport on the first morning flight. I was seriously underwhelmed at being treated like a criminal by the jobsworths that worked there. I have arthritis in my feet and ankles and the cold and damp was not helping the discomfort I was in or given the occasion, my usual sense of good humour.

Having been instructed to remove my shoes twice by separate officious little twerps, the final straw came when I forgot to remove my Breton cap to pass through the body scanner. The metal tags in it triggered the scanner bringing a sub machine gun-toting policeman rushing over waving the bloody thing at me.

Given the sombre, pensive mood I was in and my zero tolerance of bullshit default setting, I like to think that the icy stare I gave that young copper without uttering a single word caused him to appreciate how very close he had just come to having his gun inserted firmly into that dark place where the sun never shines.

I know security is safety related and important but come on guys… Newquay is a small regional airport and we were local people boarding a short local flight without baggage and in a cabin where the pilots sat directly in front of us rather than hermetically sealed in a separate compartment.

The way we were being treated was beyond unacceptable. What the hell did they think any potential hi jacker would do, crash it into one of the many SEF (Southern England Farms) broccoli rigs working like grazing dinosaurs in the nearby fields?

Apparently, there was a security exercise going on to train people from other airports but all they had to do was say so. I was not the only one who was seriously upset and the outcome was that the airport management were subsequently summoned to St Mary's to explain themselves. Some good did eventually result because there has been a marked improvement in attitude at OUR airport since.

The funeral was a sombre affair and unusual to me as the coffin had already been brought to the church when it had arrived back on Tresco. Mourners turned up and sat down and finally the close family came in and the service got under way.

I left right after not wishing to hang around as there was no reason for me to be there any longer. Catching the boat back to St Mary's the weather closed in and all flights were cancelled so those of us over for the day were marooned.

I was billeted for the night by Skybus in a guest house in Old Town but there was no food as they were actually closed for the winter so I had to walk into Hugh Town in unsuitable shoes in soft drizzle that soon made you wet only to find that I was too late for food there as well. Today, Scilly can be an inhospitable place in the off season.

I was very glad to be on a flight out the following morning tired, hungry and footsore. But the sun was shining and I was sitting on the starboard side looking down on my beautiful North Coast which was being kissed by a glittering blue sea in the breezy aftermath of yesterday's blow.

The Christopher family live at Borough no more and the lovely holiday complex they developed was coveted by the Tresco Estate who despite a secured tenancy with a lifetime left to run, applied pressure for the family to quit.

In the end the tenancy was bought out by Tresco Estate and the family moved to Cornwall. This marked the end of an era as the very last Islander tenants left Tresco – the final act of attrition in the sterilisation of a once vibrant, traditional, island community.

I want to remember that beautiful island and its tight-knit community as it was and I cannot see a reason for ever wanting to return.

Chapter 4
Back to mainland Cornwall and an introduction to fishing

Home to Woodbine Farm for a while

Back home to life on the farm and reality after the amazing summer on Tresco, we were making a living and expanding. Government policy was encouraging small farms to modernise and we had our own advisor assigned to us and a few of the other small farms in our valley.

We were owner-occupiers but many of the other holdings locally were owned by Tregothnan Estate and rented out. Many of the tenants were on the first rung of the farming ladder while young families were being reared on them and the countryside was looking good.

An enduring memory on a still morning being the sound of milk churn lids being knocked off ready to be filled or the rattle of churns on the Milk Marketing Board truck that collected the churns which were left on stands for collection at the end of most farm lanes.

The beauty of milking despite the relentless tie was that there was a guaranteed, regular monthly income via the milk cheque. With the housekeeping being covered by the income from egg and turnip sales at the gate, the Friday market held by Richards Son and Murdoch used to pay cash, so calves not wanted for rearing and litters of store pigs generally went there.

Dairy herds were small, in keeping with the small size of the farms typically averaging 20 or 30 acres. We milked 12 cows, kept around ten saddleback sows crossed with a landrace boar. We also grew 4 or 5 acres of swedes cutting the best to sell locally and fed the rest to the cows.

A couple of Shire x Welsh Cob brood mares producing thoroughbred cross foals which always found a ready trade, completed the mixed picture. The brood mares were served by stallions under the 'Horse Improvement Society Scheme.' The stallions Father used were owned by Jimmy Snell who was actually the baker in Breage. 'Arthur Sullivan' was the name of one stallion that springs to mind. Another was 'Abergwiffy' owned by the Le Grice's of Trereiffe. These fine stallions put Cornwall on the map as the top notch foals always found a ready market at the Horse Improvement Society's regular show and sales which was at Hereford Racecourse and was conducted by auctioneers Russell Baldwin and Bright.

One particularly fine two-year old colt by Arthur Sullivan was perfect in almost every respect except that he would not load. Loading was an essential element in the turnout of these

71

animals for sale and had to be taught. This particular young man just walked up to the bottom of the ramp and froze every time. It became a battle of wills which Father intended winning, and he had a rarely resorted to using the ace up his sleeve which he called the *'gypsy remedy.'*

The boy was standing placidly at the foot of the ramp absolutely refusing to step onto it. Everything else had been tried but to no avail. However, he had to be persuaded – not forced so sticks and whips were not an option which others might have resorted to in similar circumstances. Father put his hand in his pocket and got out his baccy pouch. Biting off a big piece of brown roll, he put it in his mouth before chewing it to a revolting looking pulp which he then rolled into a gooey ball in the palm of his hand. Gently patting the colt down, carefully standing to one side, he lifted the tail and inserted the baccy ball where the sun never ever shines. There were quick hints of agitation, an almighty buck and the colt quietly walked up the ramp on a slack rope where he stood doing what could best be described as an equine twerk.

Patting him down, Father whispered something in the colt's ear and gently removed the source of his obvious discomfort. The problem was solved and from then on it was possible to let go of the halter at the foot of the ramp when he would walk calmly into the lorry.

Later at Hereford, the beautiful colt made top dollar being bought by the wife of the Queen's portrait painter who had spotted him coming out of the lorry and took an immediate fancy to him. She enquired his name and Father, on the spur of the moment, replied "Profit, Mrs…" and 'Profit' he became henceforth.

Not long after this, the chance came to rent another farm with a modern, 4 abreast milking parlour, large covered yard and 30 more acres. It started well and we were milking 30 cows with plans for a bulk milk tank. There were two tractors; a Massey 135 and a brand new 165 and I was doing the odd bit of tractor work for others.

To expand, father had been buying freshly calved cows at market but one of them had 'contagious abortion' (a type of brucellosis which causes spontaneous abortion in cattle). This was not good and soon several cows were slipping their calves. Government policy also shifted and suddenly small farms were not wanted anymore.

The writing was on the wall for another piece of our rural fabric as the winds of change blasted the valley of the River Tinney and its several small farms. But it was not just us, it was happening everywhere.

Looking back at those times today it is interesting to ponder and compare the social benefits of several small farms to a parish – all keeping families and local suppliers in business in contrast to the current situation, where it is not unusual for one mega farm to occupy, in extremis, several parishes.

Is it possible that inefficiency actually had its social advantages?

The 'Michael and David'

I had been pestering my cousin Mike Rowse, who skippered a 36-foot former Breton crabber called the 'Michael and David' for W Harvey & Sons, the shellfish merchants in Newlyn for a job. I was out in the Railway Field at Woodbine ploughing when Mother came out across the field to say that Mike had rung and if I wanted the job to be ready in half an hour.

I gathered up my oilers and boots, a change of clothes and my wash bag and we were on our way to Hayle with me in the back of Mike's Mini Pickup. It was highwater on a neap tide around midday when we sailed in perfect warm weather with an almost flat calm sea.

The crewman showed me how to cut up the gurnards for bait and I got stuck in. It took just under two hours to get to the gear off Pendeen and the afternoon was spent hauling the 120 French barrel-type pots they were working primarily for crawfish, although that day there were just as many mostly large lobsters. All was fine until they stopped for something to eat in the early evening.

They fried up some megrims on the bone with sliced bread and butter. The meal was not great, in fact the cook should have stuck to the day job as it was obvious that cooking was not one of his strengths.

In the confines of the small cabin I began to feel queasy so I went up on deck while they finished their grub. Then, with me feeling pretty sick, we did a couple more tiers of pots for the second time. The first tier of 30 yielded several fine craws and a few smaller lobsters. The second close by was virtually blank.

So, being such a fine settled night we anchored on the sand behind Gurnards Head instead of steaming back up to St Ives. It was an early start the following morning and with a short steam to the gear we were well ahead of the game.

During my entire fishing career I was never really seasick. That said, stepping aboard a cold boat at the start of a trip, the fumes that came off a damp engine mixed with the smell of diesel would often bring on a clammy sweat and a queasy feeling. The remedy was to keep warm and if possible get your head down for an hour. I was very lucky that was all I ever suffered.

I was tired like I had never been before and slept well. We started again at first light and the fish came steadily with a lot of smallish cock crabs overnight to add to the mix.

We worked away steadily and completed the gear by about 09:00 when we stopped for bacon sandwiches and coffee. The sickness was gone and I was in my element. By 09:45 we started again but as we were going through the next tier there was a problem with water in the engine room.

Mike checked what the problem was and found the packing in the stern gland where the prop shaft goes out through the hull was leaking badly and we would have to go back to

Hayle and dry out in order to fix it. We got back to Hayle just before high water. The first job was to land the fish and take them to Harveys who arranged for their engineer to fix the stern gland the following day.

For a bare 24 hours work my share was £9 which was a big improvement on £5 a week at home – *at that time £9 was a tradesman's wages for a 5-day week.*

Home and away again

There was hell up and Father was teasy as an adder because I had left the ploughing. He wanted it finishing but I was off to sea again. The suggestion that perhaps he could do it himself fitchered him up even more because he hated driving tractors. His parting shot at me as we left was, "you will starve like a rat in a trap doing that effing job!"

As usual Mother was worried that this time that I might get drowned. I gave her £4 to go to Truro and treat herself but she never did. The money was put in the teapot for a rainy day. The 'dear of her.' I still had my £5 though so I was no worse off.

Off we went again… the neap tide was ending and Pendeen did not fish well on big tides so we hauled and boarded the 120 pots till the Michael & David looked like a floating hay rick piled 3 high with pots. Again, there was a bit of fish which amounted to another good day's wages.

Working the bay

We shot the pots starting about a mile off St Ives Head in a line towards the Stones Buoy off Godrevy and went into St Ives to anchor with the fish stored in the vivier tank. We had half a dozen brightly painted Breton crabbers for company that night. After a bit of food, we turned in for an early start in the morning with the gear less than 20 minutes away.

When we turned to at first light, the Bretons were long gone probably having a 3-hour steam to their gear out towards the Seven Stones. One of them was the 'Cite D'Arvor', an Audierne-registered boat whose skipper had the dubious experience of watching the Torrey Canyon plough onto the Seven Stones in 1967.

The weather was not as good and there was a freshening SE wind as the day broke in a reddish sunrise which never bodes well. We started on the gear. The fishing was patchy but good in places with several lobsters in a pot every now and again with lots of empty pots in between. But it was easy fishing within sight of the harbour and it kept turning in a good day's work.

The wind freshened through the morning with rain coming in as the wind veered S then SW which was not a problem because St Ives bay is sheltered from the East around to the NW. By mid-afternoon we had fished two full hauls for another day's work. With the wind almost certainly veering NW it might not be such a comfortable night in the Bay so it was a case of tucking in under the shore as close as possible off the pier end.

The night was uncomfortable for sure, with the spring tide running the boat lay beam on rolling like a pig in the swell. So, the mizzen was hoisted which helped a lot - to my mind a mizzen is indispensable on static gear boats, as future events were to frequently prove. These days, few boats have them which to me is akin to a woman with no knickers.

There was no sign of the Bretons that night. They had either gone to the Scillies for a bit of shelter or home to land over the top of the tide.

The next morning the blow had passed. It was cold and clear with a fresh NW breeze which was not that comfortable in the shallow water inshore but the fishing remained steady. The north coast of Cornwall differs markedly from the south where relatively close inshore you can find 40 fathoms, whereas north of St Ives, you had to go a few miles off to find better than 20 fathoms. This caused a ground sea to rear up and play hell with the fishing on occasions.

Getting a full week in before landing over a thousand pounds in weight of nearly all top quality select lobsters with hardly any craws, there was also the bonus of over a ton of good quality, smallish, cock crabs which more than paid the expenses. I picked up over £70 for seven days of pure enjoyment but was still glad to be back in my own bed again for a couple of nights.

I was happy, Mother was relieved, Father was very quiet!

Gaining experience

We had a good summer, generally working the Pendeen Rough on the neap tides and north and east of St Ives on the springs, although for six weeks during June and early July, fishing very close to the shore in Bassets Bay (between Godrevy and St Agnes) was so good for lobsters that we never left it. We worked in tight under those towering cliffs in the unbroken quiet sunny weather and it was awesome.

The interesting thing was that even though skin divers had been decimating the crawfish in recent years, the few we caught to the eastward were usually darker-coloured monsters. Some were purple when they came out of the kelp beds and it soon became clear that the further north east you found them, the bigger and darker they tended to be - so different to the smaller, lighter-coloured Pendeen fish.

The skin divers were a huge problem. They would completely clear a patch of ground of craws and move on to the next with no thought about conservation, whereas our Breton-style pots were actually so inefficient that although we caught enough to give us a good living, most of the fish didn't get caught so we could always go back again.

The proof being that our grounds had always sustained a big fleet of Breton boats that had been coming for decades. One night in St Ives, there were 40 at anchor but that was exceptional. Normally there were around a dozen regulars from Camaret which is twinned with St Ives and a few from Audierne plus a handful of Cornish boats.

Having cleaned out the shallow inshore waters, the divers edged off deeper venturing down toward the westward, but the casualty rate began to rise as relatively inexperienced divers lured by the big money took far too many risks and succumbed to the bends on a regular basis. Ratio of 'risk to reward' was moving against them without stopping them so the body count rose exponentially.

Down in the deeper water we had to learn to live with this menace but we were holding our own, despite repeated calls to Cornwall Sea Fisheries Committee and the Government, nothing was done and it remained a free for all. Luckily, there were plenty of lobsters which the divers could not catch so easily, so our catch ratios changed to a lobster bias and we got by.

Step up to the 'William Harvey' and over to the islands

At the end of the season Mike had done so well with the Michael and David that Harveys offered him a bigger, better, former Breton boat called the 'William Harvey' which opened up new horizons for us.

That autumn Mike chanced his arm and went to the Scillies with 180 pots which was 60 more than the Michael and David could carry. Arriving just before dusk, we shot 30 pots to make a bit of room on deck right by the Spanish Ledges buoy in St Mary's Sound before going into Hughtown on St Mary's for the night.

The plan was to shoot the rest of the gear on a patch called the 'Biddies Ground,' south of St Agnes in 40 fathoms in the morning. After a very sociable time ashore that evening we got away early to shoot the rest of the gear.

Having shot it all we went straight back to the Spanish Ledges and struck paydirt. The omen was good with a craw in the very first pot we hauled in Scilly. We had a few more smallish fish but nothing tearing so we took that tier off and shot it next to the rest of the fleet.

Going straight to work on the other, recently shot tiers we had steady if unspectacular fishing but certainly enough to get by well on if we could keep it up. The craws were a bit smaller than at Pendeen and even lighter in colour, but still not to be sniffed at and the water was far too deep for divers.

Over the top of a spring tide, working the gear was still easy unlike Pendeen, so we were more than happy in our work. The Biddies ground proved to be our banker. Always producing a day's work, it could be fished in virtually any weather with the pots safe in the deep water.

What we did see particularly overnight, when the craws were not so active, were worthwhile

Former Breton boat, 'La Servante' which later became 'The William Harvey'

numbers of very good sized cock crabs. For some reason, Scilly grounds never produced any large numbers of lobsters, while those it did were nowhere near the quality we were accustomed to on the North Coast grounds.

Fine weather and cutting tides saw us venturing towards the fearsome Western Rocks, Gorregan Crebinnicks, Retarriers, Bishop and Crim, were sampled always from the relative safety of the deep water on the seaward side. It was hit and miss but if we found a patch of craws they would come thick and fast.

A big hit

On one occasion, steaming up from the Bishop to the Biddies, well off outside of Gorregan, Mike spotted a small isolated pinnacle on the sounder and decided to give it a try. We shot away, stopped for a bite to eat and a cup full for certainly no more than half an hour and then we hauled it back. There were 50 craws from 30 pots.

Shooting back again we carried on up to the Biddies and hauled the gear there, returning back to the spike and plastered it with all six tiers. The following morning, we hauled the six strings for average fishing which was not unusual overnight. The second haul, they were there in numbers again and the vivier was filling. A third haul saw 3 pots in succession boarded with five fish in each pot. We ended the day with 212 craws not even bothering to count the lobsters.

77

That evening in St Mary's, legendary RNLI Coxswain Matt Lethbridge came aboard, laughing that we wouldn't catch very much where we had been that day.

Then, as always, he lifted the lid and looked into the vivier. His jaw dropped and for a moment it looked as if he might fall into the tank. All he could see was horns poking out of the water. As probably the most knowledgeable Scillonian fisherman ever, even he didn't know that spike was there.

The next day we were full and reduced to piling craws in bait boxes on deck between layers of hessian sacking kept wet by the deck wash hose as we boarded the gear to steam home overnight. We arrived in Newlyn just after high water that morning and went up ahead at the top of the North Pier to dry out.

It was three weeks before Christmas at a time of peak prices for crawfish on the French market. Ronnie Harvey learning that we were about to land a huge haul of craws panicked and cut our price by half a crown a pound to ten shillings a pound. Despite this blatant robbery, I still went home that day with £120 for five days' work.

Despite the unwelcome price cut it was a good Christmas that year.

After Christmas, high pressure built and the weather was largely fine, with high pressure continuing to predominate. It was cold with light easterly airs for days on end. Although we never repeated that record trip we continued to do well mostly at the Bishop and Biddies until in mid-March when a bit of a blow came through that shot rapidly around to the NW and blew an absolute hooley.

We had to get the pots by the Bishop aboard before they got smashed. All was going ok and we had a full row 3 high securely lashed along the port rail when suddenly a big lump of water crashed over the starboard rail putting the William over to port on her beam ends. We all thought for one horrible moment that we were gone but fortunately that magnificent little boat shook herself, bobbed right back up again and we all lived on to fish another day.

We very carefully boarded the rest of the gear and got the hell out of it back to the relative safety and comfort of the Biddies breathing collective sighs of relief. I reckon our guardian angels were working overtime that day.

A rotten plank that could have sunk us

Come late April, the William was slipped for a paint up and a bit of caulking when Raymond Peak, the shipwright, found a plank just under the waterline on the starboard quarter that he could push his finger through. It was right where my head would have been when lying in my bunk and just a few weeks previously, we had been battered by a gale.

The William was a very soundly built former Breton boat with one and a half inch Iroko planking on oak frames. Raymond Peake examined every inch of the hull and it was all very sound apart from that one, fairly short plank in the stern. The only explanation he could offer was that Iroko heartwood could sometimes be inclined to rot. The plank was replaced and all was well again.

To the Idle de Blanc

Harveys had got news that there was a lobster bonanza in the Solent and all around the Isle of Wight and that boats from Salcombe and Dartmouth were making a killing. So, at Ronnie Harvey's instigation Mike decided to give it a go as well.

Off we went, eastwards, full of optimism the first day we steamed to Brixham. The following morning saw us on the 50-mile leg across Lyme Bay toward Portland in lovely fine weather. Off Portland there is a notorious tidal race but to us hardened veterans of Pendeen a bit of tide was no obstacle… we would show them how to do it.

Big mistake!

An encounter with the Race

We shot in the Race a couple of miles south of the Bill on what looked like good ground. The buffs and wash balls were just bobbing quietly on the surface and our confidence knew no bounds. Suddenly the buff we were drifting lazily alongside went 'plop' and disappeared as we started drifting away back towards Lyme Bay at a rate of knots.

We had shot our gear right on the high water slack but now we were stemming the tide flat out and barely maintaining station on the gear. Five anxious hours later the gear plopped back up and we raced to board it before it disappeared again. Thank goodness we had only shot the 180 pots on deck, not bothering with those in the fish room below.

When we got the first end aboard the heavy grapnel made of railway track with heavy reinforcing bar for flukes had practically pulled straight and the end pots had obviously been on the move all frapped around the backline.

In the nick of time we got the last end aboard just as the tide started roaring back the other way fortunately, pushing us more or less in the direction we wanted to go. 180 pots produced one very pissed off looking lobster!

This was not going so well, we were not as clever as we thought we were!

After a pleasant night in Weymouth we were bound for St Catherine's Point on the SE corner of the Isle of Wight. We carried on around and shot the gear from under Culver Cliff up to the south of the Bembridge Ledge where, according to the chart, there was a bit less tide.

Pompey

We were based in the Camber Dock just inside the Mouth of Portsmouth Harbour on the Southsea shore. The Devon boats were there when we got in and were talking of really big fishing between the Owers off Selsey Bill out to the Nab Tower.

79

We went off across the Solent the following morning to haul. The gear was still where we left it, which was a start and pots came aboard with the odd scabby crab in them. In places there were whelks, then a small lobster, more whelks, then a couple of small lobsters and so it went on. Starvation was looming on this easy ground. Obviously, someone had been here before us.

We boarded the gear again and shot on the edge of the St Catherine's Deep in a strongish but manageable tide run inside the busy shipping track to and from the eastern Solent. It was a long hard stem back to port against the tide pouring around Bembridge Ledge. Compared to the Devon boats, our meagre day's work was highly embarrassing.

Unpalatable facts were beginning to emerge. Our gear was hopelessly unsuitable and we didn't have enough of it anyway to even begin to compete. The Devon men were working heavy inkwell pots and leaded backlines. Provided the end pots were heavy enough - as in needing two men to move them around - their gear would rarely shift in the roaring tide unlike ours.

Our pots were very light and made of peeled chestnut slats in the form of a barrel attached to floating backline designed to work on very rocky areas without constantly coming fast or chafing out on the bottom. It was a clear case of horses for courses and we were clearly on the wrong horse and on the wrong course.

Mike called Harveys for some suitable gear but all they managed was sixty, small, fragile-looking, wire inkwells from Port Isaac which soon proved to be about as much use as tits on a bull. Newlyn over the years has proven that the mindset is *'never do the job right if you can get away with a lash up on the cheap.'*

The other fundamental difference was that Devon boats worked across the tide but our gear dictated it was better to work up and down tide. Like it or not, the real game changer was the fact that they were prepared to invest heavily in the right gear and lots of it and boy were they reaping the rewards.

We staggered along for a couple of weeks just about scratching a living while our Devon colleagues were cleaning up every day. It was demoralising to say the least after being used to much better things at home.

The unexploded bomb

One day, over slack water, while sorting out yet another monumental mess of rolled up pots over the slack water in fortunately flat calm conditions, the gear felt unusually heavy.

I was on the winch and having to be careful that the backline didn't melt due to the friction. One of the crew had to keep spraying the deck hose on the capstan head so we tied the gear off on the rail while Mike cut what pots he could off the backline to try and clear the bights of rope hanging back toward the propeller.

Suddenly he yelled out and jumped back. Then it must have been the wake of a passing ship that made the boat start a steady slow roll where every roll was causing a heavy dull thud on the hull. Looking down over the side, we could see a very large bomb with our backline wrapped around its fins. We all panicked and ran behind the wheelhouse for shelter like a bunch of shy ferrets.

Then we all looked at each other and roared out laughing because if that thing exploded it would take much more than a wooden wheelhouse to save us. We gingerly lowered the mess back to the bottom to try again the following day. Luckily, that plan worked and when we got the frap back up alongside the bomb was gone and we got the mess sorted and shot away again. We were gluttons for punishment!

We should have known that the St Catherine's Deep was a former ammunition dumping ground but we were catching a few lobsters there.

To the Hamble as I get itchy

We were bumping along wishing we were back on the North Coast as June started and with no money, the novelty of nights ashore in Pompey had worn off. We then developed engine trouble. Water was getting into the lube oil. A cracked liner was diagnosed and we were told to go into Port Hamble Marina where the main Gardner agent was located for repairs to be done.

What an eye-opener that was. Hundreds of big expensive looking pleasure craft as far as the eye could see. The William was shipshape and tidy and we became a bit of a novelty to the people coming and going from the pontoons. We actually did a roaring trade with the few lobsters we had aboard which kept the wolf from the door for a few days before we went home for the weekend.

I had developed a rash and started to itch. My face and forearms were a red, inflamed mess and it hurt like hell as the rash started to weep. Getting home, I went to casualty and they asked what I did for a living as they thought it might be an allergy. One of the doctors who examined me soon put his finger on the problem. It was 'weed itch' caused by a type of sea weed that blooms in places like the Solent in warm weather.

The Bacchus days

That ended my time in the Solent because I was signed off sick, having to avoid strong sunlight while the rash cleared up. This took several weeks and resulted in an unexpected move up the ladder with the offer of a coveted berth on Cornwall's biggest crabber, the Bacchus, owned by the three Burt brothers from Newquay.

Eldest brother John, a great bear of a man, had gained the nickname 'Amos' after a popular TV programme called 'Burke's Law.' Quite appropriate really because John's word was law aboard the boat. Younger brother Mickey was a perpetual worrier who obsessively looked after the spotless engine room and its ultra-reliable 160HP Baudouin engine which was the first choice in most Breton built boats.

David, the other brother, was quiet and easy going and looked after the deck and the bait. The two other crew members were Les Carne and Rick Birch. Les was an older scrawny little fellow, very clever at solving problems - his speciality was making ships in bottles. Rick was a cool surfer dude who was a dead ringer for David Soul. Then there was me… the tall ugly one with big ears and a short fuse.

Six hands was new to me and I could not help wondering what they all did. Actually, it was plenty. The Bacchus worked in the proper Breton style. Pots were unbent from the backline as they came over the rail and the backline was neatly coiled in bights on the starboard side back aft alongside the wheelhouse with the becket to bend the pot leg onto facing out of the stack of coils.

John remained in the wheelhouse at all times, keeping the boat up exactly on the gear because a boat the size and weight of the Bacchus could be very hard on the gear otherwise. The winchman stopped hauling as the pot came over the rail, literally for a split second for the clove hitch securing the pot to be unbent. At all other times he would be hauling as fast as the back would come with at least six turns on the winch.

This set a cracking pace that could be maintained all day in any weather likely to be worked. The other hands were busy baiting, stacking pots on the huge deck and nicking fish before putting them down the vivier hatch.

Pots were bent onto the backline as they were shot. There was no danger of getting caught up in a rope and being dragged overboard and it was a very safe system of work.

A fantastic lifestyle with money to burn and trips to Camaret

One of the most satisfying things on a fine evening at anchor was to be out on the foredeck repairing a pot, maybe replacing a broken slat or mending a gash in the net ends while yarning away with a cup of tea and a cigar. The gear was always kept in tip top order.

The other benefit was a large dry cabin with comfortable, spacious bunks which had plenty of headroom. The Bacchus was built of oak on oak in Camaret, originally to fish the Portuguese coast for craws before she came to Cornwall, proudly bearing a Padstow registration.

She used to return to Camaret for maintenance at the yard where she was built. The first time I went to Camaret was fascinating. The port was on the south side of the Rade De Brest and its speciality was crawfish. With various classes of boat fishing as far south as Senegal and north to Scotland, those Bretons certainly knew where the little buggers lived.

The Bacchus alongside Ernie Stevens' 'Rose of Sharon' berthed at Newlyn's North Pier at around 1971

Camaret

Camaret was a fine harbour, a very sociable place already twinned with St Ives. We were made very welcome as we acquired a taste for pastis, Gauloise and chewing garlic. We were in danger of going completely native.

The first night we arrived we were practically frogmarched to a wedding of the daughter of one of the skippers who fished off Cornwall. It was the first time I had tasted couscous which was full of chunks of tender lamb and hot with chilli and garlic and all washed down with lusty red wine. It was lush.

The first job in the morning was to go along the front to the boulangerie to collect half a dozen freshly baked, still warm baguettes for breakfast which involved running the gauntlet of several bars where they were all hell bent on dragging you in at 8:00 in the morning for a brandy-laced coffee. But you had to, without being unduly antisocial, get that bread back to an always starving Amos.

We all went to the Fisherman's Coop chandlery to buy stylish blue boiler suits that actually looked smart unlike the horrible, ill-fitting ones at home. There were pantaloons and jackets as well as proper Breton caps, boxes of Opinel knives and comfortable, stylish, zip up boots or clogs. We really started to look the part.

I even managed to get one of the Breton skipper's wives (who invited us to dinner) to sort me out a bottle of Chanel No 5 for Mother which pleased her no end and lasted her for years.

Then there was the bar-tabac with cigars and Gauloise or Camel cigarettes at giveaway prices. When we were about to leave for home we stocked right up on everything while dreading the Revenue man back in Padstow.

As it happened, when we got back into Padstow at around midday on the Saturday and notified him of our arrival, he didn't want to know because he was off to football to watch his team Plymouth Argyle play. The contraband was spirited away a bit sharpish that afternoon.

Nomadic fishing

A typical trip for the Bacchus would be ten days. Leaving Padstow a couple of days after the top of the tide, we would normally shoot somewhere north of Newquay and work to the SW often end over end from there fetching up off Pendeen or NW of the Longships for the neap. On odd occasions when fishing was slack we might fetch up in the Scillies or off deep of the Lizard.

I used to like working these places. In those days the coaster traffic was heavy and you were rarely out of sight of at least one. Many were Dutch-owned and crewed by a husband and wife with the children aboard. They were real family affairs. Everards were also a common sight along with the Crescence Shipping, Rix and Brook boats, many were heading to Newlyn for stone from the massive Penlee Quarry.

Others were bound to or from the St Austell Bay ports on the china clay trade or headed who knows where with who knows what in a never-ending procession of trade.

We would fish the Scillies in winter just like the William Harvey, but we rarely, if ever, went ashore dropping the hook in the outer harbour ready for an early start. As previously said, you never saw many craws overnight so aboard the Bacchus in winter we would do three hauls then board the gear overnight meaning it was safe if the weather made (got worse).

Early starts and late finishes meant we were as lean and fit as racing snakes. With the freshly baited gear in the water for first light, we were one jump ahead of the others. After the first haul, we would stop for proper brewed coffee with a daily tot of rough, Algerian red wine and slabs of bread and jam in the Breton tradition. That was your lot though, no boozy nights ashore, we were there to earn money, not to spend it.

The steam back home to Trevose from Scilly at the end of a trip was around 70 miles, equating to an average ten-hour steam.

If the wind was right we would break out the forrard staysail and offset the mizzen. You would hear the load come off the engine, saving fuel as she picked up half a knot. It was a great feeling heeled over a bit with the roll damped down. Hissing along, she must have looked a pretty sight to those who could see her.

A day to remember

One trip in particular on the Bacchus stands out in my mind. It was Friday 18th June 1972. Three things were going on that day. Two were family orientated and the other was an imminent tragedy.

We were deep off the Lizard in the shipping track, the tide was starting to jump on a warm overcast morning that promised a fairish day. It was my sister's 17th birthday, my great uncle

Charlie Bennetts' funeral and the day of the Navy's annual Plymouth to Fowey Whaler Race.

The shipping forecast didn't give any warning of wind, in fact it was nearly flat calm with a light southerly air. The fishing was ok with a good smattering of big cock crabs, one monster actually topped ten pounds and demolished the pot before the neck could be cut out to remove it. The lobsters and craws were all good sized with a roughly 50/50 mix.

We stopped for our coffee and tot of vino after the first haul as usual at about 09:30. Noticing the wind puffing and a huge black cloud looming up to the south and west, it looked like oiler tops would soon be needed. Sure enough the rain came and with it a rapidly freshening southerly wind that just kept freshening throughout the morning.

By midday it had veered SW and become storm force with horizontal driving rain that was reducing visibility to less than a mile. At around 14:00 we were boarding the gear with three strings of sixty to go when the VHF channel 16 started blaring a mayday. The Navy whaler race was in serious trouble and it sounded like there were several bodies in the water between Plymouth and Fowey.

By this time, we were struggling to haul, the boat was nearly full ahead to keep up to the gear and the mizzen was bar tight as it held us up to the seas. Then a particularly large steep wave actually came over the bow and filled the foredeck which was unprecedented.

Out of the corner of our eyes we were watching the 100,000 ton tanker, Gulf Hansa, which was a regular sight on the run from the Gulf Terminal on Whiddy Island in Bantry Bay, Eire to the Gulf refinery in Rotterdam. It loomed out of the haze, passing close enough down our starboard side while also passing a much slower, Crescence Shipping coaster on the same course further inside again.

As the tanker cleared ahead of the coaster which was lightship (without cargo), an extra-large wave pooped the coaster and caused it to broach which must have really shaken the crew up. To see a 250 foot long ship pushed ninety degrees to port and over on its beam ends was an unforgettable reminder of what the sea really is capable of.

With our final end aboard it was time to get the hell out of there in the direction of Falmouth. As we were underway deep off the Blackhead in mountainous following seas, the wind rapidly veered west then north-west without pausing to catch breath. So, we tucked away in Coverack for the night instead of running the extra distance into Falmouth Bay.

That day running before those huge dangerous seas, the staysail forrard was the life of the boat just as much as the mizzen had been previously while hauling head to wind.

The following morning, we steamed for Newlyn and the only sign of what had happened no more than 18 hours before was a huge ground sea pounding the Lizard as we rounded it into Mounts Bay. The prospect of an unexpected Sunday at home was very welcome after that little lot.

Pot making

One of the best aspects of being in the Bacchus crew was that we really were like a family. We worked together as a tight-knit team to mutual benefit. We all relished the success and took the odd failure equally, while at the end of a trip, we could have a drink together then go our separate ways until it was time to go to sea again.

We used to make our own pots, a winter job when the wind was howling and it was too poor to work at sea. The Burts had a loft in an old barn halfway up Tregunnel Hill looking over the River Gannel.

It was once a farm but the developers had already moved in on what was becoming prime real estate. We had a pot-bellied stove fired by the pot making off cuts where a kettle was always boiling. Others would often drop in for a yarn so it was very social with a steady, unhurried pace.

The pliable chestnut lathes came in roughly 4 metre lengths tied in bundles from Bretagne and carried on the Plomarche, the big shellfish carrier vessel that used to collect the fish for export from Harveys in Newlyn before there were any vivier trucks.

The birth of Brittany Ferries

Around this time, a new freight ferry service was just starting between Roscoff and Plymouth initially to get broccoli from SICA, the huge farmer-owned, grower's Co-op in St Pol De Lion into British markets. Cornish farmers fearing the competition confidently predicted in a TV interview *'that it wouldn't last.'*

That typically negative comment encapsulated the introspective Cornish mindset that has always held Cornwall back. That service they simply dismissed did last. And within a few years it became the mighty, Brittany Ferries operation that today dominates ferry traffic in the western English Channel.

It is very interesting to note how the generally, much smaller, Breton farms embraced the cooperative movement with huge success, while Cornish farmers tended to compete with each other rather than coalesce into a force to be reckoned with like their Breton counterparts. It is so easy to digress here so back to pot making…

Pot making part 2

The lathes were cut to the correct length, about 2 feet 6 ins in our case for the actual bars of the pots. You would get about 4 decent bars out of a length with any shorter offcuts being saved for the neck opening. The bark was always peeled off using the Opinel knives that we all carried at all times.

Opinel knives, like Guy Coten oilers, were the best. They had the trademark cherrywood handle with a carbon steel blade that had an edge like a razor. The blade would fold back into a recess in the handle and there was a locking collar to stop the blade closing on your fingers. They came in various sizes; from tiny for net mending, to the seriously large for heading monk. We used the medium size with a blade about 4 inches long.

The inner hoops of the pot were formed in a roughly circular template although ours had a trademark slightly flattened base to hopefully sit on the bottom better, (they certainly stacked better on deck). Having fed the pliable lathe into the template (easier if the lathe had been soaked) it was tacked together with short nails made for the job. There were four hoops to a pot.

The inner hoops would be placed on a jig at the correct spacings and the lathes would be tacked to them at around 2 inch spacings. At the top where the 12 inch mouth sat, there would be shorter lathes tacked between two hoops leaving a gap between the two inner hoops for the pot mouth.

Next, the outer hoop end would be wedged between two bars and tacked to the pot bars all the way round until overlapping the beginning, also wedged between two bars to finish. By the time all four hoops were tacked in place the structure was pretty strong.

The worst job was making the necks which was fiddly. They were formed from very smooth beechwood planks that apparently came from New Zealand butter barrels and were bound by two small chestnut outer hoops to form a 12 inch circle about 8 or nine inches deep.

To finish, the necks were lashed into the hole in the top of the pot and netting was tacked into the open ends with two dollops of concrete on the base for a bit of weight. Thus, the job was a good 'un.

Then there were the bait toggles, hundreds of them, made from a 2 ft length of tarred braided nylon twine. The ends were sealed by dabbing them on the stove and a toggle, like a small duffel coat one, secured to one end of the twine. The bait was cut with a hole in it through which the twine was threaded.

When baiting a pot, the toggle was pulled up a slit in the neck, with the bait held tightly against the outer face of the neck where it would be difficult for fish to get at. It then secured with a half hitch to the pot lathe above.

It sounds complicated, it wasn't really, but presentation was everything and even back then, good bait was not cheap so it was never ever wasted.

A brush with 'The Firm'

Bait brings us to the first experience of 'The Firm.' (W Stevenson & Sons) at that time WERE Newlyn. They controlled most things and woe betide those who crossed them.

It was a balmy summer Sunday tea time on the dead of the neap. We had just finished work NW of the Longships by about seven miles and intended to steam to Newlyn for the night to take bait in the morning.

Amos got talking on the VHF to Tommy Symons (who just happened to be Ronnie

Harvey's brother-in-law). He was skipper of the Stevenson trawler, Elizabeth Caroline at the time which was working the Norrard of the Wolf ground which was prime gurnard country.

We could see the Caroline to the south south-west and it ended up with Tommy offering us the freshest bait possible which was irresistible.

The Caroline was hauling as we approached and it was so quiet we could actually lie alongside her which was very unusual in that neck of the woods.

We ended up taking 58 baskets of blood-red, large gurnards. It was hard work getting them out of the Caroline's fishroom and across to the Bacchus, but there were plenty of hands and we were well sorted. The agreement was that the financials would be sorted out through Harveys.

Bait

Instead of the three hour steam to Newlyn, that evening we went into Gwenver and dropped the hook, before setting to work salting away those stunning gurnards in the bait tank. Most just tipped gurnards into barrels lashed on deck and sprinkled salt on them.

But, as in everything we did on the Bacchus, it had to be done right. She had a large, rectangular, wooden tank lined with fibreglass down below the full width of the fishroom, aft which had a drain plug into the bilge for washing it out. The brine never smelt that good mind, it needed a strong stomach and was definitely not for the squeamish or delicate.

Starting with a clean, empty tank a layer of salt was sprinkled over the bottom followed by a layer of gurnards all neatly laid out individually in rows then more salt, until they were all put away. Enough fresh bait for the morrow had been toggled up and lightly sprinkled with salt to 'draw out the smack', that oily fishy odour that shellfish could not resist.

Consequences

When Tommy got into land he was sacked (not unusual in 'The Firm'). Unbelievably, Billy Stevenson had been sitting in his car in the car park at Land's End with a powerful pair of binoculars counting the baskets of gurnards.

The fact that they had been declared and paid for didn't matter. We were all on his shit list and the sack was a formality. Tommy soon got reinstated but Amos was seriously out of favour for a very long time to come.

In another later part of this yarn 'The Firm' and the Caroline assume a major role!

Chapter 5
On dry land... for a bit

A spell ashore

In 1972 the construction of the Camborne bypass was underway and the massive earthmoving kit fascinated me. Maybe foolishly, I left the Bacchus for a job as a semi-skilled serviceman on the heavy muck shifting plant operated by M C Pierce as sub-contractors to the main contractor Costain.

Mickey Pierce was an interesting character, an Irishman who made his first money operating rickety tipper trucks on the construction of the M4. He had got lucky and married the daughter of the W D & H O Wills tobacco dynasty which gave him the golden key to that elusive inside track into high finance.

Having worked his way west via the Taunton and Collumpton sections of the M5 and Haldon on the A38, Mickey Pierce was the biggest, privately-owned earthmover in the country.

He rocked up next in Camborne as earthmoving sub-contractor to Costains, with a complete new set of six, Cat 631 motor scrapers, Cat D8 and D9 dozers and a huge Terex 72/81 21 cubic metre loading shovel to complement six, older Terex R50 50 ton dump trucks. It was a case of, *'get out of the way Cornwall, Paddy is going to town,'* and by golly didn't they just!

The workers were largely itinerant Irish who lived in caravans on site. Real 'salt of the earth' grafters who drank like fish, swore like troopers and worked like donkeys.

There were a few local fitters who had been poached from Clay Country looking after the repairs. The foreman fitter was Gordon Hubbard, a pessimistic Yorkie universally known as 'Steptoe' who was perpetually stressed by impossible demands and unreasonable deadlines, which, with much yelling and shouting, he always met.

There was also Afro-Caribbean, Ian Elsworth, a zany, cheerful, amazingly skilled coded welder who rejoiced in the ultra-politically incorrect nickname 'Jungle Jim' which constantly amused him because he was good and had nothing to prove. He really was one of the boys.

I detest prejudice and racism but it must never be buried and allowed to fester. There is good and bad in every race. Luckily, Ian relished his incredibly un-PC nickname and he was a *'good as they come,'* great bloke who became a good friend.

The best explanation I have seen of how pathetic and ridiculous racism is was a picture of three eggs; one snow white, one the lightest brown and one the darkest brown. All very different on a plate. Next a picture of the same three eggs cracked into a basin together all looking exactly the same.

The bottom line being that no book should ever be judged by its cover, not even mine, it is what is inside that truly matters.

Like a well-oiled machine with a few warts

To watch the Camborne job unfolding was a revelation. Everything was programmed and costed beforehand. There were no computers. It was left to John (Mother) Kelley the site agent, the surveyors and a handful of administrators housed in a large portacabin in the Broadlane Compound that also housed the fitting shop, to keep tabs on everything.

Mickey Pierce was one of the boys. He spoke their language and knew how to motivate his men. He would often show up unannounced in the yard in his Range Rover and in his working clothes before driving quietly along the cut, observing the goings on.

On one occasion when he caught a driver abusing his machine, he went across and pulled the driver off the machine before showing him how to do it his way, properly. A man used to leading from the front, not to be trifled with, he was a man to be respected.

The working day began at 06:30 when a couple of us would be on site to check the machines for oil, water and hydraulic oil then firing them up to warm up ready for the drivers to start at 07:00 sharp. As long as everything ran smoothly there was no panic.

There was a short 15-minute break at 09:30 when a mobile canteen would pull up. We would take the chance to assess things like cutting edges for wear and tyres for damage. At 12:30 there would be a 30-minute break when the chuck wagon would re-appear and we might change a set of cutting edges. Finally, at 15:00 there would be another short, 15-minute break and then straight through to finish at 19:00.

Between times, I would be out in the Land Rover fetching parts or helping in the fitting shop. When the machines stopped, we would pitch in on oil changes, greasing and cutting edge changing. Wear rates varied being particularly bad at the Scorrier end which was low grade kaolin. Although silky smooth to the touch, it was incredibly abrasive, eating away at the hardened manganese steel cutting edges at an incredible rate.

This was where the fleet of six scrapers were working, running over to Treleigh underpass to tip. A fully loaded scraper with forty tons coming out of a dust cloud at you doing 40 mph was an awesome sight not to be trifled with.

There were the almost inevitable mishaps. None fortunately too serious, although one incident does stand out to highlight the danger. One of the foremen had left his car by the side of the haul road when a scraper ran over it fully loaded at full tilt in the dust. The driver had simply misjudged things and the sight of that utterly flattened wreck was enough to make anyone stop and think.

Arson

Arriving at the yard just before 06:30 one Monday morning there was a strong police presence around the still-smoking, burned out shell of a car. There had been a kerfuffle at the Flamingo Club late on Sunday evening and a policeman in a Morris 1000 Panda Car had chased the culprits back to the site.

The copper had locked and left the car to make enquiries while the suspects had sneaked back to the Panda Car and sprayed it with easy start before throwing a lighted match at it. They were long gone before reinforcements arrived. Although there was hell up for weeks, afterwards they could never pin it on anyone.

A spell in the pits

As the Camborne job was winding down, the 50 ton dump trucks were moved to Clay Country on hire to Western Excavating in North Goonbarrow pit, then over the road to Gunheath.

One day, a heavily loaded truck climbing the Gunheath haul road out of the pit on a steep incline broke a half shaft and careered backwards toward a fearsome drop back into the pit. The driver bailed out, escaping with a badly broken leg while the truck was arrested by burying itself in the sand berm at the side.

The big dumpers were powered by two stroke V16 General Motors engines which, while noisy, produced brute power and were very durable. One of the truck's engines was worn and tired and was burning a lot of oil which became a problem when oil blowing past the rings caused the engine to run away.

Nothing would stop it, not even wads of rag stuffed in the air intake. It simply sucked them in, burped and blew them out as a shower of sparks. All that could be done was to retreat to a safe distance and wait for the inevitable.

Louder and louder, faster and faster, more and more black smoke, then bang clatter bang and a strange silence. When the smoke cleared, there was the smell of burning lube oil and a big black crater under where the sump pan had been. Every last moving part in that engine was buried into the dirt smashed to smithereens.

The remaining four trucks ended up at Wheal Remfrey where they moved the original old conical burrow to the growing Melbur tip to open up further reserves of white gold at Wheal Remfrey.

The Par Harbour job

The scrapers went on hire to Western Excavating for a short while to dredge the channel into Par Harbour on the spring equinoctial tide. It was another interesting job which also involved two D9 dozers; one to push load the scrapers and the other rigged with a winch and massive towing strops in case anything became stuck.

There was a three-day window while the tides were at their very lowest and all went well shifting a massive amount of sand out of the channel onto the top of the beach. On the last load of the last day of the tidal window, having just turned low tide, one scraper driver ended up in a deep hole that had been churned up by a ship's propeller.

The driver was standing on the bonnet which had partially nose-dived into the hole and the water was rising. It was bitterly cold but we had no option but to wade in chest-deep to attach the ready-rigged strops on the scraper to the dozer.

Then, having persuaded the scraper driver to jump for it, there was nothing to do but to stand back, cold, wet and shivering to see what happened. The consequences of not recovering that scraper would have meant the closure of the port as the approach channel would have been effectively blocked.

They only had one chance. By this time, an agitated harbourmaster had arrived looking very anxious which was not really what was needed. The dozer took the strain, gently putting the power down until inch by inch the bonnet began to rise as the scraper wheels were dragged up the bank into shallow water and the rapidly rising tide began to cover the beach.

Everyone breathed a huge sigh of relief that Par was still open for business.

In many respects there were similarities between earthmoving, mining and fishing insofar as the network and camaraderie was tangible and connections strong which always seems to be the way in tough environments where real nitty gritty teamwork makes the job go.

I stayed with the job until it wound down in the late summer enjoying every minute of it. I had an option to move to another site near London but decided not to. In my book, leaving Cornwall to work when there was work on the doorstep was to admit failure.

Costains, the main contractors delivered the Camborne bypass slightly ahead of time and on budget even though it was a huge job not without some serious unforeseen problems with mine workings at that time.

Incompetence

Unbelievably since then, decades overdue, the missing three-mile link in the A30 dual carriageway across Bodmin Moor between Temple and Higher Carblake, took over a decade of wrangling to complete. At times, the wrangling descended into the realms of farce before work even started on what was, in reality, a pipsqueak job compared to Camborne almost 50 years earlier.

The eventual appointment of an incompetent contractor by an equally incompetent Cornwall Council acting as agent for Highways England remains an acute embarrassment to any self-respecting Cornish person.

The unpalatable fact that both significant cost and unforgivable time overruns resulted in massive penalties eventually being imposed on the contractor that mitigated the cost overruns, is little compensation where congenital incompetence by all concerned is involved.

Chapter 6
More from the briny

'Boom and bust' or, 'Situation normal'

Meanwhile at sea, another cycle of boom was kicking off just as the crayfish boom was going bust in a flood of crocodile tears. Despite pleas to Cornwall Sea Fisheries Committee and the Government to protect the dwindling crawfish stocks, they did nothing. In fact, they actually poured petrol on the flames by introducing generous grants for new boats. This resulted in the arrival of a new fleet of tangle netters in St Ives (in particular), with others in Newlyn, Hayle and Padstow. It was interesting to note that as usual when a grant is involved, surprise, surprise, the cost of the grant eligible item automatically increases in line with the amount of grant available. But the 'something for nothing' syndrome ensures blindness to that fact.

The new boats came on stream working miles of super-efficient gear that soon finished off what the divers had left. When the craws were done they turned to the huge packs of spurdogs in CornIsh waters, traditionally fished sustainably by longlines. It didn't take long to sort that little lot out as well!

Many days the dogs were piled up in heaps the length of Newlyn's New Pier as there were not enough kits or boxes to put them in. Unfortunately, a lot of the proceeds were splashed against the porcelain of the pubs that were enjoying a seemingly endless party.

The spurdogs like the craws had been virtually wiped out, yet again greed via overcapacity enjoyed a resounding triumph over need.

Caleb Mundy (see later) had left Nancekuke, having sold the Pteropod he had bought a new Porthleven-built, 28 foot, fibreglass, Aquarius boat called 'Gemini' which he was working out of Portreath. He had decided to try lining for the dogs that were swarming 8 to 10 miles north of Portreath at the time.

I was skippering the Lady Violet at the time with Timmy Heard, but she was laid up with engine trouble. It was late July on the tail end of the neap, the weather was grand and a day's dogging (no, not that sort of dogging!) seemed like a good day out. We went away at 03:00, an hour and half after the high water and shot 1,000 hooks at first light.

We went to work hauling at 08:00 and there they were, down into the depths, a big dog on practically every hook with the odd ling, conger and ray. As we were on the last basket the boat was seeming to wallow. Even allowing for the considerable weight of fish, it didn't feel right.

93

Then the engine started making a peculiar gurgling noise and Caleb stopped it. Thankfully, it really was flat calm but it was obvious we were sinking and the water below was half way up the engine and was about to inundate the battery box.

The automatic bilge pump was working but we had to find where the water was coming from a bit sharpish because there was more than the automatic pump was clearing. Looking over the side the boat was obviously well down in the water with the weight of fish alone, then it became obvious. The main bilge pump discharge was below water and there was no non return valve fitted, so water was siphoning back into the boat at an increasing rate. We had to get the engine running again to pump the water out, but were the electrics still functioning? Caleb tried the starter key and on the last knocking of power from a dying battery the engine started with the main bilge pump engaged.

The next life-threatening problem was that the engine flywheel was throwing water over the air intake which, if ignored, would cause the engine to hydraulic. Then we really would be stuffed.

It is amazing how you think on your feet in such life-threatening situations. I saw the teapot through the wheelhouse door, reached in and grabbed it placing it over the air intake. It did the trick. Caleb was able to increase the revs and the water level started to drop rapidly. All this time I was spread-eagled over the hatch being lashed with filthy oily bilge water off the flywheel holding the teapot in place. We got the water out and with the engine hatch cover off to keep an eye on things, headed for home.

Arriving back in Portreath around 14:00, we landed over 800 stone of huge dogs and around 50 stone of other stuff. A good day that could have turned out much worse were it not for that battered old teapot.

The obvious design fault with the bilge pump discharge was rectified, but it goes to show the potential for disaster that an undiscovered design deficiency can so easily create. If the weather had been different we may not have been so lucky. Likewise, if the teapot wasn't sitting there in sight it may have been too late to find something else.

Caleb Mundy

Caleb was a great friend and angling companion with a brilliant mind. He worked as a scientist at the Chemical Defence Establishment, Nancekuke where his role included monitoring the suitability of process water for discharge into the sea. This was done by testing the water with prawns which are ultra-sensitive to contaminants.

When Nancekuke closed, he became a full-time fisherman who was unfortunately lost when returning to his boat the Mary Amelia, anchored off St Ives on a dark cold winter's evening.

It was a privilege to be selected as a bearer at his funeral. R.I.P. Caleb.

The mackerel boom

Nature is generous even though so many humans abuse that bounty. The next boom came from the humble mackerel when, for a few years, Cornish waters sustained a winter mackerel fishery that, at times, took one's breath away. The mackerel were so thick from the Wolf to the Eddystone it seemed at times that you could walk on the water.

Hook and line mackerel fishing has to be one of the most sustainable fisheries there is. What a sight it was on a fine winter's day to see a hundred or more small boats sitting on a huge shoal. The stereo effect of VHF chatter, idling engines, the clank of gurdies and the slap of strings of jumbo mackerel hitting the deck was, and still remains, unforgettable.

Add the whiff of halitosis in your face from the breath of a breaching pilot whale almost touching the boat as it dives and then the squawking slash of hundreds of gannets diving to feed and being so engorged they couldn't fly, plus the thousands upon thousands of gulls squawking and crapping on you as they hung over the boats… and that is what the job was like.

The Bacchus had been sold to the Channel Islands due to crewing difficulties and the disappearance of the craws. The final straw was when the Scillies were closed to mainland boats big enough to work there in winter. At least the Scillonians had moved to conserve their craws!

Dave Burt had got married and taken a job ashore. John and Mickey Burt had bought a Looe boat called the 'Ma Cherie' and I was invited back as crew along with Dave Snell from Newquay, Rick Burch having gone fishing in New Zealand.

The 'Ma Cherie' was a Looe-built, 36 foot, hatch-boarded, shark boat with two engines under the foredeck, a wheelhouse just forrard of amidships with an open cockpit aft and a huge mizzen. Not my ideal boat, but 'in for a penny in for a pound…'

The mackerel job was about as near office hours as you will ever get in fishing. We would muster in the dark at around 06:30 and row out to the boat on a mooring in the Penryn River between Coastlines and the Greenbank Hotel.

Quickly underway, we would join the fleet pouring out of the river. Most would head toward the Three Mile Buoy and the Manacles, where the mackerel were often to be found. Others would head away toward the Dodman, but by the end of the day they could all end up anywhere depending on the fishing.

The VHF would be going nineteen to the dozen, mostly complete bollocks until someone dropped on a mark of fish when it would quieten down a bit. I often wonder if some of those characters had sat on a gramophone needle; either that or they just liked the sound of their own voices.

Some of them were like sponges absorbing every scrap of information but never ever giving anything back. As always, people separate out as takers and givers but that is human nature.

The kettle would have boiled and we would grab a cupful which would likely be the last for a few hours, then John would stop the boat on a mark and we would try it. Often, in the first light they would be minis, too small to be any use so they would be shaken back into the water.

Then you would drop your line and feel the thud thud pulsations of good fish and wind away on the gurdy till the top hook broke surface when you would grab an arm span of line inboard and remove the fish with a good shake before doing the same again till the weight was up. All the while you had to take great care that the thirty hooks never frapped up into a time-wasting ball.

You also had to be very careful not to let your line go slack when the weight stopped going down as fish hit the line because again, a slack line would result in a monumental frap up.

It was important to make sure as far as was possible, to keep at least one line in the water at all times to hold the feeding frenzy of mackerel under the boat.

Sometimes the fish could be flighty and you had to keep moving. Other times you could sit in one place and the fish would just keep coming. On occasions there may be a quota of say, 50 stone a man imposed by the buyer but generally it was a 'free for all – fill yer boots' job. It was not unusual when on solid jumbo fish for 4 men to have a 1,000 stone aboard by early afternoon.

The trick was then to get in and get landed before the herd arrived otherwise you could be waiting till late evening to get your fish ashore. We never fished on Fridays or Saturdays. Fridays we would scrub the boat end to end and pick up our pay which was a good steady living as a rule.

The worst enemy was the dreaded easterly wind which for some reason spelt 'death to all fishing' on the south coast as long as it persisted, which could be weeks in late winter and early spring.

The following year, the Ma Cherie was sold and replaced by the Fiona Mary, a very pretty looking, small Breton boat with a Kelvin engine.

Unfortunately, not long after she was bought, serious rot was found in several of her Iroko planks in a similar way to the rotten plank on the William Harvey previously. Repairs took a while as the insurance got involved in a lengthy wrangle with the surveyor who had previously given her a clean bill of health.

The mackerel boom inevitably ended in another bust when the Scots pelagic fleet and East Coast trawlers displaced from Icelandic waters, turned up and started hitting the shoals, landing thousands of tons to Eastern European factory ships. They broke up the shoals making them flighty and hard for the handliners to catch.

Around this time, John Bennetts known universally in the trade as 'JB' who is Glenlee's younger boy (my cousin), had a mishap that nearly did for him. He went aboard a Polish factory ship and got drunk on overproof, wood alcohol which left him blind and paralysed for several days. The Sun newspaper headline read, 'BOOZE SCUPPERS THE SKIPPER.' JB fortunately lived to tell the tale.

Another duff move

It was time to move sideways into another dead end.

John Arrow lived in Selsey and was an impresario who claimed to handle among others, Shirley Bassey's affairs. For some strange reason, he was also a shellfish merchant with a base on Lockyer Quay in Sutton Harbour, Plymouth.

Arrow Shellfish owned some rough crabbers, namely the 'Marcel Andre,' 'Bellatrix' and 'Crave Bihen.' I got offered the Crave Bihen by his manager Joe French who had appeared on the scene during the mackerel boom.

Being a naive idiot who just wanted to run a boat and make a living I took up the offer. Les Carne came with me and his sidekick Irish Joe Ryan who was a great bloke if he didn't get drunk. Unfortunately, Joe did get blind, roaring drunk far too often for his own good. We had 300 inkwell pots and the plan was to work off St Ives and berth in Hayle to land and take fuel. She would be too deep to work daily so trips were the only alternative.

The Crave Bihen had been a fine boat in her day but that day had been and gone. The hull was sound, she had a three cylinder, air-cooled Lister driving the winch which was a plus but the main engine, a 160 Baudouin, although running well enough, had practically zero oil pressure which was always niggling away in the back of my mind.

Unusually for a Breton boat she had an ugly, grey-painted, all steel, wheelhouse which was made worse by the rust that confirmed the general impression that the old girl was lacking TLC. I wanted to paint her but was told that paint doesn't catch fish – 'Get the pots aboard and get going'. That may be so, but a bit of pride in your vessel is a great morale booster and incentive.

To cut a long story short, we went into Newlyn having steamed down from Plymouth with a gale of NE wind up our arse and no sign of it letting up for a day or two. Wind from that quarter is not good around the corner on the north coast.

A couple of days later the wind eased and away we went with the wind still NE but just a moderate breeze rather than a gale. It was not ideal but workable. We went past St Ives and the Stones to deep off Basset's Bay where there was a nice bit of ground to try for starters. We shot our 5 strings of 60 inkwells which were good sound pots that I had made up myself.

The following day we hauled and there was a good showing of lobsters and three tea chests of good crabs – so far so good. We picked away quite reasonably for 3 weeks and then ventured down toward Pendeen. Bearing in mind that we were not going to catch any craws, we were essentially a one trick pony so, with only 300 pots, we were not going to break any records.

The name of the game was to keep picking away and be there for the longer term in the hope that some decent gear became available because I could not stop to rig my own. One fine Sunday morning when we were off Pendeen on average fishing with two pots to finish the tier, I put her in gear to give a kick ahead and nothing happened.

The engine was running as sweetly as could be expected, the gearbox was engaging but the prop shaft wasn't turning. Further investigation revealed that the four-inch diameter prop shaft had sheared right in the gearbox coupling as if cut by a laser. We were adrift and helpless but in no immediate danger with no wind, no shipping and a dead slack tide.

I called the Coastguard and explained our problem, there were no other boats anywhere to be seen so the Coastguard asked for the St Ives lifeboat to be launched. We saw the lifeboat coming and were ready to secure the tow. Tommy Cocking was the coxswain and I endured a bit of banter from a couple of hands I knew.

The Crave Bihen in Hayle with ships discharging at the power station circa 1975

One of the crew was a real blast from the past in the form of 'Newell Perkin' our old Religious Education Teacher back at Penwethers. He was as surprised to see me as I was him. It was 12 years since I had seen him last, what a world in miniature our Cornwall is?

The tow got under way with the flood tide in our favour and by the time we reached Hayle Bar the tide was high enough to scrape up the river where our mooring was waiting. The repair took what seemed an eternity but we were very relieved to get away again. Thank heavens the gear was all where it had been left and surprisingly there were enough fish in it to make hauling it worthwhile.

The next lesson wasn't very far away. It was a crash course in problem solving after a near miss where the mizzen actually did play a major part in saving us from a possibly sticky end. The Crave Bihen had a pumped vivier and also a large tank capable of holding a couple of tons of crabs in compartments that stopped the pump circulated water swilling around too much. It had been fixed we had assumed, securely over the steering quadrant. But the very FIRST LESSON in the school of hard knocks was to never ever to assume anything!

Where we were working it was easier to store the fish in the tank aft and land them regularly rather than in the vivier where a quick landing was much harder work.

It was a big spring tide and we had spent an uncomfortable night at anchor in St Ives with the mizzen set to minimise the roll. We had a fry up before getting going because it was going to be another uncomfortable day on account of a persistent high pressure system delivering yet another day of fresh NE wind.

The ebb was away like a river as we got the hook up and headed out toward the Stones Buoy. Just as we got underway, she rolled heavily and the steering inexplicably jammed, fortunately slightly to starboard but the ebb tide was setting us toward the Head. The bloody crab tank had come adrift and landed on the steering quadrant.

The guardian angel was working overtime, with the ebb setting us sideways as we passed too close for comfort past the Head. Without that mizzen keeping her up into the wind there could have been a very nasty ending.

As we cleared St Ives Head into relative safety there was the major job of emptying the shellfish out of the tank without harming them too much.

Getting the really heavy tank fixed securely back into place was the absolute priority. We just kept dodging head to wind out to sea while Les Carnes' ingenuity with some strong baulks of wood from the forepeak saved the day. We were an extra couple of hours late on the gear but another challenge had been overcome.

Baudouin engines were fitted with a highly effective air start system but the air start valve had a reputation for sticking if carbon built up. If it happened then all the air was lost. Unless there was an auxiliary compressor to recharge the bottles you had a problem.

One morning it happened quite unexpectedly because the air start valve did get maintained.

We had no air but we were safe at anchor so the valve was removed and cleaned however, the engine needed to be started. Les came to the rescue again with a brainwave… Our pot winch was driven by an auxiliary engine. Les thought that if we rigged a couple of pulleys to lead a rope down into the engine room and wound it around the main engine flywheel, used cold start cartridges and the decompression levers, we could winch the engine off.

So we tried it. Les gave the signal to Irish Joe looking through the engine room escape hatch. Joe said, "go" and I winched like hell. It worked spectacularly… well, sort of!

We had wound the rope the wrong way around the flywheel and the engine had fired up and exhausted through the inlet rather than the exhaust. Les had shot up the escape ladder with the black smoke chasing him. The engine had only run for a few seconds because it had a failsafe on it to stop that happening.

So back to the drawing board with the smoke clear and the rope wound on the flywheel the right way, we were soon back up and running with the air bottles charging nicely.

At the end of September, with the weather looking catchy, I decided rather than risk the gear, we would move around to Falmouth on the hen crabs, which are at their most plentiful best in the autumn before they spawn around November time.

While the gear would be safe from any weather in 40 fathoms, there was a risk from French trawlers so, to be safe, we stayed just inside the six-mile limit between Coverack and the Black Head.

We had just got into our stride when we had a call from Arrows to inform me that the Bellatrix, which had been fishing in Scotland but had lost her gear, was at anchor in St Ives with a smashed up engine and a bad leak that needed a salvage pump running continuously to stay afloat. She had been on her way back to Plymouth and needed a tow.

So, having finished the pots late that afternoon we set off for St Ives. We had the tide against us virtually all the way and the Crave Bihen's bottom was badly in need of a scrub. It was a long night.

We set off with the wreck in tow manned by a clueless crew. How on earth they had made it as far as they did from Scotland I will never know but it was clear from a terse telephone call with Joe French that Arrows would much prefer it if the Bellatrix did not make it back. In fact, what was suggested was highly illegal.

This made me absolutely determined to get the Bellatrix to Plymouth because my integrity and reputation were on the line. It was a long old tow but the weather was fine and the salvage pump kept running.

When we eventually got the Bellatrix alongside at Lockyer Quay it did not take a genius to deduce that I most certainly wasn't flavour of the month. In fact, I was about as popular as a fart in a spacesuit, because the wreck we had nursed home was an expensive liability. But my copy book was clean and that was all that mattered to me.

We steamed back to Falmouth after a confrontation about payment for the job. In the end, we took a tank-full of diesel and headed back to our gear off Coverack. We finished the season there and took the boat back to Plymouth and walked away. We had scratched a living but there was no future with that outfit.

Unbelievably, after Christmas I had a call from Joe French telling me that he had finished with Arrows and bought a boat and would I be interested in taking it (probably because no other mug would). Anyway, one word fetched another and I was persuaded to take a look at it in Salcombe.

The Lady Violet actually wasn't too bad, a 40 foot forward wheelhouse job with a sealed deck and nicely rigged for 2 handed potting. She had been built of larch on oak by J Hinks in Appledore with a 180hp Gardner 6LX and the hydraulic winch driven by a separate engine with full deck controls at the winch, a spacious deck and my favourite big mizzen, plus she steamed like a witch.

It really would have been rude not to give it a try despite my niggling doubt about Joe French who was too, in-your-face full on, in the nature of a Staffordshire Bull Terrier.

Preparations for the season

By this time Father had left Mother, having bought a house for her in Redruth. He went his own way while our relationship became more strained than usual. I continued to live at home with Mother in Redruth, while getting more and more concerned about her deteriorating health.

The minute she met Joe French she did not like him which was very unusual for her.

I had shipped a young crewman from Mylor called 'Tim Heard' whose father was a shipwright at his brother Terry Heard's Tregatreath Boatyard. Tim was from good stock. Despite being an absolute heller, he was as good as gold and the long hot summer of 1976 was a vintage one if you discounted the odd scrape he would get into.

April saw us hard at it rigging 60 extra double netted 30 inch steel inkwells in the back garden at home, having previously fetched the Lady Violet down to Mylor and touched up the smart orange and white paint, she was looking grand.

Mother thought the world of Tim but one day we were in the kitchen having a cup of tea when he spoke disrespectfully about his own mother. Mine was having no truck with that malarkey, delivering a loud slap across his chacks, with the rider "don't you dare talk about your mother like that." Tim took it like a man and he deeply respected her from that day on.

The trip home confirmed that she did indeed steam like a witch. I noticed that the Gardner sounded slightly lumpy but there was a very good oil pressure and she was not burning any oil. She slipped through the water so easily that there was no point in running the engine any more than half speed.

At the time I was inclined to think the lumpy sound was caused by the length of corrugated stainless steel flue pipe that was part of the air intake fixed to the deck head in the engine compartment under the non-soundproofed engine hatch.

Chocks away

Anyway, to cut a long story short, in the first week of May with a brand new string of 60 heavily rigged inkwells on board, we steamed from Mylor around the Land and shot them inside of Bann shoal before going into Hayle to load another string to shoot the following day.

So off we went. Weeks of fine weather with light east or south-east airs saw baking hot temperatures. With no real rain since February we were in the thick of the worst drought in living memory.

I had a Morris Oxford car and we used to take a few crabs home now and again for pocket money. One day there was a bit of a smell in the car. On investigation nothing was found but the smell became a stench till you could not bear it.

It turned out when we eventually took the back seat out that a decent-sized, cock crab must have crawled out of the basket and under the seat. This ex crab was oozing the most foul smelling yellow slime imaginable that would make the strongest stomach urge. When I tried to pick it up to remove it, it just disintegrated making the stench even worse.

I tried disinfectant and washing and it would go for a day but kept coming back just as bad in a few days. In the end, I just cleaned it one more time and used a mega dose of air freshener an hour before putting it through the local car auction. It sold and there were no comebacks.

That meant that I was riding to work with Tim for a few days. He had a 250cc Bennelli motorbike that would go like a cut cat. I just used to get on the back, close my eyes and pray. There wasn't much else you could do. He was mad but he could ride and we survived.

He also had a silage-green coloured Hillman Imp that used to burn more oil than petrol, leaving a grey smokescreen everywhere it went. One morning the bugger turned up late having already been caught speeding on his way to pick me up. We headed for Hayle via North Cliffs because the A30 was gridlocked with holiday traffic and on the sharp right-hand bend before Hell's Mouth going too fast he lost it. He rounded the bend on the wrong side.

At exactly the same time, another idiot driving a navy blue Morgan too fast, came the opposite way losing it as well. Thank heavens the road was wide enough because we passed each other on the wrong side and the split second glimpse of the demented look on the other driver's face said it all.

In July, the browse on the North Cliffs caught fire which went into the underlying peat soil and burned for several weeks. The fire brigade would put it out and it would burst out somewhere else. We could smell the smoke every day 9 miles NW of St Ives.

One day, we got in on the last of the tide. It was so baking hot in the glaring sunlight that we both jumped over the side in our jeans and T-shirts, got on the bike and rode home still baking hot.

A visit to the Green Room and a scary encounter with 'George'

Another morning we were going away at 03:00 just after high water. There was thick fog so we felt our way down the river carefully and just before we got to the Bar there was a touch of lift in the water which was nothing unusual given the hours ebb tide coming out. Then we went over a big one that broke right on the stern.

We went through the next monster, everything went eerily quiet for what seemed an eternity but, in reality, was just a few seconds. It is known as the 'Green Room' and it is a place you try not to visit if you can help it.

Water was dripping from joints in the wheelhouse roof where it shouldn't be. Then the third one came but we stood on end and staggered over the top of it. As quick as they came it all went quiet again, there was no swell in the bay.

Big swells like that are known locally as 'George.' They are very dangerous and never to be trifled with.

That is how it happens. Out of nowhere and you need a good boat to come through. Luckily, we were aboard a good one, although if that lot caught you going in instead of coming out, the outcome could have been very different.

Several years later, the 'Gillian Clare', a St Ives gig, was actually lost on the Bar entering the river when conditions were very poor in broad daylight. Her crew perished yards from the beach. Not everyone realises that a tasty crab sandwich comes with such hidden costs attached.

A broken crank

The following week we were bound in on tick over nicking crabs and putting them in the store pot when the engine literally started clanking. Not good, it kept running still on tick over and sounded bad. We just dumped the store pot off the Bar and quietly carried on in. We called Joe French and he went ape but we had done nothing wrong. He had best get the 'Gardner Man'.

This set me thinking… what if it had happened in the Green Room? Fortunately for us it didn't! It turned out that the crank had broken on the front main bearing which in a Gardner is practically unheard of. What the hell had I done to deserve this?

It turned out from the serial number that our engine had come out of a Plymouth Citybus double decker. Joe French then admitted that it had been reconditioned by a well-known cowboy in Plymouth.

The crank had broken because it had been ground wrong and we were very lucky that it had lasted as long as it did. The rest of the engine proved to be fine, but finding another crank and getting it back together took valuable time.

One step forward and two steps back and Joe French was speaking with forked tongue.

Back to Falmouth

When we got going again it was that time of year when you are liable to get a big blow so discretion being the better part of valour, I decided to move back to the Falmouth crab ground where we had done OK with the Crave Bihen the previous year. Being fine weather we moved the gear around in 3 trips over 3 days.

The fishing deep off Coverack was steady if unspectacular. We were working out of Mylor Dockyard which back then was a sleepy backwater and not at all like today's booming marina complex.

One morning towards the end of October, we got on the ground and couldn't find 3 tiers which, given we were just inside 6 miles and not on trawling ground, was strange. We went to the other end and the buffs were all where they should be so we started hauling away. When we got to the other end the gear was a bit of a mess but all there.

Then we heard that the Big Five were in Falmouth landing a huge shot of mackerel caught off Coverack. The Big Five was a group of crack Scottish pelagic trawlers and our messed up gear had all the hallmarks of being caught up in their pelagic gear.

We went into Falmouth where they were still landing and when we spoke to them they were very good. It was a pure mishap in the dark and fouled static gear did not help them. We gave them our Decca navigation readings and to make amends and they dumped a couple of brails of mackerel aboard for bait.

We would never normally use mackerel because it was too soft and too easily ripped out by the fish, so we boxed up what we could and managed to scrounge a few bags of ice, throwing a bit of salt over the rest. There were so many we didn't know what to do with them.

The following morning the gear was all where it should have been so we went to work. The plan was that instead of a couple of bits of ray back or gurnard, we would smother the pots with bait as much as we could get around the bands. We did the first tier with probably ten times the normal amount of bait.

We did the same with the other five and we had enough very lightly salted bait left to do the same the following day. It was a case of sit back and await developments.

Full of anticipation, the following morning we went to work and it was amazing. The first pot came up full of crabs, great big deep-shelled hens. All well the top side of a kilo each, the sort with really hairy legs denoting a hard shell bursting with meat. And not only were there crabs, there were also about 40 decent lobsters - where you might see a dozen in a normal day if you were lucky.

As for the crabs, where we normally saw six tea chests in a day we ran out of the 12. We always carried and had to build a pound in the stern for the surplus which, when we got more chests off the lorry back in the harbour, amounted to another 12. Four times our normal haul! On top of that, there was over 50 stone of decent ling for Newlyn market and 50 or 60 stone of congers which we kept for bait.

The following day with the less fresh lightly salted bait, the haul was down by a third but still amazing and the next couple of days using big chunks of conger, we lost the ling and conger but still had a dozen chests a day from our 360 pots. It was our best week ever! What a buzz, proving beyond all doubt that plenty of good bait is everything.

We had our moments when it wasn't all balls ups and the Lady Violet was a lovely boat to work.

Despite that high note, all was not cool with our owner who was robbing us blind by drawing a wage as well as the boat share to make gear but was doing next to nothing. One word fetched another and reluctantly, I was gone to a job at Mount Wellington Mine to fulfil a long-standing ambition. That was the first time Joe French said to me, "if you don't like it you know what you can do," so I did!

I don't like that sort of ultimatum. Several years later, in a totally different situation he did it again and it was probably the best thing that has ever happened to me in hindsight. I had wised up considerably by then and once again called the slippery old bugger's bluff.

Tim took the Lady Violet after me but eventually had enough of slippery Joe as well and the Lady Violet was sold to Newlyn. Sometime later she sank off the Lizard. Tim went to South Crofty Mine as a miner and became a top man there but, as always, the sea eventually drew us back. More about that later in this story.

Chapter 7
Going underground

Mount Wellington Mine overlooks Twelveheads and the valley of the Carnon River. It was owned by a Canadian company who had done the necessary development work to open the old mine up again and was then ready to go into full production. I was employed as an underground labourer which meant that I did all the crap jobs like ditch digging and fetching and carrying for the more skilled crews.

The first time underground was strange. I was used to big skies and fresh air but on this job for the first three months I was on permanent night shift and being winter I only really saw daylight at weekends. Wellington was a very wet mine and they were pumping eight thousand gallons of water a minute just to keep up with the ingress.

If a pump went down they had to close the lower watertight doors and let the levels flood to protect the shaft.

I knew a few of the other miners but it was still very strange. I was only labouring for a couple of weeks when a trammer* had an accident on his motorbike and broke his leg. So that was it… when I picked my tag up to go underground that night the shift boss told me that I would be tramming on 5 level which was the main production level at the time.

The miners on 5 level broke the ore in a shrinkage stope by working off the top of the already broken ore. Underneath the stope every few yards were chutes where the ore was loaded into a train of 4 or 5 wagons pulled by a battery-powered, electric locomotive. It then went out to be tipped down the ore pass from where it was loaded into the skip for hoisting to the surface.

This work was 'on contract' where, if all went well, a bonus would be paid, which was a great incentive to crack on. As usual, all did not always go well. The theory and the practice were poles apart.

We were told what chutes to draw from, which had to be well clear of where the drillers were working.

The problems arose when the miners broke the ore in the stope and it was too big to come through the chute. Hung up chutes did not produce bonuses. The remedy was a

A 'trammer' is an assistant miner whose duties include general mining and loading materials onto wagons or belts

'slap dab,' a small piece of plastic explosive stuck on the offending rock to hopefully break it up without damaging the chute.

It was hard, frustrating work. When ore was actually flowing as it was meant to, you had to be careful not to overfill the wagons and bury them. If that happened it was down to you to dig them out. On top of this, the track and points were always shaky, often causing wagons to derail, so you soon learned to get them back on the track.

Sometimes it made fishing look like a walk in the park - working in the pitch black with ice cold water running down your neck while you were sweating your cobs off with exertion. It took a special kind of patience.

A week in the shaft

Later, as the lower levels were brought on stream, the main 5 level pump station was due to be moved to the bottom sub level.

The mine levels were 100 feet apart vertically and Wellington had 8 levels with a sub level where the skips were loaded for hoisting and provision for a new, main pump station with much bigger capacity to replace the one on 5 level.

The shaft had originally been inadvertently sunk on the Mount Wellington Fault, which meant that it had only been sunk to 850 feet where the fault was encountered, preventing it from being deepened further.

As a labourer, I was detailed one night to work with a fitter and the shift boss called 'Tiny Marsh' overseeing to start moving the pumps out of 5 sub level so that they could be moved down the shaft to their new location.

That was hair raising. We were working on the far edge of the shaft from the station, which involved walking around the shaft edge on a girder about a foot wide. Even though you were wearing a safety harness, looking down 350 feet to the pinprick of light in the sump or up at the light at the top of the shaft 500 feet above was scary.

The first night I was terrified, almost afraid to move, while Tiny was walking around as if he was in his kitchen at home. The scheme of work involved moving a pump per night shift for 5 nights. Basically, it involved getting everything unbolted and moved out far enough to be lifted by a wire hung from the bottom of the cage.

This involved Tirfor winches attached to suitably located ringbolts in the wall. Bearing in mind these were serious bits of kit with 700hp electric motors, they weighed several tons. As I began to feel more confident near the open shaft the job became very interesting.

It became even more interesting when the first one was hoisted under the cage with Tiny Marsh riding up with it to the surface, hanging on to the wire it was slung from. What would have happened if anything parted out heaven only knows. But it didn't and the job went like clockwork because we had taken our time and thought very carefully about what we were doing.

Purgatory in the loading pocket

Another time, I ended up in the loading pocket right down near the sump where ore was fed onto a conveyor belt that fed the skip, which at Wellington was actually the man riding cage with the floor lifted up. There were endless problems with water turning the ore into an uncontrollable slurry that was constantly running off the conveyor, threatening to bury the whole belt system.

Labourers were sent into this hell hole to clean up the spillage by shovelling it back onto the conveyor belt. It had to be the worst job in the world. However, there was no alternative but to crack on or quit altogether, which quite a few did on a regular basis.

One used to dread the words 'loading pocket' as you picked up your tag and were assigned your night's work.

Spillage

There was one job that was even worse than the loading pocket but it was highly paid and took place at weekends when there was no production. There was always some spillage as the ore from the loading pocket was loaded into the skip and that spillage ended up in the sump 50 feet below.

The sump had to be kept clear so volunteers worked on Saturday and Sunday to dig the stuff out and load it into a kibble*. Working in knee-deep water, the job was challenging but it was very well paid and it gave some of the younger miners with mortgages and young families the chance to literally double their wages.

The Frederick's Shaft breakthrough

Water was a constant problem but the engineers were working on a solution. Once the pumps from 5 level had been refurbished on the surface, they were sent back down the shaft to the 8 level pump station newly installed and commissioned. There was a new and massive watertight door leading to a drive where a crack development crew had been working for many weeks.

On the night in question, two of us were sent down to the bottom pump station where we were met by the mine manager and shift boss who informed us what was going on and what we must do without hesitation if anything went wrong which was both scary and fascinating.

Part of the problem was that the water was coming out of the ore body which was, in effect, a giant aquifer. The water was actually percolating through the ore body from the vast flooded voids in the United Mines set to the west of Wellington.

_____
*A 'kibble' is a type of hoisting bucket or container used by miners

The drive was within 10 metres of what was known as 'Sir Frederick's Shaft' which was the eastern-most shaft of United Mines. That night, they were going to long hole through into an 800 foot head of water which sounded like suicide to me.

The really impressive thing was the pinpoint accuracy of the surveying and the way they were able to navigate so accurately through solid rock in the pitch black. But they were not stupid and had planned well.

What had happened to prepare was that several large standpipes with suitably rated stopcocks on the end had been grouted deep into the rock face. The mining crew in there were drilling through the first standpipe and were within feet of breaking through into the water. We were on the watertight door with a loco attached ready if necessary to pull the door shut entombing those inside – a potentially heavy responsibility.

To say things were tense would be an understatement. After about 3 hours of idling at a high state of alert, with the manager coming and going from the drive, we heard what sounded like a jet engine. There was no panic, no instruction to shut the door, but the water flow coming down the drive increased by a noticeable amount.

Eventually the two miners came down the drive, they were soaking wet and looking relieved. After a quick cup of tea, one said come and have a look at this, so we walked in about 300 yards as the noise got louder.

The manager was standing to one side of a massive jet of water under terrific pressure that was boring a hole in the solid rock of the sidewall of the drive. The visibility was hazy from the water vapour generated by the pressure, and the loco holding the drill in place had been pushed back as the pressure forced the drill steels out of the hole.

Then obviously still standing to one side, the manager closed the stopcock. The noise subsided and the water was about to be tamed. Over the next few weeks, they drilled through each stopcock in turn. At this point, the flow of water was under control by being able to be regulated by opening and closing the standpipes to suit pump availability.
I am glad it went to plan because the thought of entombing three good men in that hell hole is too awful to contemplate.

Apparently, by the time Wellington finally closed, they had drained United Mines down to 8 level and it was possible to look into Frederick's Shaft from the drive, with the water pouring out under no pressure. To think that beneath that there was another thousand feet of water still percolating into the 1,700 feet depth of Wheal Jane across the Carnon Valley.

What a tragedy after all that work and investment that the collapse in tin prices forced the closure of our mines and the loss of the skills that supported them.

Stacking supermarket shelves is no job for men more used to being highly paid for doing real work.

The sudden drop

One very poor very wet night, we went down in the cage as usual. The weather above grass was immaterial because underground it never varied. Just above 5 level, the cage was slowing as normal and it was just about stationary at the station when it suddenly dropped maybe 10 or 15 feet very quickly as if in freefall. It was scary as we all looked at each other, with the cage bouncing on the end of the rope. The cage then slowly inched back up to the station and a very relieved crew got out and walked into the workings wondering what the hell had happened.

Later, when Tiny came around, we were told that the wind had blown the exceptionally heavy rain into the winder brake housings causing the winder brakes to slip when they were applied. There was actually no real danger but it felt scary in the cage that night; the really surprising thing being the amount of elasticity in 500 feet of wire rope to allow the cage to bounce up and down as it did. If the rope had parted, it was reassuring to know that the cage was fitted with devices to stop it freefalling to the shaft bottom.

A week on production

Once on a rare week of dayshifts, I helped a production miner while his partner was off. I got a real taste of the rock face and it was an eye opener for sure. Those men earned their money, and that week I got some of it.

The rounds drilled were fired at the end of the shift when everyone bar the pumpmen and the shot firer were on surface and accounted for. You would often be in the shower while a large round was fired right under your feet and the floor would pulsate as the millisecond delays in the detonators prolonged the explosion.

The great County Adit

After the end of the nightshift at 04:00 there was often the chance of 4 hours overtime working on the first level, maintaining the course of the County Adit that was an integral part of the level. Care always had to be taken that the adit didn't burst off its channel and find its way down into the extensive old workings below.

The old, worked out, shallow stopes running down from the first to the second level were huge. The scale was hard to appreciate with just miners' headlamps but, at one point, at the top, the tree roots were coming down from the roof, which indicated that we were just a few feet from the surface and right under the road above.

The great County Adit was a serious undertaking in its day, draining water from dozens of mines as far back as 'North Downs' by Treleigh. It all discharged from the actual adit via the place we were working and into the Carnon River through the portal.

Miner's revenge

An evil practical joke was perpetrated on Tiny Marsh, the shift boss who was a big, mouthy, Cockney, larger-than-life character who, beneath the bluster and bullshit, was a top miner and a pretty sound man. But he had one vice that had put him in the firing line and terrible retribution, 'miner-style', was nigh.

A lot of miners, usually those who didn't smoke, chewed gum underground but everyone was sick of Tiny pinching their chewing gum while on his morning rounds. One miner had bought some laxative chewing gum and put it in Wrigley's chewing gum wrappers. Enter Tiny… the miner offers him some chewing gum and he grabs most of it and starts chewing away.

The shift bosses would go up to the surface around 11:30 each day and they were all in the cage on the way up when Tiny grunted with a griping pain in his guts. As the cage surfaced, he burst out of it, running across the bank undoing his boiler suit as he went.

Tiny didn't make the toilet and he never scrounged chewing gum again. Miners' humour was lethal.

The end of my short but interesting mining career

It was April 1976, the days were opening out and above grass, the sun was shining. I was back to the drudge of tramming on 5 level. One nightshift, all the chutes were jammed solid and the wagons were off the track yet again. Life was shitty.

I have no problem with problems or problem solving as long as they lead to a solution rather than that endless, gut-wrenching frustration and negativity that non resolution and stagnation brings.

After popping several boulders in one chute an even bigger one came down jamming everything up once more. I put a larger dollop of plastic on the boulder, fired and the chute collapsed. The ore ran like a river, burying both the wagons and the loco.

A light came bobbing down the drive and it was Tiny on his rounds. What had just happened spelt grief for him and he was not amused. So he started hurling abuse the way that mouthy Cockneys do.

One word fetched another and I wasn't going to be spoken to like that. I lost it and picked up a 2 foot drill steel and beat him over his helmet with it knocking it off. It didn't hurt him but it did shake him because he had never seen me mazed before. He started to retreat back down the drive shouting at me, "you're mad!"

I wasn't just mad, I was murderous. I picked up a rock and threw it at the retreating form. It caught him right between the shoulder blades and he went down face first in the ditch. He then got up and legged it. It was around 03:00 when I picked up my dinner bag, walked back to the shaft and waited for the cage to go up. It was the end of my short mining career.

Interesting… but curiosity satisfied, mining was not for me.

A few years later I bumped into Tiny at Redruth Rugby Club and we had a drink and laughed about that night on 5 level when we had each, in our own way, both lost it. I like it when grown men can let bygones be bygones and move on, grudges achieve nothing.

"Cornish boys are fishermen and Cornish boys are miners too, when the fish and tin are gone what are Cornish boys to do?"

(Above) The old wall at South Crofty Mine said it all… the end of an era

(Right) The pumping station at Mount Wellington Mine

(Above) Balls of steel… would you?

Chapter 8
The sea comes a calling again

Rock bottom

That summer was spent just dicking around living the dream, working, Caleb Munday's 23 foot boat, the Pteropod (Greek for 'Winged Snail' apparently), out of Portreath.

There was trouble with some scumbag pinching lobsters from out of our store pot in the Bay. Caleb solved that problem by taking our lobsters into protective custody up in his lab at the Chemical Defence Establishment, Nancekuke where he had large aquariums used to test the quality of purified process water on pollution sensitive shrimps before being discharged into the sea.

This was probably the most secure lobster storage in the universe with probably the purest water. That said, despite the security, they had a problem with large quantities of mercury going missing from an ultra-security-conscious site on a regular basis.

Ministry of Defence Police could not crack the case and despite searches of every vehicle leaving the site, the mercury kept vanishing. It continued until one day, an elderly site labourer was pushing his bike through security when he tripped and fell. A policeman rushed over to help him get back up and pick his bike up for him when he found that he could hardly lift it. It turned out that the old man used to remove the saddle and fill the frame of the bike with mercury every day. Then he'd push his bike straight out through security. Now that is a classic example of feral Cornish ingenuity for sure.

The summer slipped by and I had no money. I wasn't earning bran for ducks and at 27 years of age it was time to shake my feathers and get real. It was so bad that I was down to my last 50 pence. The car was running on fumes and I couldn't even afford to fill it with petrol to get to work.

On the way home I dropped into the Clinton Social Club in Redruth for a pint which at the time cost 30 pence. I then did something I had never done before or ever done again since, I took the remaining twenty pence piece and put it in the one arm bandit. Pulling the handle I went to walk away, soon turning around when I heard the sound of cascading coins as a fiver dropped out.

That was my own Dick Whittington moment and it turned my life around.

The 'Firm' for real

The following day I went to Newlyn looking for a berth. Speaking to Billy Stevenson who wanted my pedigree he commented, "you were with that John Burt but I don't like him, but see… Roger Nowell wants a cook on the Jacqueline, so you had better go there."

And that was it, I was working in the 'Firm.'

Roger and his brother Frank, were legends in their own lifetime. Terrible pranksters who could not be serious if they tried, but they were damn good fishermen, which is why they always got forgiven for their frequent misdeeds which would wind Billy up no end. They probably held the joint record as the most sacked pair in the firm.

Away to sea on the Jacqueline

I was there the next morning and the first job was to light the oil-fired, Rayburn-type stove and get the kettle on. With the grub already aboard, off we went round the Land and bound north up Channel on the top of the autumnal, equinoctial tide.

I set to cooking a roast for dinner so it would be ready presumably after we had shot but I had no idea where we were actually bound. It turned out that we were bound for the 'Tanker Pitch,' a celebrated piece of ground 5 miles off Trevose.

Dinner was ready and left warming while the gear was shot. Side winding was all new to me so I just did as I was told and then went aft to the galley to dish the dinner up for the crew. Roger Nowell, Jack Blowers the engineer, Roger Lobb who was a Padstow hand and myself. They were a good crowd.

Jack had the first watch so Roger stayed up the wheel house until Jack had eaten then came down for his. In the dark, the trawl was rumbling along the bottom astern. What would be in it when we hauled?

A lot of blondes

Come 22:00 the bell went and everyone got into their oilers. Jack and Roger Lobb manned the winch, having released the towing block aft which kept the two warps under control while towing, heaving until the doors crashed up in the gallows to be chained up and unclipped from the bridles.

Roger, up in the wheelhouse, circled the Jacqueline until we were beam on to the light wind where we lay with the net streaming away from the side at an angle. It seemed heavy.

Then the quarter ropes were hauled in on the whipping drums and the Gilson lifted the ground rope over the rail inboard. The net was then hauled in by hand using the roll of the boat to help until the cod end was up far enough when a strop was wrapped around the belly with the Gilson wire hooked on. Jack lifted the cod end aboard.

The cod end knot was released and out cascaded what looked like a lot of big blonde rays,

Above: Roger Nowell (left) and Billy Stevenson

Left: An older John Burt with young Simon Porter who is now a top netting skipper in Newlyn

a few stones and starfish and not a lot else. Roger N was whooping, doing a dance on deck, so he was obviously well pleased with life. It turned out to be eight and a half, ten stone kits of big blonde ray.

That night we got another couple of good hauls in and as daylight opened out we towed away to the north where there were no ray but just slim pickings consisting of a mix of plaice gurnards, the odd cod and a few, smallish hake.

In the late afternoon, we towed back into the Tanker Pitch and sure enough the ray were there again. Apparently, they were only there for a few days around the equinoctial full moon in September, in the dark.

Another good night down the fish room and we towed away south-west before hauling around mid-morning for not a lot. That was it. Gear aboard washed down and we were bounders, a short trip for a good haul of ray.

A collision with a Frenchman

The next trip was out to the Wolf. We had fine weather with no wind at all. This did not help when sidewinding because it was hard to get the trawl to stream away from the side when shooting away. It was steady fishing with a bit of quality monk and dory plus the odd turbot to bump up the value. Get the time in and it would be fine.

It was a particularly fine morning, we had just had breakfast and had turned in for an hour because it had been a long night of mending after a big smash up. Again, Jack Blowers had the watch and was towing to the east just north of the Wolf itself.

Asleep down below, the engine eased in, which always spells trouble of some description. We all piled out just as there was a heavy thud and a ponderous slow roll that dictated we should be up on deck pronto. Roger shot up into the wheelhouse while we watched a blue, French, stern trawler circling us.

Jack had seen the trawler coming down from the north and held his course, having the right of way. When the other vessel had shown no sign of altering course to pass round the Jacqueline's stern, he had eased in to let her pass close across our bow, which was all he could do in the circumstances.

It transpired that the Frenchman was bound home. The watchman had gone below to make a coffee and when he came up to the wheelhouse again the sun was in his eyes. Suddenly, he realised that he was on a collision course with us. He went hard to port at full speed but the starboard quarter had caught our port bow with a very hard glancing blow, hence the heavy roll.

An inspection revealed the Jacqueline's stem was missing from just below the waterline to the top of the whaleback. Water was coming in on the waterline but given the fine weather we were in no immediate danger.

With the Frenchman standing by we hauled and headed slowly towards Newlyn. To avoid putting undue pressure on the gaping bow where the stem had been, water was dribbling in through the nail holes where the spikes had been ripped out by the force of the collision.

We eventually arrived in Newlyn where a grim looking Billy Stevenson was pacing the quay with the Harbourmaster, Andrew Munson, who was also the French Consul in attendance.

Both skippers gave their version of events in the presence of Andrew Munson, which beyond all reasonable doubt laid the blame at the Frenchman's door. Obviously, this would result in a substantial insurance claim by the Firm.

From my perspective it was one more example of my Guardian Angel working overtime. Had the French helmsman not altered course he would probably have hit us square on and sunk us like a stone, probably cutting the wooden Jacqueline in half.

It rammed into me how vital it is to keep a proper lookout at all times and observe the rule of the road regulations to the letter. The man on the wheel holds his crew mates' lives in his hands and that is a very serious responsibility never, ever to be taken lightly by anyone.

The Karen

The Jacqueline was slipped the following week for Raymond Peake to fully assess the damage. It didn't take the master craftsman and his men, Nim Bawden and Dudley Penrose long to fit a new stem and get the old girl back fishing again.

I was next sent aboard the Karen, a steel 75 foot sidewinder of the Sputnik class built in Berwick on Tweed originally for her Aberdeen owners.

Her and her sister ship, Bervie Braes, had come to Newlyn from Aberdeen in the late 1960s and were a vast improvement on the ageing fleet of wartime-built, ex MFVs (Motor Fleet Vessels) that were still the backbone Firm's fleet.

Leslie Lashbrook, the skipper of the Karen, was the polar opposite of Roger Nowell. Quiet, comfortable and serious, no pranks but a good skipper who was no slouch when it came to catching fish. I went there as a deckhand because they already had a cook.

Stephen (Stuffy) Stone was the cook on the Karen who doubled up as entertainments officer. He was a tall, gangly, wind up merchant, an aggravating bastard in the nicest sense, who must have given Leslie Lashbrook nightmares.

The engineer was Ernie Blake, a quiet, competent man who just got on with the job in hand without complaint.

The Dory Pitch

The first trip was to the *'Dory Pitch'* in the middle of Mounts Bay deep off Porthleven in sight of Newlyn Harbour. The target was John Dory. If they were not at home there was little else to catch. They probably concentrated in that area in the autumn because of the pilchard shoals that also concentrated there.

It was roughish ground that was not kind to nets but if it was on form, floaters of dory were not unknown and that was the object of the exercise.

The dory were there, not in huge quantities but Leslie persisted. We had a few small bits of damage, some hauls but only a bit of chafe here and there that didn't take long to sort.

Then, on the second day, the persistence paid off. The closing in haul that night produced a floater. I had never seen such a sight. The cod end bobbed on the surface full of dories, eight baskets when picked up, with a few big monk to go with them. You had to be careful handling dory because they really were prickly buggers.

Handling them it was easy to see why fishermen had given them the nickname 'handbags,' because these were that size and shape. Dory have to be one of the best eating fish in the sea and certainly my favourite fish.

Another good haul followed despite a badly smashed net. Leslie decided to whip in and land what we had while the net was being sorted out. It was a good trip moneywise but we were away again that afternoon back to the dory pitch.

Three balls ups force a retreat

There were to be no floaters this time!

Having shot away it was obvious that something was not right. There was no spread on the warps so it was a case of haul in order to sort it. The tide was jumping and that was the probable cause of the cable laid doors. Heaven knows how, but there were three turns in the warp with the heavy doors locked together.

That took a bit of sorting but Leslie was nothing if not persistent. We shot away again and soon came fast which damaged the net. It was laced together to save time and shot for the third time but it was not lucky.

Having got a full haul in when we hauled, the net was empty with a neat granny knot tied in the stocking. It was unbelievable and it was obvious that the skipper was not happy. The minute everything was aboard, the throttle went down to the stops and we were bound west.

The Dory Pitch was collecting the rent and the crew of the Karen were paying.

Squids in

We ended up Norrard* of the Wolf where several other Stevenson boats were homing in on a decent showing of squid. Having wasted the best part of the day, we needed to touch on in order to build on the good shot of dory already under our belt.

What was left of the first night produced a decent haul with squid, some flats, a few big dory and plenty of the big red gurnard that were usually a feature in this area. The daylight hauls as usual were slacker so all was hanging on the dark hauls as the fleet circled around the big tow.

Just before dusk there was hell up on the VHF. 'The Excellent', skippered by former Lowestoft man Ernie Hunter, for some reason had his portside gear in the water which dictated that he had to go round the tow in the opposite anti-clockwise direction.

On the turn, he had fouled the gear of the Roseland, skippered by Joe Brownfield who sounded as if he was about to swallow his pipe. Joe normally had two speeds - dead slow and stop. Never breaking any records, he was usually content to just rub along. One of the most placid, pipe-chewing men you would ever wish to meet. Tonight, Joe was in hyperdrive and Ernie was the target of his invective.

The squid had come on solid and we were all doing well. While the Excellent was locked onto the Roseland's gear, as the crews worked to sort the monumental frap up out, Ernie was resorting to the, 'attack is the best means of defence' strategy while Joe was having none of it. Eventually it got sorted out without too much damage and the silly buggers got on with it in sulky radio silence.

Ernie saw sense and shot his starboard gear.

After four nights ending up at the Ship (Sevenstones Lightship), there was a good bread and butter trip down below and it was time to 'go home to see Mother' (happy skipper speak for bounders or in to land), aggregated with the dory landing, we were ok.

I knew I was only on the Karen for a short time but I got on well with Leslie and was grateful for the experience and the good recommendation he gave Billy... that I had a future as a trawlerman.

In the 'Firm,' promotions and demotions were rapid to say the least, many on the eccentric owner's whim depending on how the maggot was biting that day. Given the pressures he inflicted on himself by micro managing his men, it was a wonder he never had a seizure. But at that time, he was more than good to me.

The Rusty Rat

The Belgians had been beam trawling during the winter on the Trevose Grounds for years and it was glaringly obvious that they were cleaning up on soles using beam trawls. Billy converted the 100 foot 'Elizabeth Anne Webster', a former Admiralty Motor Fishing Vessel (MFV), built in 1944, which the Firm had bought from Torbay Trawlers in Brixham some years before, along with three other similar boats.

The 'Webster' was a fine sea boat, exceptionally heavily built and was originally a mine-sweeper. She was fitted with two, four metre beams worked off the end of a heavy derrick* each side. Frankie Nowell had been the first skipper but he had done so badly that she came close to being converted back to sidewinding.

As a last throw of the dice, Billy had put David Hooper (Hoops) aboard as skipper and the job took off because David had the magic touch. He soon set a then, unassailable port record with a massive landing of Trevose soles. Hoops was so successful that Billy was persuaded to buy a second-hand, Dutch beamer called the 'Aaltjie Adriantje (AA)' for Hoops to take.

The Webster was given to Delwyn Puckey, a diminutive Padstow hand who had battled polio as a boy which left him with a bit of a limp. But that did not belie the fact that Del had something to prove given that he had the heart of a lion and balls of steel.

Delwyn Puckey

In yet another amazing thread that runs through this story, we unwittingly had previous form. The first time I met Delwyn Puckey in Newlyn I half recognised him but when the penny dropped, it was hilarious. In a former life he had been a Western National bus conductor who had thrown me off his Number 18 bus.

The daughter of the Carharrack Post Master was an absolute cracker who knew it and

*The Norrard (Northern) Rocks are a small group of uninhabited granite rocks in the north-western part of the Isles of Scilly

Below: The Elizabeth Ann (aka 'The Rusty Rat') shooting the gear and (inset); Skipper Del Puckey R.I.P. (aka 'The Poison Dwarf')

wasn't backwards in coming forwards. She used to go to Truro Girls' Grammar School and flirt with me on the bus and even though I didn't know what to do, Delwyn who was older, saw me as a rival because he did know what to do and he was doing it.

Even more amazingly the coincidence didn't end there as Delwyn's father had been a gardener at Trevince, the lovely Manor House by Gwennap Church and the home of the Beauchamp family. But he had moved from there to Padstow as head gardener at Prideaux Place, the home of the Prideaux Brune family.

One of his second cousins is currently the partner of my niece, so the circle of connection and place turns albeit unwittingly.

The Number 18 bus used to stop in Carharrack for a while and he used to meet the minx in the alley behind the Post Office.

*A 'derrick' is a type of lifting device

Delwyn had left Western National to work as a crewman on the Padstow dredger which is how he originally fetched up in Newlyn. He had shown an aptitude for fishing and rapidly made skipper on a sidewinder. He was another heller in the league of Roger and Frankie Nowell, often getting sacked.

Thanks to Leslie Lashbrook's recommendation I ended up on the Webster as cook that autumn. We had a great winter on Trevose, blighted by a couple of bouts of winch trouble because the converted sidewinder winch wasn't really up to the job but it was the best we had and we were earning money.

When we weren't working Trevose we usually fished from west-south-west of the Wolf down to the Humps and Bumps (sandbanks) on the three-mile limit south-east of Scilly. The main catch that way was sole and monk but we got a bit of everything to go with it as well as a lot of good hen crabs and scallops. It was an excellent mix that pleased the buyers on the market no end.

A bit of a mutiny in the heat and… lost knickers

Occasionally in summer we would venture east to the grounds off Start Point when fishing elsewhere was a bit slack. We gradually ventured further out into the channel.

When we went clear we were catching good numbers of big turbot and other flats but being so calm the trawls kept digging into the banks of sand taking the bellies down, which resulted in endless mending. The weather was absolutely baking hot with a flat, oily calm and stifling humidity when everyone mutinied and decided they were going over the side for a dip.

I was neither a strong swimmer or at all confident when out of my depth, but not to be outdone I got a lifejacket and put it on before jumping over the stern from the boat deck, in my underpants.

As is so often the case things did not go as planned!

I hit the water from about 12 feet high and promptly shot straight through the lifejacket because I had not secured the crotch tape. All that saved me was the tape that had wrapped around my forearm.

I surfaced spluttering and I was struggling to remain afloat and get back into the lifejacket when I discovered to my horror that my pants had come off and were slowly disappearing down into the gloom of the depths. I was bollock naked and had to climb back aboard like that to the catcalling and taunts of the others who were highly amused by my misadventure.

A few seconds later Delwyn and I roared with laughter as the others were panicked by the ominous approach of a triangular fin, with us yelling, "SHARK!" As they were scrambling panic stricken toward the chain mat to get out of the water, they were buzzed by a pair of playful dolphins.

The skull

The following day we were just north of the Hurd Deep and when we hauled there was a really awful stench of putrefaction coming from the pile of fish in the portside pound. They were hosing the pile down to wash the sand away when the source of the stench became apparent. There was a human skull with a mouthful of gold teeth looking out of the pile at us.

Del called the coastguard who advised us to put the skull somewhere safe and the police would meet us on arrival home. So, I went back to the galley, found a couple of carrier bags and a strong cardboard box which the skull was placed in as respectfully as possible. We then put the box on a shelf under the whaleback.

The fish that side had to be ditched which was a pity because it was quality stuff and for weeks afterwards it didn't smell too good under the whaleback. When we got in, the police were waiting for us and after taking statements they took it away.

We enquired later and they said that the skull structure indicated someone Chinese or SE Asian in origin. No one had been reported missing of that description and a check of dental records came up with nothing either. Their best guess was that someone had died on a foreign ship and been buried at sea as happens sometimes.

A near death experience averted by goodwill

On the Saturday before August bank holiday we went into Brixham for a bit of R & R. The bank holiday meant an extra day on the trip but we didn't carry enough fuel to do it yet still wanted to land on the Tuesday market. This meant arriving back in the small hours of Tuesday morning.

Anyway, all hands were sat at a corner table in the Crown and Anchor minding our own business, enjoying a pint, when in walks a man mountain about 6' 6" and 25 stone with a big bushy black beard and hands like shovels. Up gets the 5' 6" poison dwarf (Delwyn) and limps over to him in his Cuban heels.

Delwyn starts poking this huge man in the chest saying, "I don't like you Mister, I am going to get my mate over there (pointing at me) to come and sort you out." Like hell I was. I wanted to live to tell the tale. The man mountain then orders a round of drinks for all hands, picks up the poison dwarf, brings him over, sits him down and said, "I have heard all about you, now you sit there, drink your pint and behave yourself." He looked at the rest of us and continued, "hi everyone, I'm Chris Boyce… let's all be friends."

Then another larger than life character wandered in known universally as the 'Colonel, John Sanders.' John was another Brixham legend and a truly innovative fisherman. A vintage night was had by all. Unfortunately, the Colonel was another victim of the curse of cancer at an all too young an age.

What a gentleman Boycey was. We all became great friends and especially the poison dwarf.

Boycey was a legend as a skipper but like so many good 'uns he also went around the land far too soon.

Del really was a nightmare at times, but we all still loved him to bits and would have followed him to hell and back if we had to.

A tragic suicide

That Christmas tragedy struck. Jimmy Philips the Webster's then Mate, who was a hard-working skilled fisherman, but sadly, one of life's losers who always saw the negative side of everything, hung himself from the stairs at home.

His wife had passed away and his new partner was bleeding him dry to the point where we reckoned everything he owned could be contained in the carrier bag he used to come to sea with. Presumably he had just had enough. But what goes on in such a person's mind has troubled me on several occasions since when other instances of this awful act of desperation have touched my life.

We all went to his sad funeral and it was agreed with the family that the Webster would scatter his ashes on the Tanker Pitch when the time was right.

There had never been any love lost between Jimmy Philips and Mike Corin. The time came to scatter the ashes in March after the Webster had been blown into Padstow for shelter and got be-neaped (left aground) which caused us all to be sacked yet again. Fortunately, the wind howled incessantly until the tide made again, so being sacked was a total irrelevance.

Poachers in the storm

On the night we had got blown into Padstow there was a howling SE storm that despite being off the land became unworkable, even out on the three mile limit. We had dodged in under Stepper at around 22:00, a couple of hours before low water while the wind roared out of the river.

With a NW storm forecast the following morning, it would be around eight hours before we could get up river due to the big ground sea that would be breaking on the bar.

Next thing, Del decided to shoot, with us questioning his sanity. But being less than half a mile off the land… shoot we did. Del towed up and down under the high cliffs between the Newland and the Gulland for 3 hours. When we hauled just after 01:00 the cod ends were bulging with what turned out to be mainly oak leaves and twigs with other rubbish that had obviously washed out of the river.

The two huge piles in the pounds were going to take some getting back over the side. Suddenly, the pile started to heave and when we started to rummage, the pile was riddled with the biggest, blackest soles any of us had ever seen. So, we shot away again for another tow.

When we had finished picking up we had over 11 baskets of big soles, one of which turned out to be five and a quarter pounds in weight, which was a true monster. There were lots of others not that far behind too. We hauled again for another seven boxes by which time the tide had made enough for us to get up the river.

It was just as well we never got caught because they would have thrown the book at us for poaching that audaciously. But Del had found us a brilliant night's work which he usually did even if it occasionally meant bending the rules.

Going up river, the big ground sea on the Bar was breaking intermittently. This needed great care at dead slow speed. The big swells were sliding under us on the verge of cracking and with the wind now veering around, the rain was starting and it was good to be in out of the rapidly deteriorating weather outside.

The master prankster strikes

We were followed up river by Roger Nowell on the Trewarveneth, another of the 'Firm's' wooden sidewinders.

As we were mooring up, Horace Murt, who was Stevenson's Padstow agent, came down the quay and his first words were "Billy said I am not to give any of you subs." Never taking any money to sea it was usual to draw £20 as a bit of spending money if blown in for weather but Billy was determined that we would not be going on the beer this time.

That evening after dinner, we ended up in the Custom House, a very subdued bunch for sure. We had enough for a couple of pints each so it looked like an early night for us.

Two of Roger's crew were hippy types. They were not really drinkers but they had money yet were bemoaning the fact that they had no whacky baccy, which for obvious reasons was totally verboten at sea. It was obvious that Roger had just had one of his eureka moments. He saw a golden opportunity and moved to exploit it.

He said, "why didn't you say you wanted some, I got plenty back aboard," he hadn't but he did have a cunning plan. He rushed back aboard the old Trewarveneth as the storm roared around him. On board in the galley he had remembered a packet of damp chicken Oxo cubes two of which he wrapped in a twist of kitchen foil. The cubes were damp but not too damp.

Back in the Custom House, making a very good job of keeping a straight face, he grabbed a tenner each off them before handing over the *'whacky'* which the hippies immediately began to skin up. They rolled a monster spliff and lit it taking deep puffs.

Suddenly, the bar began to stink of the aroma of burnt chicken with black globs dropping off the end of the spliff. One of the idiots said, "wow man this is great gear, I am feeling really trippy," while Roger was rolled up on the floor in hysterics. A good night was had by all.

Even the hippies saw the funny side of it when they realised that their legs had been well and truly lifted by the master prankster.

Scattering the ashes

The wind howled for days, the fish had been landed and we went home. The fact that we were all sacked yet again was all part of the crazy game because the weather and neap tide dictated that we would be going nowhere for the foreseeable anyway.

When it did stop blowing nearly a week later we were picked up by Stones Taxi to get up to Padstow, stopping at the Blue Anchor in Fraddon on the way, where somewhat irreverently poor Jimmy's ashes were placed on the bar and a last vodka and tonic was bought for him. We got away from Padstow in the mid-afternoon on the high water, heading straight for the Tanker Pitch.

There had never been any love lost between Jimmy and Mike Corin, the engineer but when the time came to scatter the ashes we did it with as much decorum as possible. Delwyn was reading from the Mission Bible kept in the wheelhouse as I scattered the ashes carefully over the side.

As this was going on, Mike Corin was sniggering while everyone else was being respectful. Suddenly a cat's paw of wind came from nowhere and blew enough of the ash back into Mike Corin's face to make his hair turn grey, making him cough and splutter like a wind- broken horse before rushing aft to wash himself.

Did Jimmy have his revenge?

We will never know.

That evening at dinner Mr Corin was laughing the other side of his face.

Hosed down

I also had a run in with Mike. I always work on the absolute assumption that if you cannot take it – never ever dish it out. As an engineer, he used to wash the fish on deck before they were lowered down to me in the fishroom to ice away.

He was forever squirting the hose down my neck as I would go to climb down the fishroom ladder and laugh about it.

In the middle of an icy winter's night when there was already enough bloody water flying, an unnecessary extra gush right down your neck soon ceased to be funny. Despite repeated warnings to the effect of *"Michael I wouldn't do that if I were you,"* he still persisted, grizzling away in amusement, while I just bided my time because revenge is definitely 'a dish best served cold.'

Our engineer was a creature of habit especially when it came to 'number twos'. The Webster had a toilet compartment aft where there was a seat but no toilet… the actual receptacle was an empty 20 litre paint bucket with some seawater in it that was placed under the seat then emptied over the side after the business had been done.

The morning in question was bitterly cold and the unsuspecting victim having had his breakfast, as usual, moved to adjourn to the 'throne room'. The steel door had a gap at the top and there was a locking tab on the outside that a bolt could be inserted into to keep it closed from the outside in bad weather.

Hanging around until I was certain he was seated on the throne I quietly put the bolt in the locking tab. I got the deck hose and put it in over the top of the door and held it there.

There was a muffled, "WTF!" from inside as the prankster got a large dollop of his own medicine. Then came the clank of a capsized poop bucket rolling around in the rising water in the compartment. Mission accomplished!

He staggered out like a drowned rat shivering and shaking with his soaked boiler suit hanging around his waist. He was not a happy bunny and complained to Delwyn who burst out laughing saying, "it serves you bloody well right."

In future he was very careful not to squirt me again but I don't think he has ever forgiven me because Newlyners as a breed tend to be a bit sulky like that!

The South West Deeps

Meanwhile, David Hooper was going great guns with his new command 'the AA' and was working out further to the SW of Scilly in what was described as the 'Deep Water' where he was getting less sole but a whole lot more megrim and monk which was being exported to Spain to satisfy a seemingly insatiable demand.

It seemed natural that we would go that way and we did. It was asking a lot of our old winch but we were catching plenty of fish and we were also finding a few big wrecks.

Out beyond the Islands we were on the margins of accuracy for the 'Decca Navigator' (this was before the pin point accuracy of GPS). At night, the Decca could be miles out and where wrecks are concerned there is no margin for error.

Needless to say, we found a wreck that looked like Truro Cathedral, the legacy of a wartime U Boat packs ambush on a convoy. There were several more waiting to be found. We were hitched solid in the one in question but we had to get out of it without losing one or both of our trawls.

The starboard side came back easily but it felt heavy and when we tried to get the lazy deckie to the whipping head it was a real struggle being bar tight. When we did get the cod end up it was stuffed with big black lumps the size of concrete blocks. It was the finest steam coal and around 2 tons of it.

Turning our attention to the port side, it was obvious that it would not yield easily. For safety's sake, we were going to have to let the quick release gear go and this let the derrick end towing block go so that we could get a direct pull from the fore gallows which was a much more stable point to haul from.

Eventually the gear did let go and we had it back. This time, instead of coal, we had a floater of the biggest pollack and ling I had ever seen and not a mesh in either trawl was broken. We lost a haul getting it back by the time we got the quick release gear rigged back but that sort of thing is all part of the trawling trade.

No one was hurt.

A blocked pump

On another piss-poor night at Trevose, I was in my warm, cosy bunk down below in the cabin when suddenly I was doused in ice-cold, oily water and there was the sound of water swilling around in the bilges. Something was wrong for sure. As she was rolling, the water was rolling up the side and spilling over the top of the lining into the forrard lower bunks.

The bilge alarms went off and going into the engine room through the cabin access door, the aluminium chequer plates were all but awash. After lifting the bilge pump access hatch it did not look pretty but the cause of the problem was clearly evident.

While we had been in harbour between trips, the shipwrights had been working in the fishroom and had not cleaned up the shavings and sawdust very well which had ended up washing around in the bilge.

The automatic pump suction filter was badly clogged with the saw dust and wood chippings which needed to be cleared sharpish.

The engineer, while working on it, was alternately doused in icy-cold, oily seawater whilst being exposed to the baking heat of the engine room. Fortunately, the main bilge pump driven off the auxiliary generator engine was not blocked and, once started, soon cleared the flood.

With the automatic bilge pump filter sorted things soon returned to normal. Those old wooden boats would see you through any weather but they did leak a bit as a matter of course, so a fully functioning automatic bilge pump on a float switch was vital.

Back to school at Captain Howell's

The 'Firm' was short of skippers as in, 'men with DTI (Department of Trade and Industry) certificates of competency.' Some of us were given the offer of a wage while we were taking ours in return for agreeing to stay with the 'Firm' for two years. That seemed more than fair considering that six weeks' accommodation was thrown in while we studied.

You had to have a minimum of five years' sea time in a deck capacity in order to be eligible to take the DTI exam which was no problem.

Captain Howell's place was located just outside Kingsbridge in the South Hams. He was a sprightly, septuagenarian, ex–Cunard Line, extra master mariner who, in retirement, enjoyed preparing fishermen for the exam which, if you passed, led to your coveted certificate of competency.

Captain Howell would not tolerate failure and if you lasted the first day while he shrewdly assessed everyone you were in. If he didn't think you were capable, you were sent home, no ifs, no buts. However, if you did make it through that first day, provided you did the work he set, you were virtually guaranteed a pass.

I wanted my ticket so badly it hurt. This was deadly serious... no messing about here.

The Board of Trade specified that the course should take six months. We didn't have six months, we had six weeks – 10 hours a day during the week and six hours a day of homework at the weekends.

Suddenly, I realised what trigonometry, logarithms and cosines were actually for. This was not a boring maths lesson at school, this was the real deal, so we all sat up and listened very carefully to every last word the Captain said.

It was a cracking pace but the captain made it all fascinating. He was a born teacher who inspired you to do well. He had a soft spot for fishermen and it was obvious in his approach that he accepted that we all had a few rough edges that needed rounding off. He proved to be a past master at reducing rude matter into due form.

We did chart work, celestial navigation, the collision regulations, stability, first aid, fire-fighting, with the worst ones for me being, Morse code and semaphore.

We did it because we wanted to. We wanted the status a pass would bestow on us so we worked intensively and hard, testing each other constantly. For me, the stability work was most interesting but even the struggle with Morse code was worth it.

I have a slight problem (disability) insofar as apparently, I have a right-hand brain in a left hand body which causes me to see things differently which was not conducive to mastering Morse.

The exam

The six weeks flew by and we were primed up ready for the exam. Captain Howell spent the last afternoon explaining about the exam and how it worked. Marking would be severe but everything hinged on the final two-hour oral interview with the chief examiner who did not suffer fools lightly, we were told.

The key appeared to be that you really knew your subject and gave straight, concise replies to questions.

The exam papers were all two hours long. We were told to read the paper twice to clearly understand every question before putting pen to paper which was excellent advice. Finally, given that the chief examiner was such a stickler, we were encouraged to wear a suit with well-polished shoes. If anyone arrived badly turned out they could expect to get an extra special grilling!

The written papers were what they were. We had done the work and read the questions very carefully. We did the paper, checked it over twice, handed it to the examiner and left the room.

Come the final day and the oral, it was a case of taking a deep breath and walking smartly in when called, shaking hands and waiting till told to sit down. The examiner was very good, it was obvious that he was weighing me up as we were chatting. Every now and then he would steer the conversation to where he wanted it to be and we talked about boats, fishing and gear.

It was all very clever. Without realising it, stability had been covered in the course of the conversation. He wanted to be satisfied that the person he was talking to really was competent to take a ship to sea and bring it back again safely. He wanted to satisfy himself how you might cope with an emergency and that you had a firm grasp of the collision regulations.
A flash fire

Three of us had a recent experience of a genuine emergency aboard the old 'Rusty Rat' (the Webster's nickname), fresh in our minds to recount.

We were west-south-west hauling in the small hours of a hot, quiet night and Mike Corin, the engineer and I were standing port side by the open engine room door. Waiting for the gear to come up while looking down at the engine exhaust manifold glowing a dull cherry red from the heat, there was suddenly a flicker of flame that instantly became a serious blaze.

Luckily, we were there and right on it from the engine room catwalk with a fire extinguisher each. We only just knocked it down after Delwyn cut the revs to tick over. The oil pipe feeding the turbocharger had broken and was spraying hot lube oil directly onto the red-hot manifold.

If that had happened a short while previously when everyone but the one on watch were turned in, the engine room would have been lost to the blaze that would have quickly taken over before it was detected. By the time the fire alarms had activated it would have already been too late.

A good pass

That example was exactly what the examiner was looking for. Proof, if any were needed, that there is no substitute for genuine experience which could never be taught in a lecture theatre.

There were no trick questions but if he wasn't satisfied with a particular response he would drill down until he was, or 'in extremis,' until he failed you. Fortunately for all of us, we passed at a high standard.

I think the examiners realised that coming from Captain Howell's star chamber we wouldn't be in front of them if we were not fully up to speed, but it was their job to try us and prove us. It was our job to step up to the mark and prove ourselves fit and proper candidates.

I instinctively knew that I had done ok when I was out in 45 minutes.

It wasn't easy, anything worthwhile rarely is, but it was worth it. We were all qualified men and the world was our oyster.

Bad weather

One thing for sure working in the (Bristol) Channel or out in the deep water, sooner or later you would see bad weather. As long as the boat was well found and care was taken, that was not a problem in itself, it was part of the job which you took in your stride.

I have several recollections of particularly poor weather episodes and some that led to tragic outcomes that we could do nothing about.

The loss of the Union Crystal

One night west-south-west, an average poor but workable evening on the Webster had rapidly deteriorated into a north-west storm that had not been forecast. We had boarded the gear and were underway between the Wolf and Runnelstone when there was a Mayday.

Both Sennen and St Ives lifeboats were being launched, God alone knows what it was like launching in Sennen that night but they did, right in the eye of that ferocious storm.

A coaster called the 'Union Crystal' (a sister ship to the later, ill-fated, Union Star) was sinking NW of Pendeen. I was in the wheelhouse with Del and we were about 12 miles away from the position given so he decided to try to assist.

We changed course from a beam sea to a head sea with wind against a north going tide and it was hellish. We were struggling to make headway but a Mayday call cannot, indeed, must not ever be ignored.

As we laboured toward the casualty we were west of the Longships, the coastguard announced that the Union Crystal had sunk and there were no survivors. You could see the tears welling in Del's eyes as the helm went over to starboard and we were running with the sea towards safety.

A big sea in shoaling water

Another night, we were at the radar buoy 17 miles north of Padstow Mouth with good fishing and a poor forecast when we stayed for a haul too many. By the time we started to board the gear it was another NW smeecher. The old girl was hissing through the water before the wind in towards Tintagel Head.

By the time we had everything secure and battened down we were far enough inshore for comfort. As the Webster came about we heard the shout to hold tight, as a massive swell caught her beam on and knocked onto her beam ends till again, like the day at the Bishop on the William Harvey, I thought we were going.

But with a shake and a powerful counter roll, that magnificent old girl saw us through. No hint of tenderness or crankiness there, any good boat will always roll back hard without hesitation. It can be uncomfortable but you know you are safe.

Given it was around high water and we were an hour and a half from Padstow, it was too late to cross the Bar which meant dodging in the storm for twelve hours. In reality, there was nowhere to go but onwards to Newlyn.

We dodged away quietly to the north-west, head to sea all night, keeping an eye on Frankie Nowell in the 'Sarah Shaun' abeam of us, (which was another of the 'Firm's,' steel Sputnik sidewinders). By mid-morning, we were well north of Pendeen and able to turn south toward the Longships.

When poor Frankie got in, Billy sacked him because a big sea had bent the foghorn back. That is how bad things were that night and how petty and stupid it could be in the Firm at times.

Overwhelmed

Once, working west-south-west, we had gone into St Mary's to shelter. The blow had passed through, but an even worse one was forecast, with a short lull in between. We left for home around dusk on 5th of December 1977. Rounding Peninnis, the land was disappearing in the troughs of the huge swells even though there was no wind at all.

Halfway to the Wolf we passed the Boston Sea Stallion, a new 40 metre modern, Lowestoft-registered, stern trawler, which had been recently built for the SW mackerel fishery which was preparing to shoot its mackerel gear on a massive mark.

Those marks were that thick that if a trawler ploughed straight into them it would stop dead and possibly lose its net from the sheer weight of fish. The trick was to just clip the edge of the mark.

We were the last ones to see her. Within a short while she was gone with all hands and no Mayday. It must have happened in seconds.

It would appear that the Boston Sea Stallion had turned back east, shot the gear and was hauling a massive catch with its hatches open to receive the fish when, with the weight of fish in her net weighing her stern down, one of the huge swells must have rolled up the stern ramp and inundated her causing her to sink.

It makes you stop and think for sure!

A sudden tempest

The speed with which weather can change is amazing and potentially very dangerous even for well found boats.

In 1978, Del decided to sail on New Year's Eve for a quick trip to catch the post-holiday market. We were the only boat away and left Newlyn in perfect, flat calm conditions with a cloudless blue sky steaming off to the Wolf. It was still perfect and as we were on deck unchaining the gear ready to shoot, we looked to the SE at an uncanny blackness heading our way preceded by white water.

Within seconds, we were hit by a screaming SE blow and it was obvious that we were not going to shoot the gear. We were being blown back in, just like that. It was tricky enough getting into Newlyn with the gale from the SE but great drops of icy rain had started by Low Lee and by the time we were in through the gaps and mooring up, it was lashing down.

Billy was there with the harbour boat to help us in berth when his light tow line parted and hit him in the ear. This did nothing for his good humour and it must have stung like hell for sure. Safely moored up that was it… off home again, too late to catch the New Year shenanigans.

Snowed in

By Long Rock the lashing rain had become sleety. By Hayle it was snowing and by Camborne it was a white out. Taking great care by a longer but more level route, I only just made it home to Trefusis Road in Redruth. By then, the snow was inches deep and driving into deep drifts in the blizzard conditions.

Mother in her last year circa 1985

Letting myself in, I found Mother in the kitchen listening to the radio half out of her mind with worry. News was coming through of a boat ashore and fatalities. As far as she knew, we were the only boat away and she was convinced that it was us they were talking about.

The *'dear of her.'* She looked like she was seeing a ghost but fortunately I was very much alive and kicking.

The boat that had been lost (with 3 fatalities) was the 'North Shields', a registered stern trawler Ben Asdale, which had been discharging mackerel into a factory ship in Falmouth Bay. Suddenly, conditions had deteriorated and she had let go but fouled her rudder and ended up ashore on the left-hand side of Maenporth Beach where the remnants can still be seen today.

As far as I am concerned, the old wooden wonders, with their massive planking and near perfect hull forms, were infinitely better sea boats and preferable to the steel Dutchmen any day. I only ever did a few trips on the 'Algrie' and never felt completely secure there. When a boat rolls and hesitates before rolling back the other way it is termed 'tender' or 'cranky'. That is not good but that is what the Algrie would do in poor weather.

Later, the Algrie had extra steel added to her keel and a covered-in stern which improved her stability and satisfied the DFT (Department for Transport).

The greatest loss of all

On 19th December 1981 came the most heart-wrenching loss of all.

The previous Sunday we had all been blown in from the deep water, as always in a SE gale. It was nasty entering the gaps on the high water with seas breaking over the South Pier. The Caroline was followed in by the Mousehole-crewed 'SDJ', another former Dutch beamer which was part-owned by the 'Firm' in partnership with Ronnie Jenkin and Ian (Josh) Downing, hence the 'SDJ' initials.

One of the SDJ's crew was Barrie Tory who I got on well with, often whiling away a watch chatting on the VHF. Having moored up, walking up the quay, we fell in together chatting as we went till we parted at the top of the pier. Barrie's last words to me were "let's hope we don't have to face that lot again this side of the New Year."

Little did he know!

The following Saturday a crowd of us went to Falmouth for a meal. The weather was making (getting worse) and it was increasingly obvious that this was not going to be any old storm as a shiver went down my spine.

Thinking to myself, 'some poor buggers could die out there tonight,' the way the southerly wind was hustling, little did I realise that 20 miles away as the crow flies, the Solomon Brown Lifeboat had already launched into that maelstrom.

We had a good night with great company and delicious food. On the way home, the gale was at its height and it was dangerous with dead branches dropping everywhere in the road.

Penlee Lifeboat crew from left to right: William Richards, Nigel Brockman, Charles Greenhaugh, John Blewett, Kevin Smith, Gary Wallis, James Madron and Barrie Torrie

The following morning it was bright and clear with a moderate NW breeze, so different to a dozen hours previously.

Turning the radio on, I could not believe what I was hearing. I felt sick to the pit of my stomach as the story unfolded. I also felt an irrational sense of guilt that we were out enjoying ourselves as this catastrophe had ripped the heart out of a tight-knit community where the ordinary men who volunteered to save lives did often extraordinary things in their lifeboat. Service to others before self has never been better exemplified than on that awful December night in Mount's Bay.

It was a very difficult week. On the morning of Christmas Eve the funeral of Trevelyan Richards (who was skipper of Stevensons' 'Excellent' at the time) also took place with huge numbers in attendance.

The most poignant thing was the bravery and fortitude of Trevelyan's aged mother who had lost her only son in such terrible circumstances and was now attending his funeral on Christmas Eve.

My enduring memory is of stepping out of that church. There was total and utter grim silence bar the sound of hundreds of feet scrunching on the gravel path. The cold easterly breeze and a grey sky promising more rain matched the solemn mood as rooks called eerily to each other in the high churchyard trees.

David Senior

The ex-Dutch beamers kept arriving as the 'Firm's' growth and profitability rocketed. Meanwhile, I went as mate on the Websters' sister ship, 'Elizabeth Caroline' with David Senior as her skipper.

David was a bit different. A public schoolboy with a posh accent, quietly spoken, older, but sharp as a tack. He was not everyone's cup of tea and Billy found him particularly perplexing because he never played the game by Billy's rules, often addressing the old ogre as, 'Dear Boy'.

As another fellow non-conformist, we got on like a house on fire.

David was based in Padstow and the Caroline had a mainly North Coast Padstow crew which suited me fine.

The Caroline in some respects was an even better boat than the Webster with a heavy-duty Lister Blackstone ES6 660hp engine and a decent, though not entirely trouble-free, new winch which was controlled by the mate and engineer on deck. All the Dutchmen had wheelhouse-controlled winches worked by the skipper.

I had a very near miss with the winch soon after going aboard. We had just shot and I was barring up the brake when the anchor point underneath where the brake shoes were fixed, let go, causing the winch brake handle to rotate until it jammed against the front of the engine room casing under the wheelhouse.

Luckily, I always had a habit of standing to the outboard side of the handle which saved me from being crushed against the casing. Getting the gear up and back aboard was another of those unforeseen interesting problems peculiar to the trawling trade. It was a very near miss indeed.

A different approach to the job

David's style of skippering was relaxed and innovative. Most other skippers insisted on rigid adherence to a clearly defined Decca track or tow along the Decca lanes and woe betide any hapless crewman on watch who deviated.

This information was hard won with hitches and wrecks that had been found clearly marked on the track plotter rolls, usually as clear red dots. Someone in the past had to have chucked the gear over blind and towed it around until it was either hauled back intact with the moneybox (cod end) full of fish or come fast when the hitch would be carefully recorded and avoided henceforth.

Above: The Caroline in her original condition
Left: Skipper David Senior R.I.P.

Cap'n Senior's take on things, which made great sense to me, was that fish don't necessarily swim along lines on a plotter roll so why stick to lines?

His orders were always based on what the previous haul had produced and were basically to have a wander around while carefully avoiding the red dots which could spell so much potential grief.

This approach tended to pay off while we were always adding to our growing collection of red dots. The Caroline was relatively low-powered compared to the Dutchmen which packed plenty of gee gees (horsepower), meaning they could tow their gear harder which meant that on clean ground they would nearly always out fish us.

To compensate a little, the Caroline was a very heavy boat for her size which helped keep her moving, but would usually come to a sedate stop before too much damage was done on a fastener. Because of this, we tended to venture onto harder ground that often yielded better quality fish where, if a Dutchman came fast, something would probably break.

It was a clear case of horses for courses and this time we were on the right horse, on the right course, unlike the earlier Solent lobster fiasco.

Short hauls

Another innovation that made life a lot easier was to reduce the length of time the gear was towed between hauls. The other boats in the fleet had historically towed for up to four hours which gave the crew the chance of a bit more time in their bunks if all went well.

David thought differently. As a beam trawl is towed along it will often start to fill with sand or stones which added to the endless chafe on the nets, damaged the fish in the net and could be really heavy work to get back over the side. This made the crew more tired than necessary, the worst sound imaginable being the thud of rocks crashing out of a badly chafed cod end onto the deck.

So, we went over to shorter hauls, usually around an hour and a half. This meant easier work patterns worked out at a rota of eight hours on, four hours off, so the crew got two periods of at least four hours off in 24 hours with four crew up all the time. If there was a smash up, all hands turned out to sort it. The rota was then re-set when the gear was shot.

The wear on the nets soon became less and if, heaven forbid, a cod end or belly got ripped then it was not being towed around in that state for too long. There was much less sand to deal with as well as markedly fewer stones. With the fish in much better order, our prices started to improve as buyers began to appreciate the better quality fish.

It did mean that the man in the wheelhouse had to drop on deck for a short while when hauling and shooting, which became quicker due to a lot less mending being needed. Like the song by Hot Chocolate, it was a case of 'Everyone's a Winner,' – I saw the band live in Plymouth, and what stars they were!

Hard country up Channel

I think the hardest piece of ground we ever worked was the Dardanelles, right into the 3-mile limit the Newquay side of Trevose, where the warps would grumble and rumble and occasionally jerk. The bottom was so hard. It was a place for neap tides and fine weather but if you got it right and the 'stickers' (soles) were home at the end of March/ early April, it was pay dirt for sure.

There was also the Goldfinder off St Agnes Head, right inside where the ground was a bit easier but if you got a crack up you knew it would be a good one.

Lampered with creepers

Top side of the Goldfinder back toward Trevose, about 5 miles off Perranporth, was the Perran Bank which was lovely clean ground which also had its moments, fish-wise. We were working a tenth of a Decca lane north each time we went round with excellent fishing, but then had a spectacular balls up.

Luckily, it was quiet weather with just a light offshore easterly air.

On hauling, both sides were heavy and it was very difficult to get the lazy deckie's to the winch. Finally, the reason became obvious, both trawls were chock full with creepers or brittle stars. The cod-ends* would not run out. It was one solid mass of creepers compressed and hung together.

*The 'Cod-end' is the narrow end of a tapered trawl net
*'Hove to' a way of slowing a vessel's forward progress

137

Openning the 'money box'

We got the port side cod-end aboard and tried hosing them out but that was no use. While this was going on, the starboard side net had been hanging down almost vertical in the water, with everything bar tight from the weight when suddenly there was a ping as a headline mesh parted out. With a sound like a very dodgy fart, the whole fishing circle then let go.

The entire net had parted company with the beam and chain mat and was dangling down on the deckie. Fortunately, we were hove to* and nothing ended up in the prop as it could easily have done.

In the end, we slit the port cod-end selvedge (woven fabric) and gradually shook the mess out onto the deck. Then, turning to the starboard mess, we managed to get the net back and basically do the same.

Luckily, we carried a complete spare net as a replacement, while the damaged one was dragged up under the whaleback to be put back together.

The whole episode started mid-morning and it was nearly midnight before we shot again. *Sometimes, problems exist to be solved, so best crack on and solve them.* We did stop for our roast dinner at 18:00 but other than that the job ran on tea and fags. It was not one of our more profitable days as we retreated to kinder ground for a peaceful night.

Thinking about it later, I recalled the Bacchus working in the general area and the pots coming up absolutely lampered in creepers. If I had only remembered that earlier it might have saved us a day of absolute grief. Those patches of creepers may be very localised but where they occur they must literally be inches deep on the bottom.

Good grub and a steady routine

Reading these recollections of grief most might wonder how we ever made a living.

Obviously, it wasn't all grief, mostly it was pretty routine as the individual often unspectacular hauls built steadily into lucrative trips which gave us a very good living. It's just that side of the job would make for very tedious reading.

It was a case of a breakfast of fish for those like me who loved it. Or bacon, eggs and the extras for those who didn't like fish at 06:00. Usually, there was a decent roast dinner or a stew or salad for a change at 18:00. We worked 8 hours on and 4 hours off for seven nights, interrupted by the odd gale or crack up to relieve the monotony.

A particular favourite on the Caroline for breakfast was scallop pie. 10 scallops per person were placed in individual enamel dishes with a dollop of butter, plenty of black pepper and some chopped parsley.

This would be covered with a good layer of sliced boiled potatoes and finished with two or three rashers of smoked, streaky bacon. It was baked in the oven till crispy on top and then finished for a few minutes more with grated cheese.

Landing on the eighth day would see 'Skips' all washed and shaved coming down from the office in the latter part of the morning with a brown paper bag, like greengrocers use, stuffed with bundles of cash for us. After expenses, fuel etc., 7% for the skipper, 6% for the mate and engineer and 5% for the crew plus 'stocker money' was shared around the table equally.

'Stocker' in those days was the proceeds from the shellfish and blackstuff (cuttles, squid and octopus) which were the crew's perks.

Then home, two clear days off and repeat the performance again.

Jacqueline Webster was firm but fair and highly respected

Stevenson's office was an interesting place where very significant amounts of cash were handled. On big landing days it was not unusual for £200,000 in cash to be paid out to the boats. The office was run with a rod of iron by Billy's sister, Jacqueline Webster, a widow who made the office her life.

She was firm but fair and straight as a gun barrel. Very little got past her and she would have no nonsense from Billy who would retreat if she frowned over her glasses at him. She presided over the phenomenal growth phase, keeping everything on the straight and narrow, while Billy fretted endlessly about the boats. Younger brother Tony oversaw the market auction.

Jacqueline was deeply respected by everyone.

If she gave you a bollocking, you accepted it because it was delivered without malice and you almost certainly deserved it, while Billy operated on a whim, often sacking everyone in sight for no apparent reason.

A farcical sacking and regime change

An episode occurred one fine afternoon when we came in early to land a very decent trip. The following morning, there was no gear to work on as it had been overhauled on the way in. Billy took umbrage at us going home early and having already had words with a couple of shore staff, he sacked everyone in sight, including my mate 'Dave Randal' who came to pick me up.

Dave responded "but I don't work for you," to which Billy countered, "it doesn't matter, if you did, you would be!" There is no real answer to that one.

Tragically, Jacqueline passed away and Billy's eldest daughter Elizabeth took over the office. Things were not the same anymore. The profitability was still increasing but instead of investing in building new boats, the 'Firm' was investing heavily in property. They ended up owning literally half the houses in Newlyn as well as several farms. That was their perfectly legitimate business decision but it marked the beginning of the end for the fishing fleet as a viably progressive operation.

All of the steel beamers in the fleet were bought cheaply in Holland because the Dutch considered them to be at the end of their working life. Granted, they were still fine boats but they were sure to become increasingly costly to maintain year on year.

Chasing good money after bad

The biggest folly of all was the money spent on refitting the wooden wonders which were ancient in fishing boat terms. Wonderful ships but far too old and outclassed to have any long-term future in the arduous job they were doing.

That said 'it is an ill wind.' Refits might take years and create an ocean of work for the shipwrights and blacksmiths, but at the end of the day no matter how well the work was done, an ocean of money that would probably have bought a brand new beamer was being poured into a basically worthless asset.

Billy used to make great play of the fact that he would never build a new boat. He was totally absorbed with the ageing fleet he had. Having convinced himself that they, like him, would last forever, while everyone else knew that nothing is forever, not even the 'Firm'.

At its peak the 'Firm' was a massive operation. In its third generation it had its fingers in a lot of pies, wielding serious clout in fishing circles and not unlike the squires of old. If you crossed the 'Firm' there would inevitably be repercussions.

Billy cropped up in the Sunday Times Rich List with an alleged net worth in excess of £100 million, but there were increasing signs of megalomania - the way he needed to micro manage everything. He had eyes and ears everywhere, a sure fire recipe for malice and mischief.

My detestation of the EU

During the early 1980s, the hated Common Fisheries Policy started to flash up on the horizon. The carefree days of just getting on with the job and catching what you could where you fancied trying were anathema to the new breed of grey-suited bureaucrats charged with implementing the hated, new EU-style proscriptive fisheries regime. It pitted us against them and brought such utter misery to Cornish ports.

The Naval fisheries patrols became a hostile force of, 'at the sharp end, sometimes officious, inexperienced nit pickers' out to nab their own grannies on the slightest pretext. Paradoxically, they always seemed more interested in their own countrymen's imagined transgressions than the hordes of foreign vessels we were often working amongst which they appeared to mainly ignore.

Disgracefully, some officers were known to refer to us, their own countrymen, as the 'ENEMY'.

The Fisheries Protection Squadron was where the newly commissioned, young officers cut their teeth. As always, most were fine but by golly when you got a wrong 'un they were 101% Grade A Shits.

A hostile encounter

You always knew what you were getting by the look on the faces of the experienced sailors who manned the RIB that brought them aboard.

One particular time, the Caroline had been on the slip and, as part of the work, a new stern tube bearing had been fitted. Steaming out to the deep water, the bearing started seriously overheating. Having spoken to the engineers ashore, they were certain that it would settle down, but it didn't, it got hotter.

So we turned around for a tedious return on fast tick over which was the fastest we could go without the whole lot seizing up. Between Wolf and the Runnelstone, we encountered HMS Soberton, a Fisheries Protection Minesweeper which was heading west towards the Longships.

The commanding officer, contrary to accepted protocol, announced his intention of boarding us forthwith instead of the usual courtesy of asking when it would be convenient (obviously, that was an accepted courtesy as they had a legal right to come aboard). At this early stage, it was obvious that this was going to be a very serious shit show.

Before the boarding crew's RIB was even launched he announced his intention of arresting us and taking us to Falmouth, the alleged offence being that the 'CO' had observed through his binoculars that our cod ends were attached to the trawls, which they always were, and therefore capable of being deployed inside the limit despite the fact that the gear was chained down on the rails for steaming.

Two very young-looking, obviously inexperienced officers leapt over the rail as the CPO coxswain on the RIB gave us a very pained expression. Cap'n Senior given our problems was in just the mood for them as they entered the wheelhouse.

One set about interviewing David under caution while the other insisted on inspecting the trawl meshes, as he was perfectly entitled to do despite his unacceptable attitude. It was my job to assist if necessary and observe.

Things were getting heated upstairs in the shed while on deck, with the aid of a sailor, the net gauge was inserted in what seemed every mesh in both cod ends to no avail. They were all legal. Then he measured both beams which were spot on too and this seemed to exasperate him.

Next, he demanded to inspect the fishroom. Even though we had no fish aboard he would not accept my word, so down we went where he rummaged around stacks of empty boxes, digging into the ice to rummage through our boxes of perishable stores which were also kept there.

As this was going on he started to change colour, from pinkish to white to grey to green. The supercilious little prick was feeling sick. In fact, it looked like he was about to honk up over the fish boxes.

At that point enough was enough as I snarled in his ear that if he did honk up in my fishroom I would rub his fucking nose in it. We had to get a loop of rope lowered down to put under his arms so that his sailor oppo could help him stagger weakly back up the ladder because I sure as hell wasn't going to help him out. He could rot down there for all I cared.

Up above, things had escalated to the point where David had put a link call through to Geoffrey Buchanan Woolaston, an old-style civil servant and absolute gentleman. He was the local fisheries officer in Newlyn who couldn't believe what he was hearing. I have a feeling he had then phoned Whitehall because suddenly the boarding crew were curtly ordered back aboard the Soberton.

While they were returning, David spoke to the CO coldly and politely, addressing him in his usual manner as "Dear Boy" (at which point it was obvious that the CO's apoplexy level was off the scale). He quietly recited chapter and verse, the relevant gear regulations from the book he always kept in his cabin. When he had finished (given that he never swore) he calmly suggested that they… "fuck off to the Norrard at best speed… Over and Out, Dear Boy."

There was a big belch of black smoke and a churning of white prop wash as the CO took David's advice by making best speed north. God help the next fishing vessel he encountered. Hopefully it would be a Frenchman!

We had done nothing wrong and were actually travelling under the duress of a serious mechanical problem at the time. We had not obstructed them in their work but their truly appalling attitude that day left a very sour taste in our mouths.

For my part, the sheer injustice of that episode planted a seed in my psyche of a belligerence towards wayward incompetent officialdom that has grown and blossomed with time into an art form. They must be clearly reminded that they work for us at every opportunity!

That said, subsequent boardings were generally courteous and highly professional affairs, timed to come aboard just before hauling so as to minimise disruption to us. They were conducted in an air of mutual courtesy and respect.

I sometimes wonder where the shower on the Soberton that day eventually fetched up.

They were certainly in serious need of a crash course in interpersonal skills.

Unrealised expertise

We were, without actually realising it, experts at interpersonal skills ourselves without the need for rigid, Naval-style discipline.

Those unwitting unrealised skills borne out of extensive experience were the key to a successful crew who could handle, without question, the often merciless banter, the nicknames, the hardships of poor weather and frequent sleep disruption, while still being able to work together as a strong team who instinctively looked out for each other and the boat.

That was how the often stunning results the top boats consistently turned in were achieved.

The Fastnet disaster

As had been the case in summer, we spent a bit of time to the eastward deep of the Start where quality trips could be had at an otherwise slack time elsewhere. We set sail the day of the Fastnet Race and passed the bulk of the fleet of yachts off the Lizard just as it was increasingly obvious that the weather was deteriorating rapidly.

Several hours later and east of the Eddystone, it was very poor indeed and it was obvious that the gear wasn't going in the water that night. We changed course for Brixham and shelter. Entering Brixham, the wind was screaming down the harbour as we thankfully moored up.

NW of The Longships, the Fastnet Fleet was in serious trouble. A fleet of lifeboats was launched from Cornwall, Scilly and Ireland along with helicopters from Culdrose and Ireland to assist in what was rapidly becoming a tragedy of serious proportions. It was yet another example of how lethal storms could rapidly become even in summer.

A fleet of 303 boats were caught up in the disaster and 15 lives were lost despite the heroic efforts of rescuers battling the horrendous conditions. It became the UK's biggest ever peacetime rescue.

The loss of the Isles of Scilly helicopter

The Caroline was about 45 miles SW of the Islands in very thick fog when chilling news came through that a Sikorsky helicopter had crashed into the sea just off St Mary's. We were too far away to be in a position to assist but it certainly cast a long shadow over the day.

Twenty people were killed when the helicopter, en-route from Penzance to the Isles of Scilly, crashed in thick fog off St Mary's. Only six people survived the crash in 1983 - two crew members and four passengers, including two children.

An official report into the cause of the crash cited pilot error, but the pilot and co-pilot, who escaped, were praised for their bravery for helping the survivors.

A very hairy night off Dunmore

The Celtic Sea from the Scillies north to Cape Clear in Ireland and east to the Bristol Channel can be a very lonely area totally exposed to gales from every quarter. The Caroline along with the Algrie, Annelise and AA were working about 40 miles SW of Dunmore East on the Irish side, with another very poor forecast of a classic fast moving, rapidly deepening low heading our way.

The fishing was reasonable and as the wind freshened David decided to sit tight while the others decided to board their gear and get underway. As dusk closed in it was getting really bad, with the wind veering rapidly from SE to SW and freshening even more. The seas were short and steep and hauling was a nightmare.

It was actually too poor to board the gear and follow the others so it was shot away till the ten fathom marks were just in the water where the gear acted as a combination of sea anchor and stabilisers as we ticked over before the wind.

It was a very hairy night with the huge, almost vertical seas, picking us up like a cork while an occasional monster would crash over the stern and fill the deck. As mate, I was very thankful that I had taken even more trouble than usual to batten down the hatches, bar up the winch brakes and generally ensure that nothing could come loose.

It was a case of sitting out what proved to be a very long and, at times, very scary night.

Come first light we could actually see what had been battering us in the dark. The waves were huge and so steep but we were OK. Then the sky started to clear and finally the wind flew up into the NW. We took the chance to have a quick bit of breakfast before going to work boarding the gear.

We got underway with the wind more or less in our favour. Halfway to Pendeen, we caught up with the others who had suffered an even worse night steaming into the eye of the storm. The Anneliese had a sea come aboard which took out the wheelhouse windows and electrics. Crazy as it seemed, David's decision to sit tight was proved right for us in the circumstances.

Riches from Poverty Bay

As the autumn turned to winter and the fast-moving fronts continued, we ventured up into Poverty Bay (Falmouth Bay) to try and lose the ground sea. It was not an easy area to work but the quality of the fish was an eye opener and we realised that we could be onto a winner as the rest of the fleet seemed to avoid it like the plague while persevering out in the deep water.

We were finding our way around making good bread and butter trips while dodging the worst of the weather a couple of hours from shelter. Without drawing any attention to ourselves, our short hauls were ideally suited to this dirty, difficult ground where coming fast became a routine of haul back, check for damage and shoot away again.

Chapter 9
Top dog!

She's all mine

With the passing of time, I was getting wheelhouse experience as David left me to it more and more. One night, passing Low Lee, he said "she is all yours, take her in." He then stepped back leaving me to get on with it. The berth was clear, there was no wind and she fell in like a dream. I had done it. It was a far cry from handling a nimble crabber for sure. The Caroline's gearbox had a nine second delay built in when going from ahead to astern which seemed like an eternity when you were heading towards the quay where Billy was stood glowering at you. But, like most things, practice made perfect and you got used to it.

My first trip as Skipper

A couple of trips later, David was off and I was relief skipper of the Caroline which was a whole new ball game and a very proud moment. It was now down to me to make a trip rather than just ice it away.

Billy put old Ernie Hunter aboard because the 'Excellent' was laid up. Ernie hated beamers and wasn't too pleased at first. Neither was I, always having regarded him as a miserable old sod but how wrong I was. Once away we got talking up in the wheelhouse, like you do, and his true character and wry sense of humour emerged from behind the cloud where it had been hiding.

He was fascinated when we shot the gear, so much easier and quicker than on the old sidewinder he was used to.

He was fascinated even more so when we hauled, deckie straight on the winch, Gilson in and two big bags of monk and megs swung effortlessly in over the side and flopped out into the pounds.

We had hauled, shot back and were towing again while a sidewinder would have been just about getting the cod end aboard.

Ernie was crippled with arthritis from a lifetime of hardship and hard graft just scratching a living. It was little wonder he was a moaner, he had plenty to moan about, he was a 'Pud' (Lowestoft Man), who had survived the sweepers like my own father and had come to Newlyn to work in the Firm after the war.

Useful advice

He was very useful at hauling time as he could stay up in the wheelhouse while I went down on deck. It meant that we could haul and shoot even quicker. We spent hours talking, the old bugger hardly ever slept. One night in the small hours, he looked me in the eye said something to me, one of those things that wise men with real experience say that registers and puts a different perspective on your outlook from there on in.

He said "you think I am a miserable old bastard, don't you?" I replied, "well Ernie I used to think so." Then he said this… *"life has been hard… sometimes I have had to be a bastard. Now you are a skipper, there will be times when you have to be an absolute bastard as well. That's the way it is, but always try to be a fair bastard if you want to be respected."*

Those words were another piece of the jigsaw of understanding started by Mr Duggan the day I left school. They shape you and help you understand that everyone has a story to tell and you should always try to listen to them.

The best was yet to come on landing day. I was Skips. Having seen the fish sold for top dollar, after a shower, shave and splash of foo foo dust under the armpits in the Mission it was off up to the office to settle. Billy seemed happy, good prices ensured that our considerable share was put in the brown paper bag for me to take down aboard and proud as a dog with two dicks.

Ernie's eyes lit up when I said what we had made. He was on mate's share as the second ticket but while I had been away he had made the galley sparkle which was grand while the rest had checked over the gear, stowed it and washed down till the rusty old girl was as near sparkling as possible.

Ernie didn't quite make the thousand including stocker for the 8-day trip but he was choked as he told me that it was the most he had ever made for a trip in all his years fishing and it was the easiest trip ever as well. He had a couple more trips with me. What he taught me was priceless, just as his money was to him.

Hooked

While all this was going on, I was courting and, by another amazing coincidence, the young lady was Julia Gribbin, daughter of the dreaded Youth Employment Officer, Dennis Gribbin. Fortunately, she was better looking than her father, in the old adage *'the uglier the ram, the prettier the lamb'* it was true.

My sister had married and moved to Carharrack and Julia lived a couple of doors down. She had been married before but her husband had left her while she was pregnant so she came with a seven-year old daughter. An instant family so to speak.

At that time, I drove a flashy, customised, Mazda pickup truck which I had recently bought brand new for cash. It was grand driving a decent vehicle after some of the lash ups of the poverty days. Although it wasn't the classic 'babe magnet', it was practical and suited me. Whenever I turned up at my sister's, Julia would appear on some pretext.

It was obvious that she was interested and we shared an interest in farming. Being away at sea so much, keeping livestock was difficult for me, although I had always rented a few acres and kept some bullocks which father kept an eye on for me when I was away.

I still lived in Redruth with Mother but her health was worsening all the time. She was in and out of Treliske Hospital which was a constant worry. My sister and her husband moved to a bigger house in St Day and Mother sold the Redruth house and moved in with Marie and Roy and I was living with Julia in her terraced cottage in Carharrack.

Julia's parents were staunch churchgoers who were a bit sniffy about us living together but we were happy and things had to take their course because the fishing was good and getting married would have to wait. Julia certainly seemed to like being involved with a fisherman and loved dropping me off to go to sea and picking me up at the end of the trip.

Back on the farm

We ramped up the farming a bit. She already had some cattle of her own and we rented a bit more ground so some of the money I was earning was going into the smallholding. We ended up with 30 bullocks and grew five or six acres of swedes which kept father out of mischief. He would cut them, select the best to net up for sale and the rest would be fed to the bullocks just like the old days.

Swedes were a cheap crop to grow and liked our sparry (stony) soil. With the advent of precision drills and residual herbicides they did not need the traditional labour-intensive, hand hoeing. The season would start in September and run through till late March and always did us very well as a side line. They also made the bullocks' coats shine.

One of my best swede customers was Clifford Thomas who owned Bartles, the celebrated hog's pudding shop in Fore Street, Redruth. Customers queued back down the street to buy them. He also did a roaring trade in home cooked ham, swedes and cabbage but nothing much else. He would only accept the best quality.

The trick was to turn up mid-morning to deliver the swedes around the time the hog's puddings were due out of the boiler. We'd carry them through the shop to stack out the back in the store room. He would generally take 30 to 40 nets a week and would pay the cash whilst reaching over the counter to give whoever was delivering a hog's pudding still hot from the boiler.

You have never really tasted hog's pudding until you have had one like that. Clifford had a secret recipe of spice and combined it with lean pork shoulder and finely minced pork rind.

No fat or rubbish in Bartles' hog's puddings. Tragically, when he retired, he closed the shop and his recipe went to his grave with him. What a loss to Redruth that was.

I had always kept the Massey 135 and had a power loader fitted to it. We were early users of round baled haylage which was less weather-dependent and with the fore end loader easily mechanised we were quite up-to-date in our own small way. It was heaven not having to save conventional bales in often catchy weather with all the work and stress that entailed.

147

That 'Eureka' moment

It was the need for a couple of cans of red diesel for the tractor one day that triggered a seismic event that, unbeknown to me at the time, shaped the next 35 years.

In at South Turnpike, where the road to Helston heads up Buller Hill towards Four Lanes there is a long-established oil distributor called Opie Oils. Founded in the 1920s, it had recently been taken over by my old adversary, Slippery Joe French.

The previous owner had maintained very reasonable prices, but whenever I had gone there in recent months the price had crept up each time, while fuel prices elsewhere had not been moving. Anyway, on the day in question, it would have been just as cheap to buy white diesel at an ordinary forecourt.

Me being me, instead of doing that I tackled him about his prices. His face changed like the sun going behind a big black cloud as he angrily fired back, "if you don't fucking well like it start your own oil company!" I thought to myself, that sounds like a good idea, but said nothing, paid for the fuel picked up the two cans and left.

That was the second challenge like that he had thrown down. There would not be a third for sure! He had just unwittingly done me the biggest favour any one ever had.

That winter we were doing very well up in Poverty Bay working poor weather to our advantage in relative shelter. No one else was around. We had the huge piece of ground to ourselves and as we found our way around we began pinpointing the best bits.

In the previous October, Julia and I had got married and went to Bretagne for 10 days on our honeymoon. When we got back we found out that she was pregnant.

David didn't make the wedding as he was off ill with viral meningitis and Billy was ugly that I wasn't around to take the Caroline away. There was no one else around either so she had been against the wall which was unfortunate but unavoidable.

An awful prognosis

A lot was going on. The hospital had told us that Mother's time was limited which preoccupied me, the oil idea had gained traction and was beginning to look like a goer, but a lot of research was needed and I would lie in my bunk at sea with all this going around in my head. My greatest wish was that Mother would last long enough to hold the baby boy we were expecting in the July. Thankfully, that wish was fulfilled.

The big trip

That winter we had the weather from hell with frontal systems queuing up to blast us from every direction. Whenever the fleet got away they would head out to the usual grounds only to be blown back in again before they could get a proper trip down below. To compensate however, fish prices were through the roof.

Left: Not how a beam trawl is supposed to be
Inset: Beam trawl as it should be

Thus, toward the end of January, we had slipped away to the east and tucked away in Poverty Bay. During the afternoon as we sailed it was blowing a smeecher from the NW but by the time we got around the corner it was a fine night and the sea was already flattening.

The rest had gone the other way as usual.

The first hour and half tow turned in a box of soles, a box of good monk tails and a box of huge lemons along with a kit of ling and pollack, a couple of bags of scallops and a box of cuttles… a very good start.

The next haul was much the same and so it went on, really good quality fish and steady fishing, with the scallops as the icing on the cake. The following day was fine, we lost the pollack and ling in the daylight but the scallops were steady into the second fine night with the forecast of a SE gale for the morning as another front came roaring in.

Come daylight it was freshening rapidly from the SE so we boarded the gear and dodged into Carrick Roads under the Roseland shore to tittivate the gear and see what happened. By mid-morning it was poor from the SW and by midday it was howling from the SW and soon flew NW by which time we were back out ready to shoot. The rest of the fleet were back in Newlyn.

The beauty of the east side of the Lizard was that as soon as the wind dropped, the sea would drop as well, unlike out to the Westward beyond the Islands in the deep water where the ground sea would often take days to die down, needing only a puff of wind on it to make it very poor again.

We had six nights of brilliant fishing like this. It was obvious that a bumper trip was building and we were going to run out of boxes and scallop bags. The final night, the forecast was evil, and come daylight the sky said it all, blood red with a fresh SE breeze springing up with the light. We towed away to the west for a couple of hauls and boarded the gear off Coverack. By this time conditions were very poor.

We got under way dodging quietly into the teeth of a SW storm. From abeam of the Black Head to deep off the Lizard took the best part of six hours against the storm and a strong flood tide. This was no night for cutting the corner up into the Bay.

Billy comes up with the goods

David had made a link call to Billy when we boarded the gear. Telling him what fish we had you could sense his excitement. We had the big one for sure. Cheekily, David asked him if he could get half a dozen cans of lager for everyone when we got in… there was a stunned silence the other end and then a 'click' as he rang off. That was that we thought, probably sacked again!

By the time we were round the Lizard the wind was veering, so going up the Bay it was still on the nose with spray flying everywhere, rolling like a pig with a huge ground sea on the beam there was a carnival atmosphere on board.

When we got in through the Gaps Billy was on the end of the North Pier in his white Triumph Dolomite. As soon as we were fast he was aboard like a long dog bubbling with excitement. He sat back on the mess deck and actually had a cup of tea with us.

When he went finally went ashore he stopped at the top of the ladder and said "they there things you wanted are under that sack over there," pointing to the coils of spare mooring ropes under the old mackerel shed.

Sure enough there were six cans of Stella Artois there, which we found out later he had sent one of the shore staff into the Coop for. In the 'Firm's' long history this was unheard of. Another first for the non-conformist crew of the good ship Caroline.

A new port record

At 04:00 the lorry turned up to land us, we turned out 48 boxes of soles, 55 boxes of monk, 40 boxes of lemons, 40 odd boxes of pollack and ling, 10 boxes of cuttles with 120 bags of prime scallops from 52 hauls in often very poor weather to gross £14,800 which set a new port record beating David Hooper's previous record in the Webster, by a, at that time convincing, £1,600.

Our record didn't stand for long. The following autumn the AA had a huge trip of monk and megrims from the Deep Water, again in beastly weather to break through the phenomenal £58,000 barrier.

Never the same again

The cat was now out of the bag and the next trip we turned up on the ground and there were beamers everywhere. The 'Firm's' fleet plus half of the Brixham fleet were there and while there was still a living to be made in poor weather, the ground would never be the same again. I am sure the fish we caught were biders that never moved very far and when they were gone, they were gone.

We were back there at the start of March but the wind was easterly and Poverty Bay was living up to its name. Even though there were only light airs, as always, the bottom changed and we were plagued with rocks and corruption for scant reward.

The last farewell

We had sailed on the Tuesday and before leaving home as always, I had taken the Western Morning News up to Mother in St Day and sat on the edge of the bed with her reading it, as was our way. The three weeks since she had been sent home from Treliske Hospital to die were amazing. She was looking radiant, had been to the hairdressers and bought herself a new colour TV.

She had (and so richly deserved) a miraculous, albeit short remission from her suffering. She had been spared to hold our boy Thomas, who was past eight months old. However, when I walked out of her room that morning it was obvious to me that she was ready to go. Her work done, I instinctively knew that would be the last time I would see her alive. That was really hard!

The passing

The weather was lousy, the wind SE and the fishing as usual with the wind that way was dire. Most of the rest of the fleet were at Trevose on reasonable fishing while Poverty Bay was living up to its reputation, there was only one way to go.

In the small hours of Friday morning we boarded the gear up off the 'Dodman' to steam around the land into the Channel. I had the watch after breakfast and was very preoccupied sitting up in the wheelhouse crossing Mount's Bay, it was a dark morning, bleak and cold.

At around 09:30 I lit my pipe and standing on the starboard veranda with the biting easterly breeze on our stern I was looking back in the general direction of the Mount and the Four Lanes TV mast, its distinctive red lights still clearly visible in the grey half-light, with Redruth and home behind it… just thinking as I puffed quietly away.

Suddenly, a bright ray of light pierced the clouds over 'Carn Brea' and a cold shiver passed down my spine. Mother passed peacefully away at 09:38 and a leading light had left my life. Rounding Carn Base I went below as David took over the watch. Lying in my bunk was strange, even though I hadn't been told I felt a huge sense of loss but also relief that my best friend's years of suffering had ended.

That might seem strange to some, not having been told I still instinctively knew. Falling asleep after a long night I was woken a couple of hours later to be told that there was a link call waiting for me from Land's End Radio. It was Julia and Marie calling to tell me what I already knew.

There was nothing I could do. David gave the option of going in but it was pointless so we carried on with the trip, which was a blur for me. We fished on till Tuesday evening, ending up with a bread and butter trip. We got in around 04:00 on the Wednesday, landed, did the gear and I went home with a heavy heart.

That evening I went and sat with her for a while in the Chapel of Rest which gave me the closure I needed. One last kiss on her forehead and it was goodbye to an amazing mother who really deserved much better than she got out of a very hard life dogged by a mysterious non-specific illness that just kept turning the screws.

She had a wonderful send off with her London family in attendance and dozens of friends and neighbours. Those of us who could, walked behind the hearse through St Day to the church. Father turned up looking very sheepish and I saw a tear in the old bastard's eye as we lowered her into her grave. So, he was human after all?

The 'Celtic Curse'

A few years later, Marie, my baby sister, started having similar non-specific symptoms to those that mother had suffered. Back and forth to the doctors solved nothing until she saw a young locum one day. She had a hunch and ordered a genetic test which came back positive. Marie was suffering from 'hemochromatosis,' also known as the 'Celtic Curse'.

This means that the body cannot eliminate excess iron which builds up leading to chronic organ failure over time. It was exactly what had happened to Mother and is particularly prevalent among those of Irish and Scottish extraction. I also had the test which revealed me to be a carrier but not a sufferer. Thomas, my son, will also need a test at some point to be on the safe side.

If you have to suffer from anything these days, when it is recognised as hemochromatosis it is probably as good as any because all that is necessary to control it if caught in time are regular blood tests and removal of blood by venesection if iron levels are high. I just wish that Mother had had the chance of a test but it was not understood in her time.

My personal tribute...

These paragraphs about my dear Mother have not been easy to write about. Coincidentally it is VE Day 2020 as I continue to work through this story. Many threads keep unravelling from my memory.

I would like these words to be taken as a tribute to my parents and all the millions of other ordinary people like them who did often extraordinary things in their country's time of need. The people who, when it was all over, returned and got on with their lives the best they could despite the scars, both mental and physical that so many of them bore for the rest of their days.

A salvage job

Back at sea, with the Trevose season winding down, we were working the Irish side off the Waterford Coast between 12 and 20 miles known as the Mine Head Grounds, where a feature of the catch was fairish numbers (for us) of the biggest cod I had ever seen - up to three stone in weight - as many as ten on some hauls. Amongst the soles were megrims and smallish turbot.

The second trip that way we were north of the Longships bound away when a call came through from the office. It turned out the 'Dew Genen Ny', a seine netter skippered and part owned by Robert George, (in which the 'Firm' also had an interest) was in trouble near the Kinsale Gas Rig south of Kinsale and about 40 miles west of where we were bound.

She had suffered a serious engine room fire and was drifting disabled in urgent need of a tow. We were, at about 10 hours away, the nearest Cornish vessel. The badly burned engineer had been evacuated to Cork by an Irish Coastguard helicopter but the rest of the crew were safe with the fire out.

The Dew Genen Ny was a fine modern, 80 foot, Scottish-built vessel that was making huge landings of whitefish using the seine net method which was not widely practiced in Newlyn. When we got to her we could see the heat-blackened plates in the region of the engine room which were steaming as she rolled in the low swell.

It took no time at all to secure the prepared tow and it was an uneventful 15-hour trip back. The harbour boat took over the tow outside of the Gaps and while we berthed to top up with fuel we went aboard for a look. Over 24 hours later the plates on the waterline were still hot to touch, such was the heat generated.

It turned out that the same had happened as we had seen on the old Webster the night the turbo oil feed pipe had fractured. This time it was a main hydraulic pipe that drove the winch system that had blown right onto the hot manifold of the big auxiliary engine.

The engineer and his son had been in the engine room when it happened. The father had got his son to safety unharmed but got very seriously burnt himself in so doing. The halon fire suppression system could not be fired until the engineer was out by which time the engine room was lost.

When we looked down the engine room hatch everything was melted, ramming home just how dangerous fire is at sea. The Dew Genen Ny had to be towed back to her builder in Scotland to be repaired which was a very long and expensive job. Fortunately, the engineer recovered but that too was a long, painful job.

Chapter 10
A restless period of change

New adventures – new ventures

The oil job was going around in my head. I was convinced that it would be a viable proposition. The bigger companies had more or less walked away from small tanker deliveries, leaving a gap in the market where Slippery Joe had a monopoly and was milking it for all it was worth. He badly needed a bit of competition.

The Firm was increasingly chaotic as more and more beamers kept arriving. Without Jacqueline's steadying hand it was obvious that the long decline was beginning. While still seriously profitable as a formidable financial entity, management was not keeping up with the phenomenal growth and it was showing in the inefficiencies evident.

I had been looking for a suitable site for my new venture. Father had been forced to sell Woodbine Farm and had a big offer from a developer on the table but they pulled out because Cornwall County Council owned a ransom strip of land needed for access and absolutely refused to sell it or grant a wayleave.

The County Council ended up virtually stealing the land by compulsory purchase at £1,100 per acre which was not much above its agricultural value and the farm became an extension of the existing industrial estate. So that was my obvious starting point until they informed me that they wanted £18,500 for a quarter of an acre!

That was the trigger for my 35 year, ongoing beef with developers in general and Cornwall County Council in particular, because I hate with a passion their profiteering and greed. A fair profit is what business is all about but the price asked at Threemilestone by the English Estates quango for that little corner plot was a total piss take!

Carrick to the rescue!

Fortunately, Carrick District Council were much more amenable. They were in the process of developing the Consols Industrial Site at United Downs, St Day as a place for businesses that would not be welcome on the more up market industrial sites. The site was on land contaminated by former mining activity.

The Council had an excellent development officer in the form of a St Agnes Boy called 'Roger Radcliffe' who understood exactly what I wanted to do and pointed me in the direction of an organisation that became the key to my early survival.

The Council for Small Industries in Rural Areas (COSIRA), had a local office in Truro where I was assigned a very capable person called Dave Hilliard. Dave was a management accountant who could prepare cash flows and business plans that a lender would accept. He was a quiet, unassuming Midlander who talked me through everything at every stage before the actual start up and beyond.

Roger Radcliffe's colleague, Russell Dodge negotiated the sale of a quarter acre plot to me through the District Valuer for £10,000 freehold with outline planning permission in place for use as a fuel sales and distribution depot. This meant a significant step had been taken because, with a new home secured, the venture really was go.

Back at sea, the work provided the bread and butter while the financial jigsaw for the new venture was assembled. Ashore, the cattle and tractor were sold which bought the land, while the house went back into hock to raise a mortgage to finance the actual start-up costs. With proper budgets and cash flows now in place a pretty clear picture was emerging.

In the mid 1980s the oil industry was not regulated to the degree it is now. While there were some hoops to jump through the requirements were attainable. I bought an aluminium tank off a BP truck for my first storage. It had 6 compartments with a total of 20,000 litres of storage which seemed huge at the time.

Thoughts now turned towards a suitable delivery truck which needed to be small and compact in order to service the customers targeted and the budget was strictly limited, so it was becoming an interesting problem.

Then in June 1985 I had an accident aboard the boat which could have finished me off, fortunately it didn't. We had just finished landing and I was on the deck by the fishroom hatch when the crewman up on the lorry let the landing hooks swing down without shouting a warning. They struck me a glancing heavy blow on the top of my skull knocking me backwards. The back of my neck landed hard on the bar tight port warp that jerked it back. I really thought it was broken.

There was blood everywhere and my neck was in agony. I was sitting propped up by the warp afraid to move. It didn't take long for an ambulance to arrive but by then the blood had run down my back and was soaking my underwear despite a bandage on my skull.

Luckily it was high water and easy to get me lifted ashore, strapped to the stretcher, wearing an inflatable neck brace with blood still pouring out of my head. When they got me to West Cornwall Hospital they were concerned by the loss of blood. Out of the corner of my eye I could see that they were ready for a major stitch up job and I used to be terrified of needles.

When they removed the pad that had been applied aboard the boat the nurse laughed. There was a biggish bump with literally a pin prick that had nicked a small artery and with every beat of my heart, a small spurt was squirting out which they soon dealt with so I wasn't going to bleed to death. Blood pressure and pulse were OK so they focused on my neck as I was wheeled into X-ray.

The X-rays confirmed that nothing was broken but it was obvious that there was tissue damage and it was beginning to really hurt. I looked a real sight when I left a few hours later in a neck collar and a heavily bandaged head.

I was off for a couple of trips but on returning to sea it was obvious that it was going to take a while for the tissue damage to repair properly. A couple more trips later David had a blazing row with Billy and we all got sacked over nothing. I went home still in pain and went to see my doctor who signed me off sick. I had enough of the lunacy in the 'Firm' and, without saying anything, I decided to finish.

This gave me an opportunity to concentrate fully on the business I was now in an advanced stage of planning. I never went near Newlyn or had any contact for three weeks or more. On the Sunday night at around 20:00 the phone rang. It was one of Billy's men. The message being, "Billy said you can come back now," meaning that I was needed in the morning, as if I was a hat hanging behind the door.

An abuse of power

That is the way good men got treated in the 'Firm'. It really was feudal. Sadly, most put up with it because they knew no different and it was regarded as a game of cat and mouse with people's livelihoods. It was OK for Billy because he had inherited his money and was in the right place at the right time to amass an even bigger fortune from other's efforts.

When I said, "I am not coming back," there was a stunned silence on the other end of the phone before he said, "you can't do that," to which I replied, "I just have." I didn't owe them anything. I had agreed to stay for two years, six years earlier, so I had discharged my part of the bargain on that score and that was the end of my career with the 'Firm'.

Delwyn had left the 'Firm' and ended up as the token British skipper aboard a Spanish flagship where he succumbed finally to the demon drink. He ended up beached and destitute. We even tried to kidnap him back to his Carharrack family to try and dry him out but to no avail. The last time I saw him he was drunk and incoherent, sprawled on a bench on Penzance Promenade. He didn't even know me.

He passed around the Land for the final time a few days later. He was far too good a man to end like that. R.I.P. Skipper Delwyn Puckey.

David Senior got diagnosed with kidney cancer even though he never smoked or drank. The final time he was fired, Billy plumbed new depths by telling a dying man to go home and stay home because he had no further use for him.

Given that Billy was deep down not a bad man I would like to think that in the wee small hours he has pondered upon what he said to David in the heat of the moment and come to regret it. If he has not then he ought to be ashamed of himself.

David fought like a tiger to live, but better he didn't because no one should suffer like he did. Again, a good man who deserved a better end. R.I.P. Skipper, David Senior.

I will catch up with you both one day on Fiddlers Green.

The mindset of a fisherman

Concerned well-meaning people ashore who know nothing of the mindset of a fisherman engage in much hand wringing about how dangerous the job is.

Granted there were risks, but no one was more aware of them than we were and we accepted them. No one made any of us do the job, it was in our blood to do it, so we just got on with it. We actually enjoyed it, loving it and hating it in equal measure and generally we got very well rewarded for it.

Into the unknown

It was a high-risk strategy chucking in a job that in the mid 80s paid between thirty and forty thousand a year for not much more than eight months' actual work. But once again, in for a penny, in for a pound. If I hesitated now I knew I would fail, so onwards and upwards to pastures new, for better or worse. One lesson I have repeatedly learned is, never ever to go back.

The tanker issue had to be resolved. I had studied tanker designs by watching them work and a friend of my father with the right trade contacts had sourced a very tidy, compact 7.5 ton 4 cylinder Bedford TK in Essex. It sounded like it was being sold for the right price, so off I went on the train to Paddington to buy it.

I stayed with my mother's younger brother in Eltham, SE London and what surprised me leaving London on the M11 the following day was how abruptly, compared with the M4, the town ended and lovely rural countryside began. We were heading for a place called 'Stondon Massey' not far from Ongar.

We eventually found the dealer's yard, way out in the sticks. It was the sort of place they would use as a location for a gangster film. They bought, sold and broke trucks for export, part scrap yard and part truck sales. The operator, Lenny Moss, was an obvious hard case and his guard dogs were definitely man eaters.

Deal done I set off back to St Day with the uncle following in his car. The little truck was indeed tidy and at £750 within budget. It drove fine on the test but 10 miles down the road on the M11 slip road the engine went bang.
Just like that it was a disaster!

In the days just before mobile phones I was unsure what to do, so walking back to the service station we had passed on the roundabout that the slip road came off, I rang Lenny

Moss expecting to be told to get lost. Fortunately, without hesitation, he said he would put it right as he had sold it as a genuine runner.

They came out and recovered it back to the yard. So, it was back to Eltham while they changed the engine for one out of the store that was awaiting export. Late the following day we were on our way again and, this time, faultlessly. I headed anti-clockwise round the M25 to pick up the M3 and the A303 home, a route I always prefer to the manic M4.

This was another example of not judging a book by its cover. First impressions of the man and his yard suggested 'hooky', but he was anything but. Lenny was a very rich man who worked hard and doted on his family. He was one of the most genuine men I have ever dealt with and his word was his bond even though I must have cost him money.

I didn't know how to thank him or repay him for his kindness. His reply was just, "be lucky," but when previously I had told him that I had been a fisherman he was drooling as he said how he enjoyed a good crab. So, it really was a pleasure to ensure that a very large cock crab ended up with him via my father's friend meeting him at a vehicle auction a few weeks later.

Tanker tribulations

Having got the truck home, the demountable box body was sold as a store for £150 making it an even better buy. The next job was to turn it into a tanker. I had been talking to Reynolds Boughton, a specialist tanker builder located in Winkleigh up in North Devon but they were way beyond my budget.

So, in a last throw of the dice I went to see Uncle, Roy Richards, our local body builder over at Longdowns who was more used to building tippers and cattle containers. He thought about it and said he would like to have a go literally sketching out the tank design on a piece of scrap paper while quoting a price that I could actually live with.

There was one problem with Roy Richards, his sense of urgency on a good day would make 'dreckly' seem like express delivery. Being snowed under with work, he was totally unflappable in the manner that when it was ready it would be ready but the trade-off was the superb standard of work they turned out.

While all this was going on I found a 16 foot portacabin for the office and got the storage sorted out and pumps installed by another stalwart, Dynamite Dave Hardiman of Western Forecourt Services who completed the job in bitingly cold sub-zero temperatures that marked the start of 1986.

Local family businesses like WR Richards & WFC to name but two, are the unsung heroes of trade who punched way above their weight for expertise and service levels that generally put larger, better known companies to shame. Particularly so in a remote place like Cornwall, where our economy is built around such firms much more than most realise.

A gate but no money for a fence

I had also bought a very strong yard gate for a song when the contents of the old Penzance Cattle Market were auctioned off. It was installed in the yard entrance. The fact that it was some time before I could actually afford to fence the yard did not stop the gate being opened and closed every day. Miraculously, nothing went missing in the interim despite the total lack of security.

The final thing which threw the still unsuspecting, soon-to-be, opposition into a tizzy was quite amusing after I spent far more than I should have on a whole page advert in the local Yellow Pages which was the 'oracle' before the internet. To announce that 'Consols Oils, the Cornish Fuel Company,' was trading under the banner of offering 'Prompt Personal Service and Competitive Prices…' well there's nothing like a bit of shock and awe, but what was needed was results.

This resulted in a series of drive by visits from the various local operators who took one look at the operation and decided to ignore me because like the Cornish farmers with Brittany Ferries over 20 years previously, they simply decided I wouldn't last.

That was a very big mistake on their part, because I had to last. Our house and the very future of my little family hung by the gossamer thread of survival against the odds. I was occupying a very lonely position.

Welcome assistance

The next piece of the jigsaw came with some very good news from the Government. For the first and last time in my career I was eligible for a grant. I was never a great fan of Margaret Thatcher. Her monotonous voice and hectoring manner just kind of ground my gears but she did introduce an enterprise friendly culture.

Norman Tebbit had urged everyone to 'get on their bikes' and I was just about to anyway but he then introduced the Enterprise Allowance Scheme which gave people like me £40 per week for 12 months to help new small businesses get off the ground.

That was really helpful. When I took it up in January, on starting to actually trade, which after the lengthy lead in was akin to jumping off a cliff, the Enterprise Allowance gave a guarantee of enough money to buy the groceries and pay the mortgage. Come what may, once more there was no going back.

A supply dilema

The biggest single issue for any fuel company regardless of size is 'supply.' Without product to trade the whole supply chain collapses in a heap. I had initially approached Heltor, a Gulf Oil distributor based in Newton Abbot for supply.

They were (and to this day remain) a very good family firm who had actually delivered a couple of loads to me, but in the back of my mind there was a major concern… they were also the supplier to the 'Firm', so strings could potentially, and probably would, be pulled sooner or later.

Another amazing stroke of luck intervened in the form of Andy Coleman, the sales manager of Fuelserve Ltd who were, at the time, the local Esso Authorised Distributors. He had actually made several attempts to catch up with me and had not written me off like the others had. When he did catch up he had an interesting proposition which suited us both admirably.

The authorised distributorship system was an anachronism riddled with self-interest, nepotism and restrictive practices. In fact, everything that was wrong with British business in those days.

A contracted distributor would get the most favoured pricing terms and the protective shield of the major brand they represented. But contracted distributors were unable to buy fuel elsewhere and had rigid volume targets to meet on pain of potentially severe financial penalties for failure to do so.

This was Andy's problem and he saw me as part of its solution – that is, as a potential volume buyer where he could dispose of excess product to mitigate the financial penalties he was increasingly and frequently being lumbered with, due to Esso's imposing and unrealistic sales targets.

The cashflow conundrum

The other potentially major pitfalls were cash flow and credit worthiness. Having no trading record, credit worthiness was a potentially fatal flaw in the business model.

My working capital was limited and the bank was far from helpful only giving me a £5,000 overdraft facility secured against the £10,000 value of the yard. Despite Dave Hilliard's professional input making a very sound case for more, my Nat West Bank Manger refused to budge.

Actually, as time went by, I realised that living inside the ruthless financial straitjacket this imposed was actually doing me a favour even though it never felt like it at the time. To survive you had to live strictly and within your means at all times.

This became the rule with capital expenditure. Henceforth, it was strictly a case of earn a bit, spend a bit and never over borrow.

This was freely and frankly discussed with Andy who did not see a huge problem, pointing out that as a large part of my sales would be domestic, most of the payments would be upfront and with Fuelserve not requiring payment till the 20th of the month following delivery, a deal was struck that proved to be immensely mutually beneficial for the first 4 years of trading.

Honesty is definitely the best policy

One thing that clearly emerges time and again in negotiations with genuine people is that honesty and openness helps. Telling it like it is, warts and all, enables all parties to make clear, unequivocal, evidence-based decisions. Being economical with the truth will always turn around and bite you as several delinquent customers of mine discovered to their cost as time went by.

This highlights the fact that business that does not offer some benefit to everyone concerned is not worth doing and it is far better to walk away than be disadvantaged or indeed, to take undue advantage of someone else, because everyone needs to make a living to survive.

Ethical business is about free and fair competition on as near a level playing field as possible. It is not about ripping competitors' throats out. That's thuggery, pure and simple. Far too many businesses engage in that kind of unsavoury practice simply because they can and because they are allowed to get away with it.

To be truly successful, the foundation stone of any business should be a culture where customers want to deal with it willingly. Any sort of monopoly where customers have to deal with it because there is no alternative, is in reality on a hiding to nothing. A bit of healthy competition keeps everyone on their toes.

The best and cheapest advertising has to be satisfied customers making recommendations to their friends.

Chapter 11
Consols Oils

The opening was far from grand

It was January 1986, bitingly cold on the last Monday of the month when the gate at Plot 3, Consols Industrial Estate, United Downs, St Day TR16 5HY was opened for business for the first time at 07:00. I sat in the Portacabin, knees knocking, teeth chattering in the cold, waiting for the electric heater to warm the place up while the kettle boiled and said to myself "what the hell have I done?"

There was no need to worry too much as by nine 09:00 I had my first customer, 'Freddy Odgers', who was a market gardener just down the road. He came in to fill his tractor up from the red diesel pump. There was a steady trickle filling their vehicles with road diesel and a surprising number filling cans with heating oil because their usual suppliers, buried in work, were unable to deliver promptly.

All day the phone was ringing with people wanting a delivery of heating oil, which unwittingly built a huge amount of untapped goodwill when I explained that the tanker would not be ready for a few days. Instead, I offered to help those who had run out by dropping off a few cans of oil to them to keep them going.

This proved to be an unwitting masterstroke.

Busy busy

I had been given a large number of clean 25 litre cans that had contained surgical spirit from a chap who worked at the local hospital where the cans normally cost money to dispose of by skip. Through the day, I had been filling them between phone calls and after I closed the yard at 17:00 I got to work, delivering the cans and tipping them into customers' tanks to tide them over.

This simple service quickly gained me a reputation for going the extra mile when the other firms appeared not to care. At the outset I was establishing a hardcore, loyal customer base that stood the firm in good stead for the next 34 years because the finest and cheapest form of advertising is always, without fail, the personal recommendation that comes from satisfied customers.

The tanker was still not ready, literally days away but no use until it started work. It was in the paint shop. The cab was light blue and only needed a polish to look the part. I had the colour scheme in my mind's eye for a while… light blue cab, dark blue tank with deep, reddish orange sign writing. Eye-catching and different to other operators in order to deliberately stand out from the crowd.

A fresh new, proudly independent, Cornish fuel brand and for better or worse, it was mine. It was created by me and brought to life by me as the direct result of a blazing row and an outright challenge that was meant as a stinging rebuke which actually had the exact opposite effect insofar as it motivated me.

'Start your own oil company indeed… well I bloody well did!'

Our first tanker delivery

In the meantime, it was the end of the month and Fuelserve needed to urgently shift some red diesel to meet their arbitrary monthly target. Despite the oceans of heating oil, they were selling, I was able to cobble together a group-buy from some fishing boats in Hayle on the last day of the month which was Consols Oils' first actual sale delivered by a road tanker.

This was complimented by an order for the rest of the 18,000 litre load to Trevassack Nursery just up the road who had been let down by their regular supplier which put them in danger of losing several glass houses full of early cucumbers. That customer stayed with us until the owner passed away 20 years later… the cucumbers were saved, Andy met his red diesel target and everyone was happy.

Finally, my own, home-made tanker turned up and things really got going. I was working crazy hours with early starts and often not finishing till 22:00, delivering the orders more or less as they were coming in while the opposition was up to three weeks' lead time for a heating oil delivery.

At this point I was cheated of something I was relishing. Joe French took the money and ran and Opie Oils was now owned by a chap I had absolutely no beef with, as a new competitor.

My first recruit

It was immediately obvious to my surprise so close to start up that I needed to take someone on to cope with the office and yard while I delivered.

Operation 'Minecap' was set up by the Manpower Services Commission as part of its job creation strategy. Carrick District Council administered the scheme which was winding down, having capped and made safe every known mineshaft in the Carrick District. My brother-in- law had been working on the job and recommended their office manager who was being laid off.

This was another unplanned, unforeseen stroke of amazing good luck for all concerned and became a hallmark of Consols Oils' rapid progression. It certainly proved that being in the right place at the right time solved a lot of problems that would otherwise seem potentially insurmountable.

Roger Stone had serious health issues and had been homeless, living in his car, until Vivian Vanstone, the local builder and undertaker in St Day who also owned a whole street of houses, recognised his plight and sorted a place out for him.

He now badly needed a job and was ideal for me. A pleasant, cheerful guy even though he had been dealt a lousy hand health wise. However, given his proven work ethic, I was amazed that someone else had not snapped him up immediately… another win, win situation.

By Easter the yard trade had picked up. Roger had sorted a basic computer system and each week we were showing a small profit. In fact, the magic break-even point was reached by Whitsun. It had not been projected in the cash flows until late the following year. Roger was blossoming in his highly valued role.

Throughout my tenure at Consols Oils the trade that came to the yard pumps was a bonus that kept a bit of steady profit going in quiet times when the best you could expect was to tick over. At the end of April, the heating oil trade traditionally tailed off while the balance of trade shifted to red diesel.

Cash flow management was a vital ingredient

This brought the first flashing amber light in relation to cash flow. A potentially life- threatening pitfall was lurking. Heating oil was largely 'cash on delivery' and provided a very strong, positive cash flow because we were extending very little credit. Selling red diesel was a whole different ball game because margins were much lower and credit needed to be extended to buyers.

Red diesel was a volume business but there was only a tiny truck so we had to tread very carefully indeed given the pressure on working capital that was almost inevitable. The summer prices were cut-throat, driven by the authorised distributors who had to shift fuel at almost any cost.

It really did make you realise that you were a minnow swimming around in an ocean inhabited by large hungry sharks who did not like their toes being trodden on, so a lot of work was best avoided. That said, there was the sector of work that the sharks had walked away from and thankfully for the first couple of years, that kept us going.

Credit control required a firm grip

The next red flashing light was credit control. Being obliging and understanding was interpreted by certain customers as equating to being a 'mug', a soft touch to be played. The first few times, my feelings were hurt. But this was a potentially lethal game and there was an 'element' appearing who had no credit elsewhere and were sizing me up for what they could take me for as the new kid on the block.

This marked another milestone where Julia, my wife, was handling credit control and gave short shrift to everyone. No shades of grey with her, which was all well and good but to survive we did need customers. Some were 100% genuine but struggling so were always late in paying. However, a balance needed to be struck which was not easy and led to a few rows over who was running the show.

We survived the summer of 1986 which was a very steep learning curve. The best yardstick of real, solid progress was the growing amounts of repeat business from customers who actually paid us. The bad payers had been reined in, but there were several thousand pounds which was several months overdue and that was looking very dodgy.

Debt collection and drastic medicine

We engaged a firm of solicitors to recover the numerous debts. The first letter was £3 to send and got about 75% of the money outstanding but it soon became obvious that if the first letter failed, costs were going to escalate substantially.

The biggest farce was that if it went to Court and judgement was obtained, it meant nothing in reality. The wilfully delinquent would take no notice whatsoever, knowing full well enforcement costs made the whole exercise non cost effective. They would commit to monthly instalments, pay a couple, then stop, meaning the whole sham had to start all over again.

The statutory demand

Then I came across a real shyster. A property developer with several sites running. Flashy car, flashy holidays, a classy house in a very select waterfront location etc. Having run up a bill for several full loads of heating oil for the swimming pool and diesel for his 'Princess' motor yacht, the payments slowed up and then stopped. We stopped supplying and when we chased him there was a mouthful of lip.

I am a great believer in drastic, short sharp lessons (old testament justice) and boy did this little shit need a jolt on his lead. As it transpired, there were previous judgements outstanding to other suppliers, so the County Court approach was a non-starter. He needed kicking into touch and hard.

I did a little more research and discovered that he did have money so he could pay. Then I discovered a very powerful weapon in the form of a statutory demand, which is the first step in bankruptcy proceedings. Once served on the debtor, they have 21 days to respond before full-blown bankruptcy proceedings can be instituted. It's a very serious matter which also has potentially serious implications on credit ratings for the debtor.

It had to be for a sum in excess of £750 and it cost £150 for the statutory demand to be served in person by a bailiff. There was an irate abusive phone call which Julia took, her bottom line being, "the ball is in your court… pay up or we proceed." On the 20th day, a cheque for the full amount plus a 10% late payment surcharge arrived. Matter closed.

The late payment surcharge more than covered the costs involved and from thereon in, the statutory demand was the weapon of choice in such cases of last resort where the debtor does have funds and, having called their bluff, the last thing they really want is a bankruptcy hearing.

Obviously if there are no funds it is a pointless, expensive exercise better done by someone else.

Making no secret of being prepared to take such action, word soon gets around on the grapevine to the unsavoury 'element', who are little more than crooks, not to mess with those who do not mess around where credit control is concerned. Our very survival always hinged on both paying and being paid.

There's a lesson here; never, ever under any circumstances make a threat that if push comes to shove you are not prepared to carry out.

In conclusion with regard to credit control, over the years we have worked with customers in very serious financial difficulties who have been upfront with us and nothing ever gave me more pleasure than playing a part in the long-term survival of a customer by being flexible with credit to assist them through their difficulties. But that has been reciprocated by the loyalty and friendship that builds.

David Goodey

After a year it was obvious that we were in desperate need of another tanker and right on cue an ideal one turned up in the Commercial Motor weekly. It was a Mercedes 814D, 2 years old at a dealer's in Kidderminster.

I enquired at the bank about finance and they agreed after a song and dance at a rate that was akin to banditry. A few phone calls were made but we didn't have sufficient track record being so new and with no accounts, they were not interested at a rate we could live with.

The very last phone call to General Guarantee struck oil. The manager, David Goodey, was looking for new business with growth potential. He was actually an existing Consols Oils customer and liked what he saw. He agreed finance at a very keen rate and that sealed a mutually beneficial, 30+ year relationship with David who later started on his own account as G&B Finance.

Any time from then on, whenever we needed another vehicle, it took a single phone call and the deal was done. What a difference to the way banks work and a major driver for our continuous organic growth

The tanker was bought and sent to Roy Richards (who was now also a customer) to be painted. Like G&B, Roy continued to do our vehicle bodywork and spraying until his retirement, tragically a few months afterwards he died of a brain tumour. It took his son less than two years to destroy 40 odd years of his father's work as 'W R Richards' folded.

Sir Alan Dalton

One of my earliest customers was a man I had always respected and admired who turned up as our customer after being let down on a delivery by another supplier. He was Sir Alan Dalton, the former supremo at ECC International, and had a reputation for amiability and good humour but could also be a steely negotiator.

I always regard this statement as his defining remark, "Our position is quite clear – we are keeping our intentions opaque for the present."

Sir Alan Dalton stood out as a man who made time for everyone. His time in Cornwall demonstrated that although not Cornish he was a truly great Cornishman and during his time at the helm of ECCI, the single, most influential and beneficial businessman in Cornwall during the 20th century.

He had once presented me with my school prize and having made the first delivery to him he got chatting over a cup of tea and a slice of his wife, Peggy's, amazing chocolate cake. I related the time he had shook my hand and he remembered it.

He was a customer for eighteen years until shortly before his passing in 2006 when it was distressing to see his health so visibly failing. Over that time, we had some amazing conversations. He was another of those inspirational people you are sometimes so privileged to know in the course of your work.

The next recruit

The arrival of the second tanker meant we now needed a driver and the plot thickened. A rep who worked for what was then Westcountry Oils based in Barnstaple, had started calling in for a cup of tea – probably under orders to keep a weather eye on us. Obviously, given our rapid growth, we had confounded them by becoming a potential threat.

The rep's name was 'Fred Davis' who lived in Helston. He had worked for Westcountry Oils for many years, starting as a driver before becoming the rep for the western part of Cornwall. One day he turned up in an obviously agitated state. He had been set an impossible target which he knew he could not meet and asked if there were any jobs going.

Par Docks in the days of English China Clay's 'Sir Alan Dalton'

Is the Pope a Catholic?

As it happened, there was a job as the new tanker was due any minute with no one to drive it. He had a class one licence and full ADR certificate to drive a tanker so was able to start as soon as his notice was completed. As soon as he handed in his notice he was sent home on gardening leave, but his contract dictated that he could not start another job in the industry for 3 months.

A welcome stopgap

Dave Hardiman's son Darren was waiting to take his LGV licence but he was able to drive the small tankers so he joined us as a stopgap in the few months before his 21st birthday, which was the earliest he could take his artic test so we were sorted for the time being.

Gardening leave

As a rep, many of Fred's customers called him at home to place orders direct with him. He explained the situation and told them to call Westcountry Oils direct to order but to bear him in mind next time. Luckily, his home phone number was his own but his old firm did their damndest to get it shut down.

There was hell to pop with Westcountry Oils because Fred had a very strong following with farmers in the Helston and Lizard area who they fully realised were highly likely to move over with him.

This meant that when the 3 month period of furlough ended, there was a sudden spurt of business for the new small truck. But it also meant that very soon, a third, full-blown, 17 tonner was going to be needed to keep pace with the surge of growth Fred brought to Consols.

The first big tanker

Yet again, Andy Coleman came to the rescue. Fuelserve were moving to six and eight wheelers and disposing of several four wheelers well before their normal replacement time. He offered us a very tidy, five year old Bedford KM 17 tonner at a giveaway price so, subject to getting it painted in our own livery, we had ourselves a full-blown, grown up tanker.

Looking very smart in its new livery, Fred took it over and started supplying his old customers. Volumes rapidly increased as a result, particularly on the Lizard Peninsula.

Fishing boats were a mixed blessing

From the very beginning I had always supplied several small fishing boats in St Ives, Hayle and Newquay and was beginning to pick up a bit of trade in Newlyn which created the first skirmish with the 'Old Firm' who, via Heltor, did massive volumes to their own fleet and most of the independents.

Cornwall Fishermen (CFL) was a cooperative fish-selling operation owned by the fishermen themselves. They were the only opposition to the 'Firm' and because I had begun to deal with CFL, I was immediately perceived as a potential threat.

As always, there was nothing tangible, but various boat owners were suddenly made aware that there may not be any ice available for them if they dealt with me, even though I was offering lower prices. Although the threats were subliminal, they drove some of the more timid ones back to the 'Firm' for their fuel.

It was a very delicate situation because the 'Firm' had been subject to a recent Office of Fair Trading investigation into restrictive practices, the outcome of which was a serious warning to the firm, with the matter remaining on file.

On that basis, we did what came our way without canvassing for trade, which was fine because a number of itinerant boats started to use us for our keener prices. An uneasy truce developed which suited me fine given there is no profit in any confrontation you are probably not going to win.

Chapter 12
The three grand principles – Brotherly Love, Releif and Truth

The Brotherhood

Away from work I had always been fascinated by Freemasonry, given my father-in-law was a prominent Mason, it seemed like a good opportunity to find out more.

I broached the subject with him. He was a third generation mason – his grandfather having been a founder of the highly respected, Tregullow Lodge 1006 in St Day. I was invited to an interview before that first, intimidating lodge committee and accepted as a candidate.

A few months later, I was initiated as an 'Entered Apprentice', which was a strange but fascinating experience that involved a ritual that included a binding oath never to reveal the methods of recognition about to be imparted to me and a lecture on the virtue of charity.

The first thing I realised was that I was not actually joining a secret society but rather a society with secrets. These were based on the three grand principles of brotherly love, relief and truth, revealed in three stages of ritual based around the Old Testament story of the construction of King Solomon's Temple.

What really surprised me was the number of people who turned up to wish me well, including Father's youngest brother, Jack who, as the prodigal, had after 30 odd years, returned home for the first time to a lukewarm reception from a still disgruntled older brother.

Father disliked and mistrusted Freemasonry and was seriously underwhelmed that both his son and younger brother had got involved with 'that bloody tribe'. I have a mind of my own and am quite prepared to use it. If the silly old bugger had only climbed down from his perch and embraced the order he would have loved its friendship and revelled in its teaching.

The 'second degree' or, 'Fellow Craft', was, in truth, a bit of an anticlimax after the drama of the first degree. The emphasis of the lecture was on the hidden mysteries of nature and science, while other methods of recognition were imparted during the ritual.

Next month came the big one, the 'third degree', which makes you an actual Master Mason. This involved the same ritual of imparting methods of recognition and another solemn oath not to reveal the same. The ceremony took place in the dark and involved me as candidate taking the part of the architect of the temple who chose to be killed rather than reveal the trust imposed on him.

The culmination involved me being symbolically slain and interred, the process of which required me to be lowered into a symbolic grave by designated masons. I had no real inkling that this was going to happen but it really was a life-changing experience as I lay there contemplating my mortality for a few long minutes.

I was then figuratively raised out of the grave as a Master Mason and a changed man, aware that I was not as I thought, immortal. My time was finite, to be used wisely and usefully.

I was never interested in high office or being addressed as 'Worshipful', as those who become Master of the Lodge through progressive offices are. I was grateful just to be a member and enjoy the privilege of access to the knowledge and friendship that causes one to stop and think about life in a productive manner among friends who share the same philosophy.

No free ticket to success

Those who join Masonry thinking that they will gain financial benefit from it are making a big mistake because in reality, as revealed in the first degree, you should contribute according to your means to assist those in distress without detriment to self or connections.

The one thing that, still to this day, makes my blood boil is those who play on a Masonic connection in business to gain an advantage. If you have to cynically play the Masonic card to get business you are a pretty lacklustre businessman.

Conversely, nothing gives me more pleasure than to deal with someone over an extended period before discovering the connection. Anyone who tries the handshake while canvassing will get cut off dead with me. We are there to do good by being charitable, not nepotistic or opportunistic to our own advantage.

After several years, I did get an office as 'Lodge Almoner', a job I did for eight years. While thoroughly enjoying it, it is actually unusual to be an Almoner not having first passed through the chair. But I am pretty sure they didn't know what else to do with me.

After several more years, a letter arrived one day informing me that I had been nominated for provincial honours, which is in itself a terrific honour I was proud to accept as an ordinary brother. Like lots of things in my varied life, I got there the hard way by putting in the time.

If only the people who regard Masonry with suspicion and antipathy could understand how much money is raised for a multitude of good causes outside of Masonry each year in Cornwall alone, they might change their view of the order.

Proof of the Bond

A few months later, a tragic bombshell exploded into our lives and proved how deep the Masonic Bond is in a time of trouble.

Father-in-law, having retired from the Civil Service, had bought a touring caravan. Each year, him and my mother-in-law would take off for a couple of months or so to tour Europe.

They had been away when Thomas was born, a point that always irked Julia who, like my father, was not best-known for letting matters rest.

It was a very hot, still Saturday night in July around 11:00 when we heard Julia's younger brother's 'Minivan' pass our house. The gearbox had a distinctive whine and hearing it pull into the parents' drive, we assumed he was having an early night. A few minutes later we heard him go again, assuming he was off to a party somewhere. About 20 minutes later a single shot rang out in the distance.

Thinking someone had shot at a fox we fell asleep, but at around 08:30 on the Sunday morning, a policeman knocked on our door. He asked to come in as he had some bad news. We instantly thought it was about the parents-in-law, but it was (if that was possible) even worse.

A worker at the nearby United Downs council tip had come across the body of a young man with massive gunshot wound to the right side of his head, with a 12 bore shotgun on the ground beside him.

Subject to formal identification it appeared reasonable to believe, given that a light blue Minivan was parked nearby, that the body was that of John Gribbin, who was not at home when the police had called there. Quite understandably, Julia collapsed in a heap. I must admit to being shell shocked but I had to hold it together and attempt to sort something out, quite what I was unsure.

The policeman said the first priority would be formal identification of the body and this was arranged for the following morning. However, the biggest issue was how to notify the parents and get them home. They had phoned Julia on the Saturday evening to say that they would be arriving in Carnac on Sunday so I had a vague idea where to start looking but actually getting there was the issue.

It was peak season so it was highly unlikely that there would be space on the Roscoff Ferry.

However, a call was made to Brittany Ferries explaining the situation and there was no problem. They always ensured there was space to cater for such an emergency so I was booked on the Monday night ferry from Millbay to Roscoff.

I was seriously disappointed that my brother-in-law, who had married Julia's sister and was a schoolteacher in Hampshire declined to go with me. So, it looked like I was on my own. His feeble suggestion being that we would never find them and it would be better to leave the job to Interpol. Like hell it would! They would need a family member there when told of the awful news.

I was up in the village at the post office on Monday morning when I bumped into Peter Carley, the previous Worshipful Master of Tregullow who had initiated me the previous year. He had heard the news and asked if there was anything he could do. I explained the situation to him and, without a second's hesitation, he offered to go with me.

The kindness and compassion of the offer overwhelmed me.

Hard tasks and assistance from an unexpected quarter

Then it was the grim job of formally identifying John's body in the mortuary at Treliske Hospital. The technicians had done their best but there was no disguising the fact that the right half of his head was missing. The terrible sight and the smell still haunts me; a mixture of gunpowder and burnt flesh which, while partially disguised by the morticians was tangible, reinforcing the horror of the event.

Peter was a Special Constable and the village printer. He was always busy. We used to spend hours chatting while he typeset with traditional hot metal. His printing press was an amazing, Heidelburg machine that looked a bit, Heath Robinson in a typically Teutonic manner. He turned out Lodge agendas, funeral notices, menu cards along with invoice books and delivery tickets for me.

He also did all the notices for the village organisations which he never, ever charged for.

But on that terrible day, his hand of friendship was extended to me selflessly and spontaneously in my hour of need. Just when all seemed lost, he was there as a quietly reassuring presence.

We set off just after 19:00 to catch the ferry. Both being pipe smokers, the air in the work's van was a bit thick but it kept us going. At Millbay a horrible realisation sank in, I had in a haze of anxiety and depression left my passport behind and there was no time to retrace the route to fetch it!

The staff at Brittany Ferries were amazing as I explained my plight to them. They let me board with instructions to report to Customs in Roscoff immediately on disembarkation. It was a long, anxious night with little sleep.

On arrival, I went to the uniformed Customs Officer. Brittany Ferries had obviously notified them about me and I was directed to a man in a leather jacket and jeans who most would not even notice standing by the vehicle exit. He was eyeing up the vehicles as they came off the ship and it was obvious that he had considerable authority as an officer in the French Secret Service.

He spoke good English and amazingly Peter knew him as a Mason having previously visited the Lodge in Roscoff. He made no bones about the situation. It was most irregular but I was given 48 hours to get the parents-in-law back to Roscoff or they would come looking for me. He also gave strict instructions to report to him upon return and he wished us well and off we went.

To Carnac and back

It was around a hundred miles to Carnac around the dual carriageway past Brest, rather than the more direct route over the top of Armorique National Park, but in the circumstances, the dual carriageway seemed the best option.

The Carnac area has dozens of caravan and campsites and the next problem was where to start. It seemed logical using the map that we had to start at the beginning at the first site we came across in the area. We did know that they would be staying in the area for several days and were intending to move to a cheaper site according to the last phone call. Not much to go on.

The first site drew a blank but at the second small, very basic site, the old lady patron and her disabled daughter became animated when shown the picture of the parents-in-law and their car. Unbelievably, they had not long left, having booked to move onto the site the following day.

Even better, they knew where they were staying that night. It took a bit of explaining but she drew a rudimentary map with the name of the site on it and off we went to find it. By this time it was 18:00, the day having passed in a blur.

It was not difficult using the map and the excellent signs detailing the sites along the roads. We arrived at the gate. Just inside the gate, the parents-in-law were having a barbeque. A picture of relaxed happiness. It had been so easy thus far as the hand of fate guided us. Now for the hard bit… how the hell was I going to do it?

There was only one way

Parking the van discretely to one side just outside the camp gate, we both took a very deep breath before walking forward. Peter's reassuring presence was just behind me to the left. At one point I stiffened on the verge of running away but felt gentle a hand on my shoulder and the quiet words, "come on old pal… we have got to get this done."

We were nearly up to them before they became aware of our presence. I am sure they thought I had brought the family on a surprise visit, if only!

Then they saw Peter and how serious we were and the penny dropped that we were bearing bad news. Telling them what had happened was the hardest, worst job I have ever had to do and hope to God that I never ever have to do such a thing again.

In less than a minute I had destroyed their world, reducing it to a dark place where things would never be quite the same again.

Without my steadfast Masonic Brother it would have been even harder. How do you ever repay such kindness?

After a very difficult night where father-in-law collapsed into a gibbering heap while mother-in-law retained a serene composure that utterly belied the pain she was so obviously suffering, we got going just after daybreak back to Roscoff. I drove the car with the parents- in-law and their caravan in tow, while Peter drove my van to catch the afternoon ferry home.

Back in Roscoff, our friend, the Secret Service Agent was there. He had spotted us coming into the terminal and came across to the vehicles to wish us well. Again, how do you convey adequate thanks to someone who could so easily not have helped and sent us packing back to Plymouth?

Better lucky than rich

So much of my life has turned out to be a series of potential disasters… sailing close to the wind but being held together by the bonds of friendship and good fortune that could never be foreseen or contrived. I really do believe in Guardian Angels.

John's funeral was grim. There was not a lot to be said that was positive. The boy always wanted to be a miner in the tradition of his famous grandfather, John Gribbin, a master shaft sinker who sank the first shaft at Ashanti Gold Mine in Ghana (which later became the world's biggest gold mine at that time). He was also underground manager at Killifreth Mine till its closure and worked at gold mines in India.

Father-in-law had wanted to follow in his footsteps but his mother would have none of it and forced him into the Civil Service much against his will. Young John Gribbin had been promised a job at Wheal Jane Mine by David Eustice as soon as he was eighteen but came off his motorbike and broke both his legs.

He had been doing various labouring jobs when a mining job came up at Wheal Concord, a small, independent mine at Blackwater. John relished the job and for a few months, things at Concord were looking good. But the mine became the first victim of the infamous tin price crash, forcing its closure.

We never did know if this is what tipped the boy over the edge to do what he did. There was no note and nothing to throw any light on his mindset. The 'not knowing' was the hardest thing of all and it always weighed heavily on family life from then on.

It was back to work for me. The others had been holding the fort but we were desperate for bigger storage capacity in the yard. I had something in mind but once more it was a tall order. I was scheming while I kept my own counsel because anyone else would have told me I was mad.

In the meantime, two new faces appeared. The first Judith James, a lovely person who had recently divorced, became our highly-skilled and resourceful administrator. She took some of the, by now, massive workload off of Roger's shoulders. The second was David Eustice.

The Hayle connection

In another twist of connections, Judith's father, Bill Hoskins, was the pilot boatman in Hayle and a former agent for cash disposals of our crabs to visitors and locals alike, boiling them in his pilot house on the end of East Quay. He was most famous for his skill in braving the notorious 'Bar' in his small boat to put the pilot aboard a vessel or take him off a departing vessel.

Hayle once had a power station, an Esso sea and rail-fed oil terminal, a chemical works producing bromine, a scrapyard, a timber yard, and a potato store where seed potatoes were imported from Scotland. One day in 1969, I recollect 11 vessels working cargo in the harbour, including scrap, sulphur, oil, coal, seed potatoes, timber and cement.

The Port of Hayle declined spectacularly in the space of a few years into a derelict, post-industrial wasteland which became destined to remain that way for the best part of forty years of dereliction and squalor while a succession of speculators came and went.

The Kinderence - a collier vessel leaving Hayle Harbour circa 1968

A time of change

In Cornwall change has rarely been for the better in my lifetime. Dereliction cloaks so many once-vibrant workplaces which no amount of supermarket or fast food joints can ever gloss over employment-wise.

Mass tourism never has and never will be a satisfactory substitute for the likes of Holman Bros, South Crofty Mine, Wheal Jane Mine or Geevor Mine which were the dynamos of an economy that was sacrificed on the altar of outsourcing and international financial jiggery pokery, cynically overseen by greedy, incompetent politicians of every hue, at both local and national level.

Thankfully, despite the loss of the quarry trade, Newlyn still clings on determinedly to its industrial roots as the only major show in town employment-wise in West Cornwall, with potential for significant growth in the post Stevenson era.

David Eustice – a man and a half

Then, in the St Day Inn, over a period I had got to know a chap called David Eustice. He had started work at South Crofty Mine in his teens and became a mine captain who ended up at Wheal Jane Mine in a similar capacity. He had also been a very successful publican keeping the Seven Stars Inn at Flushing and the Star Inn at Vogue with his wife Astria.

Sadly, he had suffered a serious stroke a few years previously which had temporarily put him in a wheelchair but in no time he had overcome being written off as a cripple by sheer force of personality and an iron willpower. Getting back on his feet to everyone's surprise, one day he asked me if I had a job for him as he needed some therapeutic work 2 or 3 days a week.

The interview and Father meets his match

David came over to see me in the yard and Father happened to be there. They were eyeing each other up and down like two boar pigs with nothing but a mains electric fence separating them. Father who disliked moustaches to the point of obsession, asked David,

"have you ever had a moustache boy?"

I stiffened and cringed knowing what my father was like.

David said, "no I haven't but what's it got to do with you?"

Father replied, "what would you say if I said I wasn't very struck on you?"

David replied, "well actually I am not very fucking struck on you either mister."

Father roared out laughing and said, "I like this bugger, if I was you I would take him on."

I did resist the very strong temptation to say "well I am not you" and did take David on which was one of my better moves.

Above: David Eustice (far right) with England Rugby International, Richard Sharp OBE (second from left) working at South Croft Mine circa 1960. According to David, Richard Sharp was a far better rugby player than a miner.

Left: David Eustice aboard his boat 'The Kelvin' shortly before his passing

From then on they were great friends. Two aggravating hellers with brutal senses of humour who sparked off each other but as for the initial interview format? Well, it was a new one on me.

I was cringing at first, knowing what Father was like, when he had unexpectedly turned up uninvited and started putting his oar in. But David took it in his stride, he was a man manager and mentor 'par excellence'.

Consols Oils was building a very unconventional but nonetheless formidable team.

Shared experiences

It transpired that David had suffered a similar, highly traumatic experience as I had with John Gribbin.

When he was at Wheal Jane, there had been a freak accident with a young miner called 'Jeremy Bown', who was the son of Ferguson Bown, the grocer back in Perran. Jeremy had somehow slipped stepping from the shaft station into the cage to go to the surface.

He was a big boy but had inexplicably managed to fall through the narrow gap between the cage and the station. His mates couldn't keep hold of him and he fell several hundred feet to his death. When they recovered the mutilated body his head was missing. David, as mine captain, had to go into the sump and grope in the slime to find Jeremy's head. What a hellish task for a man to have to do.

But that was the calibre of this exceptional new colleague and friend who launched into his new role alongside me with gusto. As if he, of all people, had anything to prove?

If David had something to say, he would say it without fear favour or malice. Offend or please, you knew exactly where you stood with him. Soon he was charming the customers out of the trees. Fred was very wary of his brutal, straight talking, and Father never goaded him again.

The right stuff

Subconsciously our recruitment policy crystalised. My preference was for people who were new to the industry, ideally from a fishing or farming background, who knew how to think for themselves and crack on with the job in a competent manner. Jobs were rarely advertised in that period. We would identify who we wanted and ring them up to see if they were interested. As a rule, they usually were!

The storage issue was becoming critical. We had actually got one 80,000 litre vertical tank from the Milk Marketing Board Creamery at Treswithian when it closed. It was cheap and sound but moving it was a challenge. As it was too high to go under the bypass bridges, we had to go through the centre of Camborne, which was fine but a bit nerve racking.

For the time being, our kerosene storage was sorted.

Balancing delivery capacity and administrative capacity was part of the relentless growth pattern. Either you needed another truck or the office needed someone else to deal with the work the extra truck brought in. It was a very difficult balancing act.

We needed another small tanker and bought an 'AWD' short wheelbase 7.5 tonner which WR Richards put together for us. I was driving it one day at a place called 'Mixtow' opposite Fowey Docks reached via the Boddinick Ferry.

Disaster

It was a wet mizzly day and the delivery was down a steep, slippery drive that terminated in a turning place with a fifty foot drop into the River Fowey, It was a customer's second home which was fortunately unoccupied at the time. I made the delivery and started back up the smooth, concrete drive which was covered with an incredibly slippery green algae. It was just like driving on ice.

The truck wheels started to slip. I stopped to try again and with the wheels spinning the truck started to slide backwards gathering speed. Thinking of the approaching drop I bailed out. The truck veered slightly to the left, its wheels still spinning backwards and crashed over the bank backwards through the roof of the house, with the rear of the tank embedded in the bathroom.

I was badly shaken and ran off to find help. Most of the other houses were also holiday homes and being winter they were unoccupied. Eventually and at the end of my tether, I found a handyman working in a house. He used the phone to call the fire brigade and I called the office to come and get me.

The fire brigade turned up and checked there was no one at home and stood by in case of fire from the small trickle of heating oil seeping out of a pipe under the chassis. All we could do was wait for another tanker to turn up to remove the remaining oil on board and then wait for what was going to be a very technical recovery operation.

To my further embarrassment, a TV news crew turned up and filmed the scene. We made the local news that night, with me wishing the earth would open up and swallow me but it didn't and I once more lived to fight another day.

Recovery

The barely two-month old truck was recovered back to WR Richards and an insurance assessor inspected it and authorised repairs which consisted of a new chassis and a new tank. The damaged tank was repaired and fitted to the Mercedes tanker to replace the steel one and life went on, a bit shaken but not really stirred. The AWD soon came back and went on working for many more years.

Speculation pays off handsomely

Then came the first Gulf War. It was obvious that oil prices were probably going to spike. We had recently started buying from Conoco in Plymouth as we were gradually outgrowing Fuelserve's ability to supply. As is often the case, there were unwelcome changes afoot within Fuelserve that did not bode well for us.

Conoco were very keen to supply us and gave us good terms, which included a realistic credit limit. At that time, we were renting 180,000 litres of storage from Denis Webber Services at Washaway between Bodmin and Wadebridge.

Denis was a likeable, irascible old bugger who was introduced to us by Andy Coleman. We started buying premium paraffin from him, which became another very lucrative string to our bow. The market for that premium paraffin was declining as the majors lost interest in it which meant that the demand that was still there suited us very nicely.

Denis had a very nice mobile home park which had become his main enterprise. Having had a mild heart attack, he had run the oil business down so he was glad to rent out the ideally placed storage depot.

For a few years, it became very profitable for us, delivering premium paraffin mainly to ironmongers who still sold it. Several of them were in Plymouth, and the Washaway storage meant that we could buy it by the artic load from Linton Petroleum, a London-based independent distributor/wholesaler who served us well.

In the run up to the Gulf War the rest of the Washaway storage was kept topped up with red diesel and heating oil in case of shortage. It was then that the adventurer in me took over.

We had been buying some gas oil out of Falmouth Docks where the tank farm had been acquired by Peter De Savary who had sold it to his step brother, Chris Walters. We got on very well. I did a deal and bought a complete 1,700 ton cargo of red diesel, to be drawn down within 30 days, with payment due on completion of drawdown which, if it worked out, would be a brilliant move.

The price was too good to miss and was in the nick of time, a couple of days before the balloon went up. If it had gone wrong I knew I would be toast.

Twitchy colleagues

By this time, Roger and Fred each had a ten percent stake in the business following a shitty attempt by an unpleasant rival outfit to poach them to spike my guns. The best way to deal with that was to tie them in and be even more successful.

Be that as it may you could practically hear Fred's sphincter twitching when he found out what I had done. It was just as well I was in a position to call the shots otherwise there would have been little growth or progress.

A horrified bank manager

Better still, I went to see the bank manager to tell him, still only having a £5,000 overdraft and being in for well north of £300,000 due in a month's time, which at that stage, was a mind boggling amount of money to me. The clock was ticking and lots could go wrong.

John Selley was an old-style, salt-of-the-earth, ultra-cautious, small town bank manager. On his desk was a posh, brass-bound, fag box. If you were in favour on the day, you would get offered a Players Navy Cut from it, but today, his body language said it all.

Getting straight down to business I put him in the picture and watched his knuckles tighten as the fag box snapped shut. No joy there… hey ho… the story of my life. I was on my own with a twitchy bank manager and twitchy partners fretting away.

As Harold Wilson famously said *"a week is a long time in politics"* and it was the same in the old oil job as the tension racked up overnight.

The balloon goes up!

The next day brought news of anxious traders, suit-speak for an impending rip off as prices started to surge. Most of our rivals bought their fuel 'ex-tank' on that day's price but we had around 2 million litres in hand in local storage and accessible. It was time to start moving it.

All we needed to do was lag slightly behind the others on price and the stuff sold itself. The only stipulation being cash on delivery, no ifs, no buts. The price ended up nearly quadrupling in the next fortnight and within three weeks the cash was in the bank to pay the huge fuel bill we were owing. The rest was honest profit which really put us on our feet.

This was trading in the raw. A hunch had been played bang on cue. Product had been secured that everyone wanted on a rapidly rising market, which turned in a 40% profit in less than the monthly credit period allowed. Risks of that magnitude were not to be taken lightly and I became noticeably greyer.

Fred may have been risk averse but he was not averse to grabbing his share of the profit. That said, most of that was re-invested, buying us another brand new truck. The sting was a serious tax bill, which was heading our way so sadly, provision had to be made for it.

Our bank manager was suddenly all smiles and the fag box re-opened. To my surprise, without it even being asked for (because I had no intention of grovelling) we got a £50,000 overdraft marked up! It still wasn't enough, but was certainly better from a day to day perspective.

Bernard Pooley

It was obvious that we had outgrown our original accountant who was a one man band in Redruth dealing with local, small tradesmen. Given the increasingly serious cash flow swilling around in our system, we were not a small operation anymore and we needed to look to the future.

The bank made a determined effort to steer us toward a significant firm of accountants in Truro but the 'hard to ignore gut instinct' persuaded me to look elsewhere.

Some enquiries among colleagues came with the same name twice which seemed a very good starting point given the highly favourable recommendations. The name cropping up was 'Bernard Pooley', senior partner at Kelsall Steele also based in Truro. Coincidentally, he was the grandson of the butcher and Mrs Pooley from my childhood.

An appointment was arranged for Bernard to visit us. He arrived and formalities completed took a look at our accounts and then our computer system. He said he'd be happy to act for us as long as we put into practice the systems he wanted in order to maintain control of a very lively operation which I was the first to appreciate needed very firm handling.

Bernard became the company accountant for the next twenty eight years and we never really looked back. Despite passing through several hoops of fire along the way, the advice always proved to be impeccable. The opposition may have sniggered at us previously but soon they were sniggering on the other side of their faces.

That was the greatest favour they could have done us while we got our feet firmly under the table. If they had come in hard on us in that first year things might have turned out very differently.

Another bully kicked into touch

John Selley had retired and the bank regime was changing. We had a very good manager for a time who was also retired, then, without being informed, the rapidly growing turnover dictated that the account got moved to the corporate department in Truro.

We had a new manager called 'Brian Grant' who had been recently promoted and moved up to Truro from Falmouth where he had a reputation as a hatchet man, prone to pulling the plug on businesses at the drop of a hat. We had a phone call as he wished to come out to see us. He arrived with two minions in tow and from the outset I sensed that this was not going to work.

Our personalities were at variance and it was obvious that he did not like the business, pointing out that our indebtedness to our suppliers did not sit well with our percentage margins. He ignored the fact that as a high turnover, low margin business, we were actually turning in healthy profits year on year.

He continually fretted about payments and inferred that he could bounce a direct debit any time he chose which would effectively kill us. What he was actually trying to do was force us down the road of factoring our invoices receivable, which effectively meant the bank would cream off most of our profits in commissions. This created an uncomfortable stand-off and there was no way I would be doing that.

Speaking to Bernard Pooley, he suggested trying another bank and recommended HSBC. I approached them and an appointment was made for a business manager to see us and look us over.

Glyn Wilkes, the HSBC business manager assigned to us duly arrived and looked at the accounts and the operation at work. He listened carefully to my reason for wanting to change banks and said, "I like what I see and will be happy to have your account." I had taken an immediate liking to him on arrival and it really was liberating to see light at the end of what could have been a very long dark tunnel.

He admitted to being aware of the reputation of our present manager and suggested that we make the change ASAP. Having spoken with Bernard, it was vital that Grant did not have wind of what was afoot. Incredibly, appreciating the delicacy of the situation, Glyn arranged for an unsecured £20,000 buffer fund to be paid into the Nat West account on changeover to forestall any potential hiccups.

On the day of the changeover there was a morning call from Brian Grant pointing out that a large direct debit was due out and funds were tight. I took huge pleasure in informing him not to worry because as of midnight we were not banking with him anymore. There was a gulp on the other end of the line, then a pregnant pause before he replied, "you can't do that." Famous last words, which I have heard many times from such men of straw.

Well we just had done it so without another word I put the phone down on the bully.

He had not noticed the £20,000 HSBC payment into our account to cover what he was carping on about. While knowing full well that there were more than adequate funds in the pipeline to cover every commitment we had, I went to ground as he repeatedly called to speak to me for the next week about reconsidering my decision. As always, there was no going back.

Feeling wanted for a change

For the first time ever, HSBC gave us an adequate £250,000 overdraft facility which stood us in good stead until things changed again a few years down the line. I would imagine Mr Grant needed to do a bit of explaining to someone higher up the greasy pole as to how a basically sound, £12 million turnover account suddenly went walkabout to a rival bank.

The repeated message about facing down bullies reinforces the lesson that there must always be a Plan B and a credible exit strategy when faced with the sort of situation described if you want to survive.

An enemy in the shadows

My policy was always; *never to rubbish the opposition.*

Sadly, a third generation local firm who were the Shell distributor at the time in question and in all honesty, a class act, easily capable of much better, was discovered casting doubt on our credit worthiness to our supplier and the provenance of our fuel to customers they had lost to us.

This was a bit rich considering the fuel in question generally came out of the same tank as theirs. Conversely, we were mining a rich seam of loyal customers of theirs who had been consistently ripped off by them for years so it was 'tit for tat'. They were looking for a row and they had sure as hell found one.

I had far more to fight for than they did because I was building my business from scratch on my own, whereas they had a thriving business handed to them on a plate. My biggest asset was my utter disdain for passive, aggressive bullies, incapable of straight talking and who fought in the shadows.

David Eustice was the perfect wingman, picking their customers off in what, at times, was effectively a turkey shoot.

One thing after another

The next issue was office space. We had outgrown the original 16 foot portacabin a while back and like a hermit crab changing to a larger whelk shell, we moved into a 40 foot portacabin with 2 offices and a central reception area that seemed enormous. Well, for a day or two that is!

But it was increasingly obvious that this was a stopgap measure and we were badly in need of a proper building that included a warehouse to store the increasing amounts of lubricants we were selling. I always like a windfall and lubricants provided the next, very unconventional one.

We had always sold some lubes without putting in a lot of undue effort. It was seen as a useful bolt on addition to the business mix.

One day I was at Macsalvors, who were the local government surplus outlet which to me was akin to being an Aladdin's Cave, as you never knew what might turn up next. I was actually looking for some blue paint for the Portacabin but ended up with something I didn't bargain on… another of those out of the blue deals not to be missed.

I got chatting, like you do, to one of the directors, a very likeable Scotsman known for his thrift. In the course of the conversation, it transpired that he was trying to move some helicopter turbine oil but having no luck.

I enquired how much and he replied that there were 21,500 US quart cans of Chevron, Esso, and Mobil military spec synthetic turbine oil. This was a significant quantity of such a highly specialised lubricating oil which was eye-wateringly expensive to buy but could also be very expensive to get shot of as waste, due to its potential toxicity.

The price indication he gave belied his Scottish blood and more so for something they obviously thought that they were well and truly lumbered with. Nice try, it often worked like that when buying at government surplus auctions – they sometimes had to take something they didn't really want in order to secure the items that they did want which would make them a really good profit.

No one was losing out unless they were forced to pay to dispose of it. So, there was obviously a deal to be done if I could identify a buyer.

I made no commitment to anything other than to try some contacts, (I didn't have any so I needed to find some pronto) and then I'd get back to him. Back in the office the others were left to get on with the day job while I Googled… 'HELICOPTER OPERATORS'.

There were not many, but hopefully I only needed one. The first two I called suggested 'Foxtrot Oscar…' they obviously thought my first name was 'Arthur' and the second one 'Daley'. But I did glean one vital piece of information which was that everything aviation-related had to be accompanied by CAA certificates of conformity and there were none in this case even though the product was the real deal.

Big problem and a potential deal breaker. But if at first you don't succeed… keep trying.

It was, however, a classic case of third time lucky. A call to a celebrated wheeler dealer who also operated helicopters in the Plymouth area got a bite. He wanted samples and a price indication. Obviously, being fully aware of the true price of the stuff, if the samples were as described, we were on.

I went to the seller saying that they could have a deal if the price was right and he said "make me an offer." I bid ten pence a can. The Scots part of him winced because he obviously knew the true price as well, but the realist part of him, without the vital CAA certification was clearly ready to breathe a huge sigh of relief at having gotten rid of the potentially costly problem.

He also added as an aside that there were two further shipping containers holding 40 pallets of 32 x 25 litre cans of finest military spec glycol antifreeze for £4 a can available. The going wholesale buying rate at the time being £12.50 a can.

I went straight to the potential buyer with a sample case of each brand of turbine oil and he carefully examined the specs on the cans and asked the price. Given there was no CAA certification, when I said, "40p per can" he practically snatched my hand off. Apparently, the true price of the stuff was in excess of £20 per quart can.

I casually mentioned the antifreeze and he also took 4 pallets of that so 10% was already gone at £10 per can which was the icing on the cake.

The deal was done on Thursday afternoon, with delivery on Saturday morning and the cash waiting on delivery. Fred had arranged for his nephew to make the delivery.

The pallets were loaded at Macsalvors on the Saturday morning and my Scottish friend did his damndest to find out where it was going. All the driver said was "I don't know but I have to be in Southampton Docks tonight," which was true, but he was delivering the stuff to the buyer's premises in East Cornwall on the way through.

On delivery, the buyer counted every last case as the pallets were unloaded and then counted out the cash. Everyone was a winner, not being greedy moved it on easily and to everyone's mutual benefit.

A few phone calls and a half a day's highly enjoyable work turned in another very useful windfall profit tacked onto the normal week's work at virtually no cost.

Opportunities like that must be seized with both hands when they occur. Those windfall deals, where you have to use your loaf, really were the fun aspect of the job and you got a real buzz from being in the right place at the right time.

Appreciating stock

It took 3 years to move the antifreeze but at a higher profit each year as the price of glycol climbed, always at a couple of quid lower than the current going wholesale rate which saved our buyers a little a bit and kept them coming back for more. In the third year, the going rate was £25 per can.

Once again it is so easy to digress. However, the outcome of the turbine oil deal was that the profit was ploughed into the purchase of a 75 foot by 30 foot second hand, galvanised, portal frame, steel building to sit on the next door plot that we had recently purchased from Carrick Council for £15,000. This more than doubled the size of our site.

Someone much richer and wiser than me once told me that it is nigh on impossible to generate meaningful capital out of income, but I proved him wrong because I had no choice. My modest lifestyle helped. Far too many people want to run before they can walk and do so by borrowing far too much.

Proper offices

Over the next year, the building went up which was a very costly job and the day we moved out of the portacabin was typically during a busy time as the phones were going mad. The phone lines had to be transferred to the new building with minimum disruption, with Roger and David hanging in there till literally seconds before the crane lifted the old portacabin onto the waiting artic to take it away.

Within an hour what at first seemed a vast new building was up and running with a heap of black bin liners containing paperwork and files dumped in the middle of the floor. These would be sorted out as time allowed. We now had a large shop area, proper toilet, shower and messroom downstairs.

Upstairs there were two toilets, a large stationary cupboard, two small offices and a spacious main office.

Office and shop-wise, there was 900 square feet on each floor as well as a 45 foot by 30 foot warehouse. By golly, that really made life easier for everyone.

One issue sorted – another one waiting

It was crunch time for our storage. Tragically, Wheal Jane Mine had recently ceased underground operations and was left to flood. While continuing to mill ore from South Crofty, the mine had a power station as part of its infrastructure which included two x 200,000 vertical red diesel tanks to supply the generator. These were due to be cut up for scrap, but they were far too good for that.

The problem was that they were massive (23 feet in diameter and 24 feet high). Having expressed an interest in them, I had to be quick because the scrap men were chomping at the bit. Time was of the essence.

The first task was to establish the feasibility of the move by surveying the route. As the crow flies, the distance between Wheal Jane and United Downs is around two miles, but the only feasible route to take was almost seven miles, with the narrowest width of road being ten feet. At first sight this was daunting.

However, on reflection and after a careful inspection, all was not lost. The widest part of a 23 foot diameter cylinder on the low loader would be about 14 feet off the deck. In the short 30 yard very narrow section, the hedges were about four feet high, with about six feet of light thorn growth above that which would easily brush aside.

There were several overhead electricity and telephone wires along the route that would need to be lifted by a cherry picker, so the next thing was to involve the utilities for their input. I also spoke with the local police traffic department who, along with the utilities, could not have been more helpful.

Then it was over to Brian Hoskin, the haulier of choice, due to his expertise in moving large fishing boat hulls from the builders to the quayside for launching. He had no serious concerns about taking the job on. His partner on these jobs was usually Jim Boyd of Falmouth Crane Services who had a look at the tanks to specify where he wanted the lifting eyes welded on.

The job was a goer, a deal was finalised with the mine and the tanks were ours for £1,100 each. An absolute steal if they could be successfully moved.

The final job was to engage PT Marine who had done all the fabrication of pipe work in the yard over a period. Their work was excellent, so they set to work cutting of the tank railings and access ladders off before welding on the lifting eyes as specified by Jim Boyd. The local team all knew each other and that was a huge asset on such an unusual job.

In all, six weeks' work went into the planning before the big day came. The previous afternoon, Jim Boyd arrived on site to tip the tanks onto their sides, but would they collapse in the process? There was only one way to find out, just crack on and do it. I watched with

Hauliers 'Brian Hoskins' moving the two giant tanks with Police escort on standby

Entering the gates at Conols Industrial Site, United Downs near St. Day

Now the really tricky bit... tipping the first tank on its side by crane prior to loading

bated breath, hoping for the best but ready for the worst. Everything was fine, then the two artics arrived. Brian Hoskin had subbed the second tank out to Cooks Transport from Hayle and the tanks were carefully loaded and chained down. By golly... they did look big. Then that was it till 07:00 the following morning.

I was on site at Wheal Jane at 07:00 and one by one everyone turned up. The front police escort led the way followed by the electricity and electrical staff. We actually left the mine entrance at 08:00 on the dot. On the road, the two tanks were a spectacular sight and at 200,000 litres each, they were probably the biggest loads by volume ever to be moved in the local area.

Given that progress was slow due to the need to lift telephone wires or, in the case of one 11,000 volt high tension line, chop the lot down, the trip was uneventful, with everything going to plan in copybook style.

When we eventually got to United Downs it was 18:00 so it had taken 10 hours for the 7-mile journey. I was mentally drained but elated by having pulled another job off against considerable odds. Including the cost of moving and installing the tanks, we had them home and in place for £5,000 each – an absolutely massive saving on buying new tanks.

They are still in use today and following refurbishment in 2018 after 26 years' of service, they should be good for another 20 years.

Paul Tonkin

As a bonus on that job, we acquired a highly competent general manager to cope with the Health and Safety Executive (HSE) legislation, computer system and RDCO (Registered Dealers in Controlled Oils Regulations), a clear indication of the stringent regulation coming on stream which seemed endless.

Paul Tonkin was a Redruth boy who had joined the army REME (Royal Electrical and Mechanical Engineers) branch as a boy soldier rising through the ranks to be a Major. On leaving the army, he had gone into partnership with his brother, Peter, who ran PT Marine. As is often the case with brothers sadly, it was not working out. Peter's loss was our gain.

The very first Consols Oils tanker

Chapter 13
'Big Boy' battles

Under attack from the corporate clones

The local authorised distributor mafia made absolutely certain that we never got access to the Falmouth BP Terminal at Ponsharden. But we learned to live without it, relying more and more on product delivered in from Conoco in Plymouth as the Fuelserve connection that had served us so well ran its course with the departure of our trusted friend, Andy Coleman.

They say that imitation is the sincerest form of flattery and the local Shell Distributor, seeing how well we were doing as an independent, fled the Shell coop and built their own depot on a disused filling station site just off the A30 between Scorrier and Blackwater. They had also operated from a Shell-owned depot just outside Newquay which they promptly got unceremoniously booted from.

Under the Shell Direct banner, a revenge mission was then launched by an irritated, vindictive Shell which immediately triggered a price war which no one was going to win apart from the customers. Shell Direct was a cumbersome dinosaur that from the outset was an inefficient confounded nuisance. In all honesty, it didn't know its arse from its elbow.

The first thing that happened was that they put bigger trucks into the depot… very efficient no doubt, but the awfully clever suits at Shell Direct HQ had, in their infinite wisdom, lost sight of one crucial issue… the width of Cornish roads. This actually brought us a bit of work where we bailed them out of an embarrassing and potentially very expensive problem.

Shell get a visit from a bailiff bearing a brown envelope

Shell Direct had the national contract to supply Trinity House lighthouses, but the first attempt to make a delivery to the Lizard Lighthouse had to be aborted because the road to the lighthouse was too narrow. If the lighthouse ran out of fuel, Supershell's reputation would be shredded. They asked us to make an urgent, third party delivery on their behalf at an excellent rate.

On receipt of the official order number, the delivery was made the same day and the delivery note was sent to the head office as per very clear instructions. We made 4 full load deliveries over a two-month period using the official order numbers supplied. We sent signed delivery notes after each delivery as instructed, with an invoice at the end of the calendar month for settlement by the 20th of the following month as agreed by fax.

We waited for payment, none came. Order numbers were queried, invoices were queried, this put them out of terms so they went on 'stops' with a 10% late payment surcharge applied. Still there was no payment. Apparently, they then sent a smaller truck from somewhere else in the network to do the jobs every fortnight until a suitable truck was sent back to Newquay. And still... no payment. We were being messed around like fools. The fact it was the mighty Shell Direct we were dealing with meant nothing to me. I wanted our money, so after six months of this nonsense, we lobbed a statutory demand at them for the amount outstanding plus a 10% late payment surcharge as detailed in our terms of business.

We had a message from our solicitors saying that the statutory demand had been served and a few minutes later the office phone rang with a very irate Shell Direct 'suit' leaping up and down on the other end insisting that we could not do this to Shell Direct.

My reaction was, "well actually we just have chap and that is why you are leaping up and down on the phone to me." After more than six months of being nice, ten minutes of being absolutely beastly had focused his undivided attention on resolving a matter entirely of their own creation.

In less than half a day the money was in our bank, the 10% surcharge had covered our costs with a useful bit of interest but crucially, we had been paid. Needless to say, we never dealt with them again. What we did was nothing more than they would have done to anyone else were the boot on the other foot.

Not long after that they were gone as quickly as they came and good riddance.

The lesson being that David beat Goliath in the Old Testament and the same still applies today. If you are right, never be intimidated by size. It really is a case of 'he who dares wins.' So always fight your corner.

The Federation of Petroleum Suppliers experience

We may not have been allowed to access the BP Terminal in Falmouth, but after a couple of attempts we did get admitted to the Federation of Petroleum Suppliers (FPS), which was the industry trade association headquartered in Knutsford, Cheshire.

Over an extended period, this proved very beneficial for networking and keeping abreast of the seemingly endless tide of new legislation and regulation that was descending on the fuel distribution industry.

I became the South West Regional Director for five years, (nobody else in the region wanted the job) which led to another very interesting experience as the board meetings were held in the Knutsford offices except for one meeting a year which was in London.

The high rate of excise duty on road diesel had created a clandestine fuel laundering industry involving serious criminal elements that was costing the Exchequer billions in lost revenue. It also affected legitimate hauliers who were being hit hard by cowboys, running on hooky-laundered fuel undercutting rates.

Everyone agreed that something had to be done, especially after Customs Officers had raided a laundering plant in the Manchester area (allegedly operated by Ulster paramilitary elements) and were threatened with firearms. A proposed piece of draconian legislation called the RDCO (Registered Dealers in Controlled Oils Regulations) was rushed out for consultation.

The draft RDCO legislation as proposed by HMRC did not make pretty reading.

A serious confrontation

The FPS were the distribution industry consultees and at the first meeting in the 'Custom House' in Manchester it was pretty obvious that Senior Customs Officers saw us in the same light as the launderers. In their view, it necessarily followed that the criminals were buying their red diesel from somewhere and it had to be the distribution industry.

From the FPS perspective, the first thing that had to be established was that our membership was, at that time, largely legitimate family firms like my own who were most certainly not crooks. The FPS had strict criteria for membership as I had experienced when we joined.

Grudgingly, the Customs delegation conceded that point, but the talks broke down when one particular senior officer called Paul Gerrard started banging the table insisting that there would be no compromise on what was being proposed. Indeed, it would be imposed without further ado.

Eventually the fractious, ill-humoured meeting broke up and was adjourned to a date yet to be agreed.

It was obvious that they needed to adopt a more conciliatory approach by accepting that what was on the table really was impractical, unreasonable and basically unworkable if, as was increasingly likely, it was arbitrarily imposed and the industry retaliated by refusing to cooperate.

At the end of the day the threat of withdrawal of RDCO registration was effectively an idle threat which, if implemented, could bring the country to a standstill, so there was an impasse.

The general, off-the-record consensus between the parties was that something must be worked out that fulfilled the stated objectives without completely alienating those charged with administering it at their own expense.

The nub of the problem being, in true bureaucratic fashion, that the awkward buggers would not say exactly what it was they wanted from us and, to make matters worse, they kept moving the goalposts while Paul Gerrard continued to make blood curdling threats.

Paul Gerrard was being seen as a difficult rather unpleasant fly in the ointment.

My take on the situation as it then stood was that Paul Gerrard had been given a massive task that he was struggling with given the time constraints. He was buckling under the pressure that those demands were imposing on him and needed to step back and have a re-think. Alas, he was probably too pig headed, inflexible and bureaucratically institutionalised to do so.

The next meeting did not get off to a good start, with Mr Gerrard again thumping the table. I had just made a point and he snarled back. I suggested that he ought to learn some manners and he practically leapt across the table. We were eyeball to eyeball and he was quivering with rage when I said, "speak to me like that again and I will fucking well head butt you." Mr Gerrard sat down. Then I sat down.

In disgrace but so what? It cleared the air

There were gasps around the table, much shuffling of paper, then the Chair coughed and suggested a comfort break. I was not proud of my outburst but I was being deliberately provoked, I felt, by yet another bully who needed to be put back in order. We were both in the wrong but feelings really were running high because there was a lot at stake for both parties.

The others left the room. Gerrard and I looked at each other and actually apologised to each other. As I said, we were both in the wrong, a few minutes brutally straight talking put together the bare bones of a scheme that could work without being too onerous on us.

The Customs delegation were coming back and I left the room to report to my colleagues through the executive secretary.

I wish I hadn't sworn but as a former fisherman there were occasions where an expletive has been all that stood between me and a heart attack. It is my safety valve. This explosive episode was definitely one of those occasions.

The 'F' word broke the log jam

When the meeting reconvened there was an entirely different atmosphere. Another hour and the proposed compromise had been knocked into workable shape without any further input from me. Had the confrontation not taken place in the way it did, the rest of the FPS board would have been beaten into submission and that would have been no good to anyone.

I look back on this episode with mixed feelings. My colleagues were obviously horrified by my behaviour, perhaps they had never been bullied in a past life like me, but what they thought of me was immaterial, results were forthcoming and a satisfactory outcome was bigger than the egos or sensitivities any of the individuals involved.

The Customs are their own worst enemies. We all have a job to do and the rule of law is important, but their tendency to regard everyone as crooks allied to their inability to actually come clean on what they actually want, is a nightmare to deal with. They were bureaucrats –

I was a trader. Without traders they would not have a job.

If only HMRC had been upfront

The conversation with Gerrard after the blow up finally defined what they actually needed rather than what they were unreasonably demanding and it was quite simple when reduced down to basics:

Firstly, they HAD to stop fuel laundering, no ifs, no buts. Agreed!

Secondly, they wanted to know how much heating oil and red diesel we were buying. Easy!

Thirdly, they wanted to know how much heating oil and red diesel we were selling. Easy!

Fourthly, they wanted to know who we were selling it to. Easy!

Fifthly, they wanted us to have our computer systems set up to supply this information electronically in a monthly report, at our own expense, potentially expensive. Not that easy, but needs must!

If they had put these requirements in plain English in the first place a lot of wasted time and ill feeling could have been avoided.

A few months later the RDCO scheme was introduced and fuel laundering went into rapid decline as the Customs men acted decisively on the data the industry was supplying.

While it was another pain in the arse to live with, we collectively buckled down, got over it and got on with it, like you do when there is no alternative. Good, well-framed legislation is no bad thing but there is far too much badly framed legislation with far too many loopholes out there that make everyone's life a misery for precious little benefit.

The Oil Barons' Ball

The highlight of the FPS year was the conference and exhibition which gave the FPS the bulk of its yearly income. It culminated in the Oil Barons' Ball, a black tie dinner on the second night of the two day event. The first one Fred and I attended was at the English Riviera Centre in Torquay.

There was an extensive trade show where new innovations often first saw the light of day, seminars on various oil-related topics and a chance to socialise (party hard) with kindred spirits. There were many great characters who, over the years, gradually disappeared to be replaced by characterless, corporate types in grey suits, by which time, for me, the organisation had lost its appeal.

For the next several years the venue was the Norbreck Castle Hotel located at the Clevelys end of Blackpool sea front. It was a rambling, castellated institution that had seen better days, with peeling woodchip wallpaper in what passed as an en-suite bathroom and the smell of boiled cabbage and dust pervading the lengthy corridors. But, the monumental booze ups in good company more than compensated.

In between, we had the odd conference at the Telford International Centre and one mega bash in Dublin at the Royal Dublin Showground, swelled by the Irish membership. In total, 1,100 sat down to a superb, highly congenial dinner served in the most efficient manner I have ever seen.

As a regional representative, like everything else in life, you only get out of it what you are prepared to put in, the frustrating thing being that there was a proportion of members who only wanted to take from the system. I call them 'the sponges', and they invariably absorb every snippet of information available but never ever give anything back.

My time in that capacity certainly broadened my horizons and my extensive network of contacts, but interesting as that was, the day job demanded that I needed to focus on operations back at home base.

Conoco treachery

One of the things that needed attention was our relationship with Conoco who had made strong hints about us becoming their local, authorised distributor. The idea did not appeal so I left it on the back burner. Then, the subtle pressure started being applied in the form of stricter credit limits, which we complied with because there was no choice and the cash flow could easily cope.

The next thing, without warning, our 'friendly' rival, the long-established Opie Oils became the local Conoco AD, which was a proper job for them and certainly, at that point, no skin whatsoever off of my nose.

We had not long before acquired our first 44 ton articulated tanker so that we could haul our own fuel out of Plymouth along with increasing volumes of red diesel out of Falmouth Oil Services at Falmouth Docks where MD Chris Walters had ambitious plans to revitalise the terminal.

We had also done a lucrative fuel throughput deal with Westcountry Oils who had tied up French oil company, 'Total' as their supplier and eventual, albeit transitory, owner. They were using our storage to load their trucks working in the local area. Having patched up our former serious differences on the basis that co-operation was more profitable than confrontation, we had access to the former Fuelserve Depot in Bodmin which they had taken over. This meant we could shed the overhead of the rented Washaway storage as a result of the reciprocal throughput deal brokered by Fred with Westcountry Oils MD, Paul Rhuleman.

They put more through our depot than we drew from Bodmin and the throughput rate was 0.3ppl which mounted up at the end of the month the more so with not having to pay the rent for Washaway.

It was early December and the run up to the Christmas peak order period when Conoco dropped a bombshell in our lap. A perfunctory call from some minion in their Warwick sales office announced there would be no further heating oil availability ex-Plymouth until 7th January, just under a month away.

This was a classic stitch up.

Pragmatism works

Paul Rhuleman, the fiercely straight, highly pragmatic MD of Westcountry Oils happened to be in the office later and we discussed the problem. A few phone calls were made which confirmed that heating oil was in genuinely tight supply due to an unscheduled refinery outage compounded by bad weather affecting shipping movements.

That clearly illustrated how finely tuned the oil supply chain is. It depends on product moving smoothly through the supply chain from the oil well, via the refinery and to the end user. There are limited buffers to avoid supply shocks if something like a refinery outage or prolonged bad weather delays the coastal shipping movements that supply terminals like Falmouth or Plymouth.

But the newly anointed local Conoco AD was crowing about unlimited supplies of heating oil. Well of course he was, because he had been allocated ours until the stink that caused forced a Conoco rethink.

The art lies in raising the right sort of stink because random abuse only makes the situation worse. A classic oil industry stitch up was confirmed when we had been selling three times as much as them as confirmed by a friendly Conoco delivery driver!

Westcountry Oils had had the opposite problem to us in the form of a tight supply of red diesel so, an exchange agreement was quickly worked out where Judith and her opposite number at Westcountry Oils would keep track of stock being exchanged and the prices exchanged at to be sorted out when the dust eventually settled.

Then something happened that really presented a serious challenge in exchange for a huge opportunity to dig ourselves out of a rapidly escalating supply black hole. We had a phone call via West Country Oils from the terminal manager at Total's Langley Terminal who had a different issue again in the form of plenty of heating oil but an absolute famine of tankers to move it. He desperately needed to move heating oil because he ran a rail-fed depot and had to have the capacity to unload the next scheduled train. If we were prepared to fetch it, come and get it.

When the going gets tough, the tough get going!

A huge advantage we enjoyed as such an effective, small, tightly-knit management team was the ability to discuss something and, if necessary, be doing it in minutes without the need to refer to higher authority. In this instance, it was another clear cut case of crack on!

Langley is not far from Heathrow. A distance of circa 250 miles which seemed crazy but needs must. It involved a 13 to 14 hour round trip with the truck double manned. The 36,500 litre load would go a long way toward our then, 50 to 60,000 litre daily heating oil requirement.

The artic had just unloaded the last load out of Plymouth and it was fuelled up ready to roll. Fred and Richard Angove our fleet engineer, set out for Langley at 16:00 and were back in the yard at 06:00 the following morning.

Fortunately, given the growing nationwide fuel delivery crisis, the FPS had negotiated a temporary relaxation of drivers' hours, which was a huge help to everyone as snow was forecast which added to the woes. Thankfully, at a local level, Devon and Cornwall had little or no snowfall, while on the third night of the Langley run they were driving in tramlines of frozen slush on the M4.

I fancy that our demonstrable resilience was a huge embarrassment to Conoco. The following Monday after the truck had left for Langley again, there was a call from the excellent Plymouth Terminal Manager to say that heating oil was once more available from Conoco as required.

We had recently had cellular radios fitted in the trucks which had coverage in the whole of Cornwall and Devon and as far as Exeter. Judith tried calling the artic and they came back loud and clear, they were at Tedburn so it was easy to divert them back into Plymouth to load heating oil, then home for an early finish.

That was yet another potentially disastrous set back dealt with by well-timed, decisive action. It more than vindicated the purchase of the very expensive artic and the installation of the cellular radios.

A few days later, thanks to the radios, we made a delivery in less than five minutes from the receipt of an order. It was an emergency involving a care home in St Agnes that had been let down on a promised delivery from another supplier. Our truck was actually passing the gate when contact was made and delivery effected which really did give me great satisfaction.

It always happened that whenever the pressure came on, the wheels would often fall off of the bigger corporate distributors who lacked the resilient infrastructure to take the strain. Assets were pared back to the bone for efficiency and during quiet times they would throw their weight around and clean up all the price-sensitive work.

This suited us because it was better to park up than work for nothing, but we would clean up in busy times. Never taking advantage of customers and getting deliveries to them promptly, was winning the campaign of attrition with the big boys and led to vigorous, organic growth. We had the storage and enough trucks to get the work done when the chips were really down.

Rip off merchants come unstuck

A major factor in gaining work was price rip offs where some work was done for new buyers at what must have been zero profit, while another longstanding loyal customer would be paying way over the odds. This was illustrated by a mother and daughter who were part of a large farming family.

The mother and married daughter obviously had different surnames but lived next door to each other. The daughter always bought on price while mother was loyal. The company in question delivered to both properties without even moving the truck. When the daughter checked her mother's price it was 12ppl more than she had paid.

To say that there was hell up did not begin to describe the situation and she rang us to confirm our price which was admittedly more than she had paid but 10ppl less than her mother had paid. She then rang the supplier who said her mother's price was a 'mistake' and promptly refunded the difference but the daughter was wise to that one and she checked back several years confirming her worst fears.

The result was that the entire family became our longstanding customers. Three farms and several houses. That is how wars are won and business is built by being fair to everyone. Because we all live in the same small, close-knit community, people do talk and compare notes and still have long memories.

Falmouth Oil Services

The Conoco debacle led to talks with Chris Walters at Falmouth Oil Services about making heating oil available in Falmouth. Chris was keen to do this and put together a deal with Texaco Fuel and Marine Marketing (FAMM) who were happy to put heating oil into the terminal's product mix. This meant hardly any trips to Plymouth and a very pissy Conoco, having lost our rapidly growing volumes.

This instigated yet another phase of attrition, with rivals throwing their toys out of their prams by refusing to buy from Falmouth. Proper job for us, but the Chinese whispers about fuel quality intensified and it was hard to resist the temptation to fire back. However, it was much better to just keep doing a good job at a fair price and ignore them.

It is a very bad policy to steer your ship by another man's compass. Our strategy was working and loading out of Falmouth which was less than 10 miles from St Day. It meant that our artic could haul in four 36,500 loads in a ten-hour day as against a 58 mile haul from Plymouth where it was a case of two loads in a nine hour day.

This seemed a very good proposition where we could promote our environmental credentials by keeping our truck off the A30/A38 Plymouth corridor which was becoming increasingly congested and often closed due to accidents and road works. Plymouth fuel was marginally cheaper but to me, Falmouth was a complete no brainer and well worth the small premium.

FAAM quickly became an excellent firm to work with. The Falmouth stock was theirs and the sales manager, based in Canary Wharf, was a real pleasure to deal with. We had a really useful facility to forward buy when we felt it was right and one winter, we forward bought half our anticipated heating oil requirement and it really paid off.

The following winter, a Somerset-based distributor knowing how well we had done, took the plunge and bought most of their projected winter requirement forward. The market moved the wrong way and a mild winter crimped volumes and it took them down. They had to sell out to another competitor. It was a dangerous game and we got away with it twice but that was it, no more.

Another innovation that made a great difference to smooth cash flow was a move to a rolling credit. Historically, what fuel you bought in a calendar month was paid for by direct debit on the 20th of the following month, which meant building up huge credit balances in the bank only to see them vanish when payment was taken.

With the rolling credit, fuel lifted on a daily basis became payable 30 days later, so the bank credit balances were smaller but much more stable, with no huge swings. This made cash flow much easier to manage, with 30 days' real time credit on everything.

Texaco's predominant interest in Falmouth was actually heavy fuel oil (HFO), that ghastly, thick, black, residual fuel that ships and, at that time, heavy industry, still used. It was interesting because EU regulations dictated that ships operating in the English Channel east of the 5 degree west line had to run on more expensive, low sulphur fuel oil (LSFO).

A prime location

Coincidentally, the 5 degree line ran from St Anthony's Lighthouse south to Ushant, dictating that Falmouth was the perfect pit stop for inbound ships to load LSFO before proceeding east. In peak months, Falmouth's throughput of all grades of HFO could be as much as 60,000 tons compared with maybe 3,000 tons of diesel and heating oil.

Esso in its infinite wisdom then decided to withdraw HFO from its rail-fed, Plymouth storage facility which supplied a limited but lucrative inland market. Seizing the opportunity to fill the vacuum created, FAMM asked us if we were interested in being their contract HFO haulier.

This meant buying another artic tractor unit and two dedicated HFO trailers. Within a short while, we were hauling HFO to the Dairy Crest cheese factory at Davidstow, ECC's Wenford Bridge dryers, St Austell Brewery, Ambrosia at Lifton, Wrigley's chewing gum in Plymouth and a large nursery at Ermington that produced practically every poinsettia plant sold in supermarkets at Christmas.

FAMM had also cornered the Brittany Ferries contract when Esso walked from Plymouth. They usually managed this by barge from Falmouth, but on several occasions, we were called in to bunker the ferries by road. Esso then decided that they wanted Brittany Ferries back and spent a fortune building a tank farm at Millbay that they sea-fed by barge from their Fawley Refinery.

This HFO haulage work was steady and predictable. Both artics were very busy and the haulage rate was lucrative. All went well for five years when suddenly Texaco got taken over by Chevron, FAMM was no more and the HFO job got moved to Cardiff. We did have the option to work out of Cardiff but being a Cornish-based company with no territorial ambitions it did not appeal.

Another course correction

Given the way things appeared to be done by major oil companies, often, seemingly just to be vindictive, I sometimes marvel at my own macro level how they ever made any money. By golly, they certainly did though!

All good things come to an end and Chevron proved to be another thoroughly unpleasant company to deal with. Chris Walters also struggled with them, having committed to rebuild the ageing tank farm dating from pre WW2 with the aid of a Freight Facilities grant. We were looking forward to a great new facility, but that now looked decidedly dicey, with Chevron calling the shots.

A minnow in the shark tank

As one door closes then another one opens and this seems to have been the story of my life. It certainly seemed to be that way within the oil industry, where once, laying in my bunk up in the old Caroline's wheelhouse, I thought I would be lucky to run one truck and make a living.

Heeding my gut instincts and following hunches that involved taking carefully calculated risks, this thing was getting bigger than in truth I would have liked.

My rule of never turning back had taken me on a journey of discovery where open doors were there to be entered. The wheeling and dealing was exciting and Father's old 3/5 rule was proving to be true.

My father could have been a tycoon were his horizons not so narrow. He was shrewd but not being greedy, he operated on a needs-based manner, his maxim being that if you pulled off three deals out of five you would be fine. If you messed up three deals out of five you were headed for trouble.

Not all deals paid off, so while it was good to be bold, being cavalier was a recipe for disaster.

Where risk management was concerned, not having had any formal business training was proving to be no handicap, and a combination of that priceless gut instinct, a hell of a lot of neck and a bit of luck were seeing me through. It certainly took a bit of neck when dealing with the major oil companies, but it was so easy to offend them and get dumped on the top of their shit list.

The most powerful weapon in a minnow's armoury within a corporate environment is embarrassment. Those anally retentive, grey-suited, corporate clones certainly had a chink in their armour because the last thing they needed was an embarrassing blot on their copybook that could send them sliding back down the greasy pole they were clawing their way up.

The biggest problem for me was their almost total lack of humour. They certainly seemed to regard me as a bit of a loose cannon, the more so given my pronounced Cornish accent and fisherman's approach to life and sometimes, a colourful turn of phrase when telling it like it really was.

They were hard to read for sure given that I was sometimes way out of my comfort zone in their presence but that old gut instinct always carried me through. The outcomes confirmed that most of the time things were being pitched at the right level.

Going that extra mile

At grassroots level our interactions with buyers certainly seemed to be pitched exactly right. We were approachable and happy to tailor our service to their specific needs.

One case, dealing with a major potato grower Rowe Farming, illustrated this perfectly. Mark Rowe called Fred at home at 22:00 on a Saturday evening for an urgent delivery to a dozen tractors that were going to be working on throughout the night.

Those boys worked hard as did we and that had to be respected. We were obliged to respond to a situation like that, which set us apart from our competitors.

This was an extreme example of emergency out of hours working. The weather had been wet and they were struggling to get the early potato crop in. It was January and it had turned cold and dry for a couple of days, presenting a valuable weather window which could not be wasted.

By this time, we had an operating centre with a couple of trucks based in Helston at Water Ma Trout near Fred's home. Consequently, it was easy to get in the truck and deliver to the fields three miles away in Porthleven.

The advantage of this was twofold. We could react promptly to emergencies as described and the two Helston-based drivers started and finished work near home meaning they did not have to drive their own cars to St Day to drive a truck back to start work in the Helston area. It was another of those win, win situations that delivered great benefits for all concerned.

We always made a point of ensuring that the trucks had fuel on them for just such occasions. Fred turned out and within the hour they were fuelled up. That really cemented our business relationship with Mark and Edward Rowe and that sort of thing tends to grab the attention of other potential customers, often creating a snowball effect.

Another attack dealt with

This is what the zombie rep working for the Brinkworth-based outfit with red trucks could never get his peanut brain around… service levels matter. He chipped away at Rowe Farming endlessly, offering suicidal prices which Mark kept throwing at David (they had been at school together so it was effectively banter with a message). But one day David said to Mark, "I can't afford to deal with you, best you take that price you have."

It lasted less than a month. At first, the service was impeccable but then, in a busy time, a scheduled Friday delivery didn't turn up and word got back that Rowe Farming tractors were queued up at Turnpike Garage to fill up with much more expensive road diesel because the other lot were not answering their phones. Mark apparently was too embarrassed to call us at the time.

That pillock of a rep even took to following our trucks around farms then calling in once the delivery had been made with a price designed to make us look foolish. This was the final straw. He was in our sights.

One day, Dave Whistle, a pugnacious little devil and one of the drivers who worked out of Helston, noticed the offending rep was following him. So, he turned into a blind lane and sure enough he was followed. A short way in there was a wide space so Dave pulled over and the rep had no alternative but to drive past into the narrow bit beyond.

Dave then drove ahead so the road beyond the wide bit was blocked, got out and tilted his cab and stood there with a cup of tea. A few minutes later, the rep, having come to the dead end and turned around, was wanting to get back past our truck. Dave told him he was broken down and couldn't move. He said he had called for help and the fitter would be two or three hours getting there.

In the meantime, having been told what Dave had done, I called Brinkworth to tell them that their rep who had been following our truck around was currently trapped by it because it had broken down. I added that if their rep was ever seen following our truck around again there could be consequences.

That idiocy ceased forthwith.

Chapter 14
ONWARDS!

Consols Oils small delivery tanker perfection at Cadgwith sporting the new livery (which is still use today)

A corporate makeover

David Eustice's son Paul was a graphic designer who owned his own company based in Bristol. Through David, we commissioned him to work on our branding and what he came up with based on our very distinctive colour scheme was stunningly simple, as all the best brands usually are. The new company branding included the strapline 'Expect the Best', which said it all really.

'Consols Oils' the movie is on YouTube

We also met a couple of local boys just starting out in business, namely 'Jack Clinton' and 'Adam Barbary', a very talented pair who ran XPY Films Cornwall. They shot us a stunning, 3 minutes 25 seconds promotional video featuring our day to day operations where I got to

Son Tom and the big artic

Fuelling the Grey Funnel Line at Falmouth Docks (also with the new Consols Oils branding)

Fuelling the Spirited Lady' which is skippered by Bracken Pearce, one of many talented, young fishermen to emerge from Mevagissey

do the voice over.

It must have been good because our hostile neighbours out on the A30 soon fired back with their own version. Naturally, I am obviously biased because I still prefer ours.

The Island connection

We picked up a major piece of core business around this time in the form of the oil distributor on the Isles of Scilly. The Isles of Scilly Steamship Company had been supplied by our A30 neighbours who'd been doing them no favours pricewise. They had been dealing with the same supplier since the year dot.

The Steamship Company manager responsible for purchasing fuel had long been an institution and it would seem that the relationship with the fuel company had been far too cosy for far too long. He had recently retired and his misdeeds soon came to light.

The former buyer's replacement smelled a rat where fuel pricing was concerned. The new marine superintendent who assumed responsibility for fuel purchases went through the system like a dose of salts and on the recommendation of the highly satisfied Scillies' distributor contacted Consols Oils.

The upshot being that having both agreed that everyone needed to make a living, a deal was done whereby we sold them fuel on which a mutually agreed fair margin was added to our buying price which we actually shared with them on a daily basis. They would decide when to buy and that price would be locked in for a specified volume.

This deal worked on the premise that it was bread and butter work where a regular fiver over time was much better than a quick fifty quid and getting caught with your fingers in the cookie jar. No rip offs, it was business based on mutual trust within a long-term trading relationship between two ethical Cornish companies. It really worked for all concerned over a lengthy timeframe.

This meant that all petroleum fuel used on Scilly with the exception of petrol was now supplied by Consols Oils and sourced from the Falmouth Terminal. It was a substantial, long-term, volume increase for us and very satisfying for me on a personal level. Exactly as all sound business should be.

A near miss

In the early days, we had been dealing with a Lincolnshire grower called 'Gosperton Farm Produce' (GFP), who had set up a substantial Cornish operation based in Leedstown. They were very worthwhile seasonal buyers but were never the fastest of payers.

I got to know Greville Richards, the Gosperton forklift driver who was the son of a highly respected local farmer friend of mine, Tony 'Skipper' Richards. Tony was an old-school farmer whose land was the most amazing permanent pasture most of which had never been ploughed in living memory. A true rarity in the west Cornwall broccoli zone.

One day, Greville tipped me off that things were shaky and I should watch the payments. They were in to the tune of just over £12,000 which I could not afford to lose, so going back to the office I made a phone call to Lincolnshire.

The manager on the other end was a classic bullshitter so it was time to call his bluff. Getting straight to the point I said, "a little bird tells me you are in trouble and about to go bust?" This resulted in a shocked, irritated denial, my response being, "OK prove it to me by paying what you owe in full."

Fair play to him, he obviously didn't want this out there so that day the full amount was in our bank, proper job and we had no further beef with them. The following week, Gosberton Farm Produce went into receivership and we were very lucky to have bailed out just in the nick of time. I certainly owed young Greville a debt of gratitude.

The rise of the Cabbage King

Greville moved quickly to fill the vacuum that GFP had left. We started dealing with Southern England Farms (SEF), his new enterprise which he and his wife founded. From the smallest beginnings, SEF Ltd has become the biggest, specialist grower of brassicas and courgettes in the UK. It just shows what vision and hard work can achieve.

We were pleased to be able to repay Greville's past help at one point in the early days and proud to have worked with him through many years of supplying fuel. We witnessed their phenomenal growth and the benefits that rippled out to landowners who rented their land, 500 plus staff and a host of suppliers to this flagship, Cornish Enterprise. It's a huge success story.

The likes of Greville, Mark, Edward Rowe and a handful of others had the drive to take the job by the scruff of the neck in a period of painful changes and great difficulty for Cornish farming. They learned to deal with the supermarkets on the scale they required and ensured the quality and consistency of supply they demanded.

Cornwall is a great place for local firms to work together in a substantial network of mutual self-help and benefit.

A tough operator

Another company involved in this process also began from very humble beginnings, with just two trucks in the haulage trade. 'Conway Bailey' was a legend in his own lifetime. A larger than life, cantankerous but hard-working character. Underneath his gruff exterior, he was kind and generous of spirit with a wicked (evil) sense of humour. He used to haul broccoli, cabbage, potatoes and flowers from Cornish growers to the upcountry wholesale markets.

This involved grinding toil, with days spent loading from around anything up to a dozen

The realm of the Cabbage King - Southern England Farms (SEF Ltd.) moving across the fields harvesting broccoli like grazing dinosaurs

One of Cornwall's huge success stories - Conway Bailey Transport, the hauliers who get the job done

farms in all weathers then home for a quick wash and meal before leaving in the early evening for London or markets in the Midlands. They'd arrive in the early hours of the morning to unload and then drive back to repeat the following day... three trips a week being the norm.

Conway had seven children, six brothers and a sister. The firm's office used to be a plank across the arms of the settee in the living room and the paperwork was contained in a collection of dog-eared duplicate books. While it was chaotic, it worked. But times were changing and four, hard-working brothers (all consummate drivers) were involved. As is often the case, one eventually stood out.

Paul, Alan and Gary were drivers but Mark had what it took to take this competent but rough and ready little firm and drive it forwards. This caused a few convulsions along the way but, like me, there was no going back where Mark Bailey was concerned.

First, a proper office was built on the side of Conway's bungalow and new, ERF tractor units started replacing the Leyland Roadtrains that had done them so well for many years.

A bit like our own experience at St Day, this was soon outgrown as was the wooden garage across the drive where the meticulous maintenance was done. The couple of acres at the rear was bought and rapidly expanded into and in no time, there were 20 trucks and a large new workshop followed in quick succession by proper offices.

Then there was a big setback when they got prosecuted for a number of drivers' hours' offences. Taken to court, Conway was heard bemoaning the fact that one of the magistrates, another haulier was 'a bigger bloody rogue than he was.' It ended up at the Crown Court where the fine was several tens of thousands of pounds.

The Department of Transport prosecutor was a former classmate of Mark's at Tolgus School called 'John Carpenter'. Outside of the court, Carpenter was expecting a blow up with Mark for doing his job, but instead Mark went straight up to him and said, "Carpenter you bastard I could have done without this today, whatever you are earning I will pay you double to come and work for me to sort the job out."

John Carpenter took the offer and Conway Bailey Transport (CBT) became totally legitimate. They could never, ever get them on maintenance because, in Mark's books, a broken down lorry was costing money not earning it.

Conway Bailey Transport always did Southern England's work, so our three firms were flying the flag of Cornish business acumen, each in our own way to mutual benefit collectively and creating hundreds of decently paid jobs between us.

Today, the trucks are more than adequately powered. They are air conditioned, with comfortable sleeper cabs and run mostly on dual carriageways and motorways. Having backed onto a loading bay to have the pallets of produce loaded by forklift, the doors are closed at the start of a journey to a supermarket hub. One pick up - one drop - job sorted. Today's drivers have it so much easier. What a difference to Conway's original overloaded, underpowered lorrys, which were without sleeper cabs or even heaters. They were handballing broccoli crates aboard from multiple farms in the rain before roping and sheeting them down and driving them through the night to the upcountry markets.

The immaculate fleet now numbers more than a hundred distinctive orange trucks that rarely stop for longer than it takes to change drivers. CBT operate throughout the EU area mainly on refrigerated produce work, but if the price is right the company has never been known to walk away from a challenge.

Brassica crops are very big business mainly in the hands of two grower/packers, with some smaller growers feeding into that system. The total acreage will be approaching 20,000 acres mostly rented in the short term. This is a Godsend to many farmers who could not earn what they get in rent from the growers by farming the land themselves.

Latterly, they have diversified into courgettes or zucchini where, as a trial, the timid would plant say 10 acres, SEF planted 600 acres. I cannot picture that many courgettes. It worked well however, and the acreage is now several times that. It's a similar story with daffodils and potatoes, again grown on a huge scale.

These men have balls like Bengali tigers and deserve every last bit of success that they have.

Two legends and the boy... Conway Bailey (middle) with Edwin Richards (right) both R.I.P.

The loss of a legend

I was heading out toward the Lizard one afternoon and, by Culdrose, I passed Conway Bailey heading the other way. We put our hands up as we passed and that was the last time I saw that amazing character and friend of my father. He got home and having had his tea he complained of feeling unwell. He then went to bed and passed peacefully away soon after. At the age of 87 it was the end of an era for sure.

I was amazed and greatly honoured when the family asked me to deliver Conway's eulogy at his funeral. It was a moving scene to see him carried into Gwennap Church on the shoulders of his six sons, united in their grief.

It brought back memories of my grandfather being carried on the shoulders of his six sons, one of whom was my father.

When it came time to mount the lectern my throat went dry at the sight of the packed church, with a couple of hundred more standing in the rain outside. But, after a gulp of water and a deep breath, it was easy to speak about such a remarkable man. A real friend who left such a formidable legacy.

R.I.P Conway.

Hell on wheels

As is often the case, the best stories came at the wake held in the Penventon Hotel. Hedley Curtis, another former haulier, told of the evil Friday night, with horizontal, gale-driven rain, when homebound loaded with straw (in pre-bypass days), they got stopped in the main street at Okehampton where a Ministry road check directed them to the station goods yard weighbridge to be check weighed.

There was a queue waiting to be weighed. It was the height of the 1970's mackerel boom and they had caught an Irish truck loaded with mackerel in a bulk trailer bound for the fishmeal factory which was ten tons overweight.

They didn't know what to do because there was no way of getting the weight off owing to its putrid nature and close proximity to a river. The queue was lengthening as the Irishman caused chaos, while the Ministry men were soaked like drowned rats and teasy as adders.

Hedley was first in line in front of Conway. The Ministry man questioned why two loads of straw were waiting to be weighed when they couldn't possibly be overweight. He asked Hedley for his weighbridge ticket which showed him to be four tons underweight. So the stressed Ministry man waved him and Conway on, assuming all was well because straw was never overweight.

A few miles down the road at the Whitehouse Café, Hedley was puzzled why Conway was so keen to buy him dinner when the truth came out. Conway was six tons overweight because he had 20 tons of stainless steel sheets for J&F Pool in Hayle under the straw and the

Ministry would have thrown the book at him if they'd known.

No wonder those old, underpowered trucks sometimes struggled up hills, but that was how it was back in the day.

Another Conway story concerned a woman who used to sit on a seat in a very provocative manner when the old A303 used to go through Wincanton. Descending a hill, there was a right hand bend where a bench was located. On the day in question, there were temporary traffic lights just around the bend and Conway's gaze was fixed on the woman sitting on the seat. Suddenly, there was a loud crash of all the vehicles to tail end, in this case, it was a Rolls Royce. The driver was not happy.

Conway, working on the theory that attack is the only defence in that sort of situation, blamed the angry Roller driver for the accident. "What on earth do you mean?" said the Roller driver. Conway fired back, "of course it is your fault, you have that beautiful car with marvellous brakes and all that technology that stops you dead, you stopped dead in front of this truck of mine that can't stop that quick so I hit you and it's your fault'!" "Don't be ridiculous man," said the Roller driver, "look what you have done to my car, I want your driver and insurance details." Conway replied, "if you give me something to write on you can have them" and the Roller driver produced a business card saying, "use this." Conway wrote down his details and handed the card back and they both went back to their vehicles.

Suddenly, Conway realised that he didn't have the other driver's details so he ran up to the battered Roller just as it was about to drive away saying, "here, hang on a minute Mr Bugger, you have my details but I want yours." The exasperated Roller driver said, "oh very well, here is my business card" and drove away. Conway looked at the card and it was the one he had put his own details on. Needless to say, Conway was out of Wincanton like a cut cat.

Home to die

The bitter winter of 1963 had seen Conway Bailey supplying fodder to moorland farmers, much of which he never got paid for. Things were so bad that he could not pay his drivers' wages. Mickey Coad, who married my cousin Jenny, (the daughter of Willy Bennetts - one of Father's older brothers) worked for Conway without wages for three months and they became like blood brothers.

Mick and Jenny emigrated to Australia and ended up keeping a fine herd of South Devon Cattle in Tasmania. They had been home a couple of times over the years so contact was always maintained mainly through my sister.

Mick became ill with bladder cancer which was terminal. Against his doctor's strongest advice, he made up his mind to come home to die. He held his own wake with his mates before he left Tasmania. He wanted to see the South Devon Cattle at the Royal Cornwall Show one last time which was a pretty tall order considering how ill he was.

213

Their youngest daughter Jessica, born after their son Adam was tragically killed in a motorbike accident on the farm road while on his way to college, was a talented dress maker and amateur model. She had won a competition at the Melbourne Show to design and model a dress for a formal occasion. The prize was $1,000 and two return airline tickets to London which got Mick and Jenny home nicely.

He made it home with Jenny and elder daughter Tracey in mid-May albeit against the considerable odds he was facing. Jessica was touring Europe but made it to Cornwall in time for the show at the end of the first week in June.

I arranged the hire of a mobility scooter for him at the show and we had a great morning down on the cattle lines. We had lunch as a family group in the members' restaurant. By this time, Mick was visibly flagging. His last act of defiance was a wall of death, flat out lap on his scooter around the table before being taken home. He had seen what he had come home to see and was content.

The following day he was admitted to Treliske Hospital and two days later he went to Mount Edgcumbe Hospice. He passed away two further days after. Conway and another old mate, Mickey Rodgers, were with him as he faded. We all arrived outside his hospice room to gales of laughter as he was rolling his last fag and telling a pretty raunchy joke with his last breath.

Somehow it wasn't that sad at the time. We stayed with him for a while and then left Jenny and the daughters with him to say their goodbyes. Waiting out in the vestibule chatting about the ironies of life, Mickey Coad had died as he had lived – well and full-on to the last. A very brave man indeed and back to Tasmania in an urn.

The brothers are reconciled

Mickey Coad could take the considerable credit for setting the stage for my father and his brother Jack to finally make their peace by persuading father to go to Australia.

When father was invalided out of the Navy he got nothing. However, a few years before he died, my sister got wind of the news that those in father's position were then entitled to a pension so we went to the British Legion for assistance. Sadly, they were worse than useless and did not seem to want to know… I thought that was why we all bought poppies?

We did find another organisation, the 'Soldiers, Sailors and Air Force Association (SSAFA)' who, to their great credit, got right on the case. Within six weeks, father had been awarded a £250 per week pension. It was the first time in his life that he ever had a copper-bottomed, guaranteed, regular income and the security that gave him apart from his meagre state pension.

At the Royal Cornwall Show -
Pimms O'Clock with Billy Kneebone from
Bude and Phil Trebilcock from Newquay

Better late than never

Father got his passport and visa and set off Down Under for three months. It was the first time he had ever flown or even been out of the country since his involuntary wartime trip to Murmansk on a Russian convoy escort.

Jack had done well in Australia and had settled in Melbourne. His first wife had left him with three children to look after and he had employed a young Dutch lady as housekeeper while he ran his business. We had already met Liesbeth when she spent a summer in Cornwall before they got married. They got married despite a considerable age difference and some in the family said it would never work, but it did. They were very happy and they had 2 children, a boy and a girl.

When father arrived in Australia he had the time of his life. He even met Jack's ex-wife who had also remarried and who Father had held responsible for burning the family bible all those years before.

Over the three month stay, the brothers mended their fences and parted the best of friends as brothers should be. Jack was ill and died not long after, so closure and the reconciliation was just in the nick of time.

Jack Bennetts was the kindest, loveliest of men who would never intentionally harm a fly. I knew my stubborn, pig-headed father had fretted over the years of division although he would never admit it.

There was one more amazing and joyful coincidence to come that cemented the ties between St Agnes and Cubert parishes on the other side of the world via the incredible Cornish diaspora.

Father had a soft spot for Jack and Liesbeth's daughter Laura, who was little more than a toddler when he was there. He predicted she would do well for herself and he was spot on. Laura grew away and went to University where she met a First Nation boy called 'Scott Kneebone', the clue being in the name.

One of Scott's forebears was a Cornish miner called 'Kneebone', from St Agnes who had married a First Nation wife. Laura's roots meanwhile were by way of her father in Cubert. For them to meet, fall in love and marry in Australia… well, how uncanny is that?

They now have three children and I met them all when they spent time with us while they were on a round-the-world-trip a few years back. I love their approach to life and admire them for their achievements. They both work in the Department of Native Affairs in Canberra and Scott's father is a celebrated, First Nation artist. What an amazingly cosmopolitan diverse family we are all part of.

Last man standing

One by one, the thirteen Bennetts' siblings dropped away until there were only two left; Aunt Clarice the eldest and Father. Clarice went first. She was into her nineties, a ripe old age for sure. Father's time came six weeks from his eightieth birthday. He had been going downhill for a while. It was gradual but increasingly noticeable. He then had a nasty fall in the garden, impaling himself on a broken fence stake. It was a horrible wound in a very tender place and he declined rapidly after this. The wound was not healing well, but even though his time was fast approaching, his dodgy heart would not stop beating. He was obviously in agony and not an easy patient to deal with.

Marie cared for him by day, while for several weeks I tended him by night. Eventually, he went onto morphine and rested easier until finally he beat his demons and fell asleep like a baby. Truly the end of an era and a very rocky road.

I miss him dearly but, in all honesty, Mother's passing hurt me more. We buried him in St Day Churchyard with Mother and walked away. All of a sudden I was the senior family member.

Chapter 15
The fund raiser

A bit of a break

I have never been a great fan of holidays, but in 2002 I went on a trip to raise funds for the Fishermen's Mission. It all kicked off in Newlyn on Fish Festival Day, August Bank Holiday. I had a 19 foot, outboard-powered, Orkney fishing boat that had a wheelhouse and a small cuddy with 2 bunks under it.

The plan was to leave Newlyn on Fish Festival Day, round Land's End and head up to Bristol, thence up the River Avon into the Kennet and Avon Canal and on to Reading. Then, down the Thames and home along the south coast back to Newlyn. It would be a total distance of 840 miles involving 139 locks between Bristol Docks and Teddington.

Fish Festival Day saw a near gale of NE wind which delayed the start until the evening when the plan was to make Padstow. The Western Shore was fine and taking the inside track around the Longships was OK but once around Pendeen it was not so nice. We met the ebb tide off St Ives and the light was failing. My main concern was a fouled prop on a crab pot buoy rope in the dark in the poor weather.

Into Newquay for the night

Discretion being the better part of valour and having my 16-year old son with me, I decided to run into Newquay for the night rather than face Ramsey Alley in the dark and the Doom Bar at near low water. I informed Falmouth Coastguard of the change of plan and stuck our nose on the sand in the harbour just after half ebb, quickly drying out in safety.

The following morning the wind was gone so we went on to Padstow, but by the time we got there the strong NE breeze was up again so we sat tight because it was no weather to be rounding Hartland in.

We had a lovely day in Padstow, feeling like emmets as we wandered around and took a walk out to Hawkers Cove, while that bloody wind freshened into the afternoon as if to taunt us.

To Watchet Marina

The following morning it was good to go with the wind gone. We had a grand run up to Hartland rounding the treacherous place in fine style. We were heading for hopefully more sheltered waters, bowling along at eighteen knots and with the tide in our favour, we crossed

Bideford Bay and past Ilfracombe. We were soon running under very high cliffs by Lynmouth.

Past Lynmouth the lighthouse on Foreland Point marks the start of the actual Bristol Channel as it begins to narrow. Suddenly, the sea turned from blueish green to brown as a line of debris heralded the ebb tide pouring out of the Channel and progress slowed markedly.

We pushed on past Porlock heading for Watchet and a rendezvous with Paul who was supporting us on the run up to Bristol. Paul's youngest son Nigel, joined us there for the ride up the River Avon to Bristol. With the tide running hard, we decided to anchor off until the tide turned before getting under way again.

Engine trouble

When the tide turned, the wind was fresher from the west and when we went to get the anchor up we had engine trouble. It ran very roughly and stalled as soon as the revs increased. By now the tide was roaring and we were potentially in serious trouble so I called Swansea Coastguard who tasked Minehead inshore lifeboat to assist us.

They were soon with us and one of the crew had a look at the engine but he couldn't see anything wrong either, so we were towed back to Minehead. Paul was waiting there and he had a look. We'd changed fuel tanks in Watchet, but dirty fuel was ruled out as the inline filter was spotless.

Problem sorted and on to Bristol

Paul had a hunch and disconnected the fuel line from the engine, that was the problem. The 'O' ring seal on the connector was pinched and letting air in. There was nothing wrong with the engine… it was that simple. Another lesson learned at the cost of half a day which could be ill afforded. We had a pleasant hour buying the lifeboat crew and shore helpers a pint then had an early night.

Catching the flood in the morning, we were soon at Portishead and the mouth of the River Avon. Passing under the M5, we were soon in the Avon Gorge and on the way up to Bristol City Docks.

The lock into Bristol City Dock seemed enormous to a 19-foot boat. Mooring to the pontoon at the entrance, I went to the Harbour Office to see the procedure for entry, but Paul had beaten me to it. The Harbourmaster arranged for us to lock in and, given our charitable mission, there would be no charge.

Once in the dock and moored up, Julia joined us for the trip to London. We got going in the early afternoon with the intention of entering the actual Kennet and Avon Canal at Bath where we would spend the night. Tom went back home with Paul as he was needed at work and Paul's youngest son Nigel joined us for the trip to London.

Bristol to Bath

I never realised how far the docks went in Bristol, but eventually we were back in the River Avon again and on our way to Bath. Often narrow and windy, the river continued to Hallam lock where we had to report to the canal office and pay the fee to use the actual canal.

We got to the deep lock in Bath which marks the start of the canal proper and the first of 139 locks between Bath and Teddington. Once through the lock we found a place to moor for the night where Nigel could pitch his tent. We then walked into town for a meal.

Bath to Caen Hill

We were on the way not long after dawn, stopping for breakfast in Bradford on Avon, then began the steady climb toward the top section between Devizes and Pewsey. We had a late lunch at the Barge Inn, Seend where we were approached by an old chap in a blazer and cravat who said, "by jove I recognise that accent anywhere." It turned into a bit of a session for sure.

It transpired that Wing Commander Trahair was an old Penzance Boy who had been stationed at RAF Lyneham before he retired. We got chatting over a few G&Ts and, having had a grand couple of hours, I suddenly realised that we needed to get going again if we were to make Caen Hill before dark. Ten minutes after leaving the Barge I had a panic attack, I had left my pipe in the pub.

I thought Julia was looking highly amused. As I started to turn the boat around she couldn't contain herself any longer and burst out laughing saying, "you silly bugger, your pipe is in your mouth!" That is how chilled out I was. Mind you, the G&Ts may have had something to do with it.

We made Caen Hill in the early evening mooring at the foot of the 29 locks in the flight to be tackled the following morning. By now we had a strategy. Nigel and Julia would go ahead, getting the locks ready following an earlier mutiny when she demanded to know why I was telling her what to do. Put simply, it was because she didn't have a clue herself and someone had to be in charge and consequently that was me!

Caen Hill towards Wooton Rivers

Julia had her bike with her which was very useful. She rode ahead along the tow path and often I could motor straight into the prepared lock. We got lucky at Caen Hill because there were a lot of boats coming down which meant we could go straight into the lock as they came out. We did the 29 locks in just over five hours so it was an early lunch in Devizes.

In the afternoon, part of the section between Devizes and Honey Street was surreal, real 'Wind in the Willows' stuff. We were pushing through reeds for about a mile, with kingfishers flying in front of us like butterflies. I had never seen so many. We were now nearing the top section of the canal 450 feet above sea level on the Marlborough Downs and we pushed on to Wooton Rivers for a dinner of excellent rabbit stew in the Royal Oak pub.

A crazy idea and another dare

We could hear the trains in the distance as the railway line was soon to converge with the canal towards Reading.

It was on the early morning train to Paddington on one of my day trips to Texaco in Canary Wharf that I first had the idea for this crazy trip. Having enjoyed breakfast in the dining car, I was reading the complimentary copy of the Telegraph when an article caught my eye while passing through Pewsey alongside the canal.

It told the story of the restoration of the canal and how with the last lock at Caen Hill being completed, through navigation between the Thames and Avon was again possible. This set me thinking how theoretically the land south and west of the canal was actually an island and, as such, ripe for a circumnavigation.

A while later, I was talking about it in the village pub like you do when someone said, "I dare you to do it." So, the following year I did. As far as I can tell, I was the first and only one to do the 840-mile round trip certainly in such a small boat.

Wooton Rivers to Newbury

The following Sunday morning we again made an early start. Ascending two more locks, we were at the top and through the eerie 502 yard long Bruce Tunnel ready to start the long descent towards Reading.

It was here that I was stopped by a young man wearing a bobble hat and anorak and with a badge announcing he was a volunteer. He was brandishing a stopwatch and he had measured my speed which he decreed was 4.2 mph against a limit of 4 mph. He wanted my details to report me for speeding.

I clearly understand that the bankside wash from vessels is a serious issue but my boat would not go any slower even on tick over. It slipped through the water with scarcely a ripple but he wasn't easily persuaded. He was a 'classic rules are rules' man, which resulted in a bit of a stand-off. Eventually he relented and after a lecture, which I took in good part, we were off again.

The next point of interest was Crofton Pumping Station at the bottom of a flight of several locks where a Cornish beam engine once raised water from the River Kennet up to the top section of the canal.

From here on we were in the canalised River Kennet stopping at Hungerford for a bit of lunch and a walk around the pretty little town. We made Newbury just before dusk where we stopped for the fourth night.

Newbury to Reading

The next day was a slog. The locks were becoming tedious and the pace we were setting was beginning to tell. We made Reading and stopped at the bottom of the last lock before the Thames in preparation for what was going to be a mammoth next day if we were going to make Teddington as planned.

Reading to Teddington

We faced a 59 mile run involving 21 locks estimated to take over 12 hours if we were not held up in any locks. Luckily, the weather was glorious and approaching the equinox, there was only around 12 hours of daylight, so it was highly likely we would get to Teddington in the dark.

We left before daybreak and turning into the actual Thames it felt like we were turning for home even though we were not halfway there by any means. The Thames locks were attended and passing through was much easier. We stopped at Henley for breakfast and to top up with petrol from a boatyard with a waterside pump.

From Henley it was a long hard day passing Cliveden, the seat of the Astor family, which was perched up on a hill overlooking the river. The Fat Duck Restaurant at Bray had lots of expensive cars and boats nearby, reflecting the wealth of its patrons… Windsor Castle and Hampton Court.

By Hampton Court the light was failing and we had to be very alert for numerous rowers without any lights out on the water. The fact that our navigation lights were clearly visible did not stop them dicing with us. They were obviously completely oblivious to the rule of the road regulations.

Reaching Teddington in the dark, tidal water once more beckoned on the other side of the final lock. We were saddle sore and hungry but we had reached the end of the beginning and tomorrow was another day back in tidal waters once more.

Teddington to Limehouse

That morning there was no great rush, the plan being to enjoy the journey down the tidal Thames to Limehouse Basin Marina. An easy day and hopefully the highlight of the journey, with a stopover to get some washing done and square away for the long haul home.

Leaving Teddington behind, the thing that amazed me was how wild and remote the river banks seemed. Huge weeping willows interspersed with marshes belied the fact that we were fast approaching central London. To make it even more surreal, some of the willows were teeming with large flocks of noisy, green parakeets. We could have been up the Orinoco rather than down the Thames.

Then around Barnes, civilisation re-asserted itself and the scenery became more familiar.

Fulham, Chelsea to port, Battersea to Starboard, then Millbank and Parliament with the spidery London Eye on the other bank.

Then it was the Tower of London and Tower Bridge. Passing under the Bridge, a Navy Minesweeper was moored by St Catherine's Pier. Touchingly, seeing our big cross of St Piran flag flying proudly on our stern they dipped their ensign. I wonder if one of them aboard was Cornish? Consequently, we dipped ours and exchanged waves, then all too soon we were in Limehouse to be met again by Paul.

Julia and Nigel went home with Paul and that was it. With no more locks to negotiate I was on my own for the long open water haul back to Newlyn.

I found a launderette where a real old-style Cockney lady did me a service wash which freed me up for a walk around the streets where my mother lived as a child. I marvelled at the changes from how I remembered them as a child myself. They were now gentrified and very upmarket compared to the dockers' homes that they once were. The industry was largely gone and the soul with it. The place now felt sterile.

I had a grand meal in the Grapes in Limehouse owned by actor, Sir Ian Mckellen which was the watering hole favoured by my Texaco colleagues on my regular trips to their Canary Wharf HQ. A huge portion of perfectly-cooked ray wing with capers and black butter went down a treat.

Time constraints precluded a courtesy call to Westferry Circus but in typical Texaco style, they made a generous donation to the Mission in recognition of the trip which was reported in their house magazine.

Limehouse to Ramsgate

The next day it was time to crack on… destination Dover. A deep breath and out into the tideway picking up the first of the ebb towards Greenwich where crossing the meridian it was weird to see the GPS registering 'Easting increasing' rather than, 'Westing decreasing.'

This was the first time I had been east of the meridian in a boat under my control. Past the Cutty Sark and Greenwich Palace in a loop around the Isle of Dogs with the Millenium Dome to Starboard and then past Woolwich Ferry. There was a quick VHF call to the Thames Barrier Control before passing through the designated portal and it was all systems go, picking up on the ebb tide towards the North Foreland.

Under the striking Queen Elizabeth bridge at Dartford, (the last resting place of Richard 'Cap'n Dick' Trevithick, the man in all history I would most like to have met) and then to port past Rainham Marshes which loomed and the wharves at Thurrock and Tilbury Docks which had made London's Docklands redundant.

This is where the big ships now dock benefitting from the efficiencies of containerisation which the traditional London dockers fought so hard to stop. The Thames Estuary was now widening out as the low Essex shore faded away to the north east in the haze.

The phone rang and it was Vic Stimson, our Texaco contact in Falmouth enquiring how things were going. Vic was a former tug skipper with the Sun Fleet which was a Thames legend and he knew the Thames like the back of his hand. I remember him telling me how they used to swing a big ship in the Upper Pool of London above Tower Bridge.

The tug would beach itself bow first, hard in the mud of Tower Beach and as the big ship passed it would swing with the tug as the anchor. As the tug was pulled stern first off the beach it was perfectly aligned to get the big ship's bow now facing downstream against the tide alongside Butler's Wharf on the opposite bank. An absolutely masterful bit of seamanship. I had the Reeds Almanac open beside me to confirm the buoys as we came to them. Off Sheppey on the Kent shore at the mouth of the Medway there was a wreck marked with a big exclusion zone around it.

It was the Liberty Ship SS Richard Montgomery which, in 1944, while loaded with a full cargo of munitions, was sunk in that spot and was considered too dangerous to attempt to salvage. So, the wreck remains there to this day still in a highly dangerous, potentially unstable condition.

The tide was carrying me along at a cracking pace in the flat calm conditions with a slight easterly swell. Approaching an extensive area of shallows known as the 'Kentish Flats', I was aiming for a small gut that would save me a nine mile detour in the deeper channel to the north. It had been mentioned in Bob Robert's book, 'Coasting Barge Master' which had been my school prize.

A long way away in the smoky haze off the port bow I spotted what looked like a copse of very big trees. Were my eyes playing tricks on me? But no… looking at the chart they proved to be the WW2 Maunsell Forts located on the sinister sounding, 'Shivering Sands'. It was a weird sight indeed, several miles to the north.

The water was rapidly shoaling up and you could see riffles of tide flowing over the edge of the bank. I was beginning to wonder if I had made a mistake. How humiliating to end up high and dry five miles off Margate.

There was now less than four feet under me, then three feet and I was drawing two feet six. I could see the deeper water about a hundred yards ahead. Tilting the outboard so as not to harm the prop, I felt a couple of bumps and could hear the keel grinding on the shingle but the tide kept the boat going and with one final bump we were over the bank and into ten feet of water. A close shave.

It was a clear run past Whitstable and Margate to the distinctive chalk cliffs of the North Foreland. I stopped just before rounding the Foreland to change fuel tanks. I had run the seventy miles from Limehouse in just under three and half hours and it was good going if I could keep it up. But the oily calm and low easterly swell was deceptive.

In a few hundred yards, rounding the sheer chalk cliffs that mark the southern extremity of the Thames Estuary, it was another world. I came straight into a force five to seven south westerly blowing against the still strong ebb tide, and boring over an uneven bottom in nine fathoms it was not looking pretty. It was clearly obvious that I was not going to make Dover as intended that evening.

A quick check on whether to turn back or continue showed Ramsgate about five miles off. The conditions were horrible but the little boat was fine. Just ticking over, the tide was pushing the boat in the right direction at six knots. It was a case of sit it out and run into Ramsgate which took just less than an hour to reach.

Ramsgate was a lovely harbour with a good marina to berth in. Mooring up I took a walk ashore and had a meal and a pint. However, compared with home, where there was always someone to talk to, it was the most unsociable place I have ever been. I felt like an alien. Walking back, the rain had started and the wind was howling. The forecast for the next couple of days was lousy, so I was weather bound.

Having arrived in Ramsgate on Thursday evening, Friday and Saturday were absolute purgatory with the wind whistling through the clanging halliards* in the marina, it was noisy. I spent the time mostly reading, drinking tea or walking. On one occasion, I walked out of town towards the broad expanse of Pegwell Bay, but otherwise it was around the dreary town which had obviously seen much better days.

I was itching to get going. The days were closing in and the weather was, to say the least, 'catchy' for a nineteen foot boat making long open water passages.

13th September… Ramsgate to Gosport

First light on Sunday saw fine weather, so off I went, heading for Gosport across Pegwell Bay past Sandwich, Deal and then Dover. With the ferries coming and going, care was needed but visibility was excellent. Past Folkestone, Dungeness and across Rye Bay by 09:00, I was then off Eastbourne, progress indeed. I stopped to make a cup of tea off the end of the pier.

Then it was off again past the massive chalk cliffs of Beachy Head and the lovely Seven Sisters and then back across the Greenwich meridian, making actual Westing once more at a rate of knots. Just off Newhaven, a green-hulled, Brixham beamer was working which was a strangely comforting sight.

Leaving the chalk cliffs behind, the coast became flat. Passing Brighton and Littlehampton the next objective was low-lying, Selsey Bill and the tricky channel inside the Owers, with a clear run across to Gosport beyond. Looking at the east side of the Isle of Wight brought back memories of our unsuccessful lobster fishing there on the William Harvey.

---

*A 'halliard' is a line (rope) that is used to hoist a ladder, sail, flag or yard.

I was aiming for the Premier Marina in Gosport and called them on VHF channel 80. They were very helpful and fixed me up a berth inside, near the exit, so not a lot of walking was involved. The place was huge. When they found out my mission for the 'Mission', they waived the fees and gave me enough fuel to top both tanks right up. Thank you for your very kind gesture Premier Marinas, it was greatly appreciated.

Mooring up completed, my brother-in-law was waiting to take me back to Fareham for a Sunday roast, a bath and a couple of pints of the superb George Gales Horndean Special Bitter. Then it was back aboard for a good night's sleep and hopefully Salcombe the following day.

Alas it was not to be!

14th September… Gosport to Weymouth

Monday dawned grey and cold in contrast to yesterday's baking sun. Away early, off down the Solent chased by an unpleasant easterly lop, the weather was not looking good. In fact, I was weighing up the option of going into Lymington. If I did, that would be it, mission aborted and home on the trailer with my tail between my legs.

Reaching Lymington Bar Buoy, it was 'make your mind up time.' Conditions were horrible and comfort and safety beckoned. I circled a couple of times, then a voice inside my head said, "crack on." So down went the throttle and I was bounders past the Needles and out across Poole Bay.

Conditions were truly awful but again but it was obvious that I would give up before that little boat would. In that highly unpleasant quartering SE lop, that day was some of the weirdest weather I have ever seen. Salcombe was an absolute no no for sure, so the option was Poole or Weymouth.

As I was pondering, the wind was backing rather than veering in the normal manner. It was now NE and blowing hard. Even though the sea was menacing and horrible it was more or less in my favour and reaching St Aldhelm's Head, the wind was now northerly and effectively offshore.

The next potential pitfall was the Anvil Ledges, a tide race that ran over shoal ground for a good five miles off. If there was firing taking place on the Lulworth Ranges I would be stuffed because that might mean a detour outside in the weather. The range safety boat was visible to the west of the ledges while I was hugging the shore.

My luck held, the range safety boat ignored me and in the relative shelter, flat out under the cliffs, I was soon across the firing range and abeam of Kimmeridge where the real fun started.

By this time, the wind had shot back into the NW and was blowing an absolute smeecher on the starboard bow. Short, splashy little waves that hit the boat slap, slap, slap, with spray flying everywhere. It was making my teeth chatter.

By Lulworth it had backed westerly bang on the nose, with continual spray from the short, vicious lop and an absolute torrent of freezing, horizontal rain. Going up Weymouth Bay in the early afternoon everything was on the deck and I was freezing cold. I was gagging for a cup of hot tea. As Weymouth entrance loomed, I was very thankful that comfort was increasing by the minute and going up the harbour to the marina above the bridge, I surveyed the sodden mess on the wheelhouse deck.

Luckily, I had some newspapers in the lockers to soak up the wet in the wheelhouse. The actual bunk space and bedding was thankfully dry but my holdall of clothes was on the wheelhouse floor and the contents were wet, so it was off to the laundrette. No matter though… the little tiger had got me through.

Clothes in the tumble dryer and the wheelhouse dried out, the outside needed no attention as the vicious spray had seen to that. She was spotless.

I went for a walk to the Lifeboat House. The rain had cleared away and it was a bright early evening with a biting NW gale blowing down the harbour. Rounding the Bill was concentrating my mind and the best man to ask for advice was Andy Sargeant, the celebrated cox of Weymouth Lifeboat. He was brilliant and put my mind at ease.

Andy explained that the way to go was right in tight to the rocks and keep up along the shore towards the Chesil Beach until the Admiralty oil storage tanks in Portland Harbour opened up before turning west, otherwise, the tide would push you out into the race. Thank you Andy Sargeant.

It was then time for a meal, a couple of pints and another early night for an early start in the morning. Weymouth has always been one of my favourite harbours and this visit did not disappoint.

15th September… Weymouth to Salcombe

The following morning dawned fair with a light northerly breeze which was in stark contrast to the maelstrom the previous day. Away in the half light of an autumn dawn, the run out to the notorious Bill was smooth and quick. Rock hopping my way round as advised by Andy, I was soon heading for the Start about 50 miles ahead. In the middle of Lyme Bay I would be up to 20 miles from the nearest land.

It was a grand day. The water was cloudy with the dying remnants of a very confused sea that was not that comfortable at full speed, but needs must. I was shortening the distance to Newlyn and that was all that mattered.

Just after midday, I was abeam of the Start and an hour later I was in Salcombe where I topped up with fuel from the barge. Then I was instructed to moor up to a pontoon above the harbour in a place called, 'The Bag'. To go ashore, it was necessary to phone a water taxi.

Having had forty winks, I did just that for a quick run ashore in what I always regard as 'bullshit central', a rather pretentious place.

The forecast was fine, with a mention of a typically high pressure-induced, easterly wind.

16th September… Salcombe to Falmouth

First light, creeping out of Salcombe, there was not a breath of wind and it was flat calm. Perfect, but not for long. By the time I was abeam of Bolt Head, that bloody SE wind was freshening by the minute. Turning back again was not an option. By the time the Eddystone was on the port bow it was blowing force five, gusting six, with a horrible foaming lop on top of a biggish swell. Fortunately, it was again in my favour.

This weather, despite its unpleasantness, was much better that the usual westerly weather where it would have been bang on the nose all the way down channel. Every passing swell was effectively pushing me home in relative comfort.

Visibility was again excellent. Passing well off the Dodman, the by now, hissing swell was pushing the boat along the downhill run to St Anthony and the safety of Falmouth Harbour. By midday I was alongside in the shelter of the Falmouth Harbour Commissioner's Marina where Paul met me to take me home for a night in my own bed. The forecast was for continuing easterly wind.

17TH September… Falmouth to Newlyn

This was it. The last leg. The final dash for home around the Lizard and up Mount's Bay. Paul went with me. The wind had dropped overnight but as we rounded the Manacles true to form, it was freshening with the daylight. Again, fortunately, it was helping us rather than hindering and we stormed around the Lizard a couple of miles off. There, before us, was the final, sixteen mile home straight.

Unbelievably on the west side of the Lizard there was hardly any wind!

Motoring up the bay, deep off Porthleven, there were a lot of splatts of fish showing on the sounder. They had to be pilchards and the marks were everywhere. I slowed down to watch as the balls of fish started to drop to the bottom and disappear. It's not every day you get to see pilchards going to bed on the Dory Pitch. Were the JDs at home I wondered?

Then it was Low Lee and the final mile, in through the Gaps and tied up alongside the fish market where it had all began 19 days previously. My old mate Phil Lockley, the Fishing News Correspondent, happened to be there and he took a picture of me at the top of the ladder coming ashore. Then along came cousin JB who just happened to be there as well.

That was it. A crazy idea had grown legs. I set myself a task which I soon realised again, was bigger than it looked, but it was a case of picking it off in bite-sized chunks until accomplished. It would have been easy to have given up several times but when the chips are

The Blue Damsel at Caen Hill

really down, I don't do that. If in life I had given up along the way I would not be enjoying the fruits of my labour as I am now.

In the light of experience

It really was weird at the end. There was a feeling of emptiness and depression that lasted for around a week. It actually felt a bit like bereavement. It was all over and there was no more left to do. That was it.

I raised just over £2,000 for the Fishermen's Mission which was a great disappointment really because had the Mission taken the trip more seriously and promoted it properly, I am sure it could have been very much more. However, that was their loss. For my part, I had a wonderful experience that tested my resolve almost to destruction once or twice along the way. And in the process, I saw our country from a perspective that only the lucky few get to.

228

Chapter 16
The Company continues with unending surprises

The pace of change accelerates

Back at the ranch they had held the fort very well during my absence.

One of the casualties of the insane market mayhem created by the big boys had been long-established, J H Bennetts (JHB). It had been absorbed into Great Western Oils (GWO), this being BP's version of Shell Direct who had long since exited stage left.

It was plain to see that it was doomed to a similar fate from the outset but that did not stop them. It was run by the bumptious buffoon of a manager who had previously done for JHB.

Time and again I witnessed such buffoons who could talk the talk to insinuate themselves into positions of relative power where they invariably failed to walk the walk. They usually created chaos before burning out and crashing in flames and the oil industry seemed to attract them like moths to a flame.

I didn't get where I am today!

I once got summoned to a meeting with this person at the Bridgewater regional HQ of GWO. His office was ankle deep in pink, shag pile carpet and the eye-wateringly expensive executive desk covered about an acre. The self-important twit was sitting behind it playing with one of those 'executive toys' where one ball swings into the rest and they all move back and forth, highly impressive! There were distinct undertones of *'The Rise and Fall of Reginald Perrin'* insofar as this comical shit show was also a complete load of balls.

Apparently, he wanted to buy us. He saw us as an ideal fit with his operation. In truth, given that we had pinched so much business from him, he wanted to buy it back. They were so incompetent at grassroots level that had we been paying someone on the inside they could not have done better for us. It felt like shooting fish in a barrel.

It all came to a very sticky and hushed up end when the Plymouth manager and several BP dealer sites were implicated in the disappearance of several artic loads of petrol from the Plymouth Terminal. There was no police involvement but a couple of BP pensions didn't get paid out which, from a BP perspective, probably more than covered the cost of the lost product.

In the midst of this corporate mayhem we survived in the longer term and actually dared to prosper despite their best attempts to bury us without trace.

We buy my namesake company to shut it up

The really ironic thing here was that J H Bennetts was reincarnated by a former employee back in Penzance. For a while, it became yet another confounded nuisance that carried virtually no overheads because a couple of cheap old tankers were drawing from Falmouth and delivering direct. We ended up buying them out for the hell of it to shut them up and probably did everyone else a favour in the process. I did get a perverse kick out of being the poor relation made good though.

JH Bennetts was integrated into Consols Oils just in time for the next confounded nuisance to arrive in God's Country. However, this one was made of much sterner stuff!

The alien invader

Even though, if I could have gotten away with it, I would have put a hit man on him, I still had a grudging admiration for Colin Owen, a London 'barrow boy' who wanted to be a Welshman. He had formed an unholy alliance with a Welsh barrister who wanted to dabble in oil under the style or title of 'O J Williams.' They operated from St Clears in Carmarthenshire.

Colin Owen may have been small in stature but he was another of those characters who, when testicles were dished, got given someone else's share as well as his own. He also sported a neck like a giraffe and the skin of a rhinoceros. He came looking for a row and like a few others before him, he had well and truly found one.

He employed a form of oil distribution blitzkrieg, bursting out of Wales and down the M5. His forward bases were portacabins, with trucks based in haulage yards and he operated a 'stack it high – sell it cheap' strategy. He was disruptive and his firm was getting noticed by potential customers. How he did this was miraculous, I had enough trouble keeping proper tabs on one depot.

This also initiated a staff merry go round where they poached personnel from other firms. They had one of my drivers for a time but when the novelty had worn off he wanted to come back. Breaking an absolute rule never to take someone back, I did and we got some high grade intelligence as to how shambolic this unwelcome competitor really was.

The price war battered everyone to a standstill, even O J Williams. If Colin Owen had realised how close I was to chucking it in at that time he would have kept going for another month. It really was that close to the wire. It was so demoralising to be working your guts out for nothing. While we were not actually losing money, we were not making any either, and that over time is pointless.

But blow me, the irrepressible Mr Owen showed his hand, paving the way for an even bigger menace to descend on us. He had been building his operation up to sell and it was eventually bought out by DCC, an Irish conglomerate that for a time kept Colin Owen on to run it. This ran its course as Colin Owen departed under a cloud to start his own 'Oil for

Wales' operation which thankfully remained in Wales.

DCC had considerable financial clout and continued the market mayhem. In a short time, by the acquisition of often struggling firms at knockdown prices, it became the UK's biggest distributor operating over 1,000 trucks. We were ready for this but the several years it took for this insane market mayhem to run its inevitable course cost everyone a lot of money for no tangible gain.

Eventually, DCC, having presumably achieved its objectives, gradually quietened down and we emerged from that particular battlefield in surprisingly fine fettle. It really is true that what doesn't kill you actually makes you stronger, it just never feels like that when you are in the thick of it and battling for your life.

I have always seen oil distribution as a cake that can be sliced in infinite ways. However, it is a mature marketplace where potential growth inevitably comes at someone else's expense. There is actually plenty for everyone if the participants behave sensibly, but sadly so many are not sensible and often come a cropper as a result. For the likes of me, it presented opportunities for year on year organic growth.

Effectively, being lean and hungry, as small operators who knew our territory and customers inside out, we could always move quickly and survive very well on the crumbs falling from the bigger operators' tables.

Our business model had been tested to the verge of destruction and not found wanting.

The Stevens family

One of my greatest friends is David Stevens. Originally from St Ives, his father was the legendary Ernie Stevens, another of that formidable breed of men who survived the mine-sweepers in WW2. He became a top, longline fisherman aboard the 'Sweet Promise' and the 'Rose of Sharon' and the 'Rose of Sharon 2'.

Tragically, like many so many other good men, Ernie Stevens died far too young from lung cancer, leaving David at a very young age to skipper the Rose of Sharon 2. David did well in her until a bitter family row saw him working in the 'Firm' skippering the beam trawlers Algrie and later, the James RH Stevenson. David was another top man who had enough of the 'Firm' and bought a former Scotch trawler called the 'Crystal Sea'.

He did exceptionally well with the Crystal Sea and with two sons coming on, another bigger, newer, Scottish boat called the 'Good Design' was bought and renamed 'Crystal Sea'. The boys blossomed a few years later with a Scottish-built, 10-year old, steel boat called 'Rebecca' which became the next Crystal Sea and the pride of the Newlyn fleet.

During the boom years while so many fishermen were whooping it up in the pubs 'pointing Percy at the porcelain' (where a lot of hard-earned money was splashed), David and the boys were at sea, earning away and investing the profits in every last bit of quota they

David Stevens (centre) with sons David (left), Alec (right) on arrival of the new 'Crystal Sea' in Newlyn circa February 2020

The Stewvens family's original boat 'The Sweet Promise' leaving St. Ives circa 1960

could get their hands on while they planned for the future.

The quota they accumulated was necessary so that there was more than sufficient to ensure the long-planned, latest incarnation of the Crystal Sea could fish to its full potential.

In February 2020, all that planning came to fruition when a brand new, state-of-the-art, fourth Crystal Sea came through Newlyn Gaps after a storm-lashed trip home from Macduff Shipyard on Scotland's Moray Coast. A £3.5 millon vote of confidence in the future of Cornish fishing in general and Newlyn in particular.

David and I both came up in a very hard school and over the years have supported each other in times of trouble which we have often talked each other through. His two boys skipper the boat on alternate weeks so it very rarely stops for more than a few hours to land and refuel. This means that they still manage to get quality time at home with their families which was not always guaranteed in the early days.

It is this sort of commitment and enterprise that we need more of if Cornwall is to pull itself up by its bootstraps and prosper in the bracing winds of change post-Brexit.

Yet more insane competition with no real winners

The opposition all wanted to be bigger. We however, just wanted to be better. Sticking to what we knew best worked for us. I was once accused of a lack of ambition because of my absolute determination not to expand into Devon, but subsequent events proved that we were doing fine as we were.

There was another creeping menace in the form of the outfit that operated those confounded red trucks out of Brinkworth in Wiltshire. They were no friends of mine. 'Watson Petroleum' was the company in question and had spent many years making several attempts to take us out.

I only met with the principal once and to his credit he was a very successful, self-made man. But in my books, he was a snob. We shook hands and his distaste was barely concealed. The handshake was limp, in fact it was akin to shaking hands with a stale whiting fillet.

His son took over the operation, I never met him but he did come across as a firm but fair, tough operator. Not being for sale, nothing went any further until, in the not too distant future, a major dummy spitting episode cropped up because of me.

Just because you are small does not mean that with a bit of insight and forethought you cannot influence the agenda out of all proportion to your place in the scheme of things. Such was the situation at the time of the fuel protest in the autumn of 2000.

Every problem presents an opportunity

My gut instinct had been working overtime again and it was clear that a storm was gathering as an irresistible force was about to ram an immovable object. Again, it was obvious to me that there was going to be money to be made if we got things right, and timing was going to be everything.

There were rumblings of fuel blockades, so we set about filling our storage and keeping it that way. A tipper haulier customer who was the local coordinator of any potential action kept taunting me that they were going to 'shut the job down', which I interpreted as a direct threat to Consols Oils.

I called him and suggested that he drop in and see me immediately. When he arrived he was a bit cocky and it was clear that he was the ringleader who would decide when a blockade would go on at Falmouth Docks.

This needed firm handling. Firstly, I sympathised with the blockaders. As a transport operator myself, fuel prices had a direct, serious impact on our operating costs as well and the Blair Government really was taking the piss with respect to the fuel duty escalator which was crippling us all.

Having let him have his say I was going to have mine and my deadly serious threat drew the teeth from his. I pointed out that there was £10,000 out of terms by three months on his account with us and that we had been nursing him by continuing to supply, so he owed me big time.

I went on to tell him that if he initiated a blockade before it suited my purposes, I would have a statutory demand on him so fucking fast that his arse would catch fire and I would take him down. No one wanted that but it grabbed his attention and he listened to what I was saying very carefully.

We needed another day to get more fuel out of the docks so that we were absolutely brim full. We also needed a very clear and unequivocal understanding that the black oil we were hauling to Dairy Crest on Texaco's behalf must be exempt because it was for vital food

233

production to keep milk producers going. I was more than happy for one of his pickets to accompany the loads to verify that.

On that basis we shook hands, the blockade would be preceded by peaceful picketing of the dock gate until I was ready. The opposition did not appear to be aware of the potential seriousness of the situation until the Plymouth Terminal was closed down, leaving Falmouth as the sole supply option for Cornwall and most of Devon.

Intelligence suggested that Plymouth-based tankers were heading west 'en masse' on a mission to raid Falmouth.

I arranged for a friend's catering van to turn up at the dock gate to dish out hot drinks and bacon butties for all hands involved in the blockade as a gesture of goodwill as the scene was set for a very satisfying trap to be sprung.

We were brim full of stock and the very last artic load had barely left the docks as a convoy of opposition tankers rolled up to be confronted by a very determined bunch of bacon butty munching truckers blocking their way. That was one of those awesome moments when you knew that in one fell swoop, it was payback time for the dozens of dirty tricks you had suffered at their various hands over the years.

I walked over and joined the blockade grinning from ear to ear just to ram the point home.

Not credit worthy?

Out of specification fuel in Falmouth?

Then why on earth were your tankers there to load the stuff?

Revenge is most definitely a dish best served cold!

The companies with no storage were dead in the water. Tough luck guys, you should have invested in your infrastructure like I had to because you kept me out of your terminals!

As always, the traders became anxious and the price of fuel went north at a rate of knots. We carried on working, confident that we had enough fuel in tank to serve our customers as normal for the anticipated duration of the blockade. And yes, we did make a trifle on stock appreciation without being greedy based on the premise that no fuel is always the most expensive fuel of all.

A picket rode with every load of heavy fuel oil. Obviously enjoying the ride, they kindly agreed that Wenford Bridge Driers could also be supplied to keep the men there working and clay production going. It is amazing how much goodwill a few bacon butties can generate, but at the end of the day we were all working men and in the same boat together.

The protest ended triumphantly with a massive convoy of trucks, ours included, driving from Trafalgar Roundabout in Truro and out to Chiverton Cross on the A30 in a carnival atmosphere where even the police stationed along the way were cheering us on.

The best bit of all just had to be the sight of Blair and Prescott on the television news that night. They were incandescent with impotent rage. Their mouths were opening and closing like a couple of goldfish with no sound coming out. Just for once, well-coordinated, ordinary working men had made them listen. Like it or not it was clear for everyone to see that they didn't like it one little bit.

Two outstanding candidates for one vacancy

Geoff Smith was our rep whom we acquired by accident. We had a vacancy for someone to run the shop and sell on the phone. In total, 48 people applied for the job. We shortlisted six. The first four were hopeless but Geoff was next. I was impressed, especially as he had worked for Agricultural Central Trading and Cargill as a commodity trader. He knew his way around farms.

I liked him and had made up my mind to take him on but Fred preferred the next candidate. His name was 'David Nicholas' who was a mere youngster at just nineteen. He was nervous but he shone out. This presented a dilemma for me, with two very different but excellent candidates to choose from and we couldn't agree who to select so we decide to sleep on it.

I woke up the following morning and made a snap decision to take both of them on. Paul and Fred were agreeable, subject to a month's trial and that was it. Two for the price of one! Geoff spent most of his time out on the road collecting payments and taking orders around the farms. He became our trouble shooter and he was good at it because he was non-confrontational, diplomatic and popular.

Geoff Smith gets threatened by a thug

We used to sponsor the Pirates Rugby Club before they went professional and out of our league. We'd encountered a fellow sponsor who ran a skip hire firm at Castle an Dinas near Ludgvan and he had run up a fair old bill. It was obvious that he was becoming a bit dodgy. Geoff called in one day to collect an overdue cheque and was abused and threatened by the scrofulous, so-called manager.

Our staff were not paid enough to get threatened with violence or abuse of any kind for doing their job so I intervened. Phoning their office, I said that I would be calling the next day for a cheque and I would like it to be signed by the owner ready for me to collect… oh… and that I'd be fully prepared for trouble if necessary.

On the way down I was mulling the situation over and decided to cover my arse just in case. So, I drove into Penzance, straight to the police station and asked to have a word with the sergeant. When he came out I explained the situation to him, saying that I feared my visit to the site in question could trigger a breach of the peace.

The sergeant agreed with me and said he would detail a constable to follow me to the site to ensure that there was no breach of the peace. On arrival, I went first up the steps into the seedy portacabin that passed as an office. As I entered I was challenged by the sweaty, greasy thug who had threatened Geoff previously. It was a hot, humid afternoon and he was wearing a grubby string vest, with body hairs poking out in the finest tradition of 'Rab C Nesbit'.

I informed him that I had come to collect the cheque that I was expecting and he said, "why don't you fuck off before I throw you down the stairs." At this very moment, the policeman came through the door. Having heard everything, he read the riot act. As this was going on, back in a dark corner at the far end of the portacabin, the owner was suddenly busy writing what looked like a cheque.

I went back and took it off him. Thanking him I said, "Michael, I sincerely hope that this cheque is good because I would hate to have to come back again." That was the end of the matter and the cheque cleared. Within a few months, the tatty, disreputable company was gone.

Another cheapskate gets his comeuppance

It is strange how certain locations often harbour nests of scoundrels. The neighbouring 'Castle Quarry' used to buy from us on a fairly regular basis but it was common knowledge that the owner would max his credit by spreading his orders around and always delay payment for a couple of months which everyone knew about. This was reflected in the price charged.

The red truck outfits rep had gone in and pinched the work at a suicidal margin. At the time, we were owed a month, which was two months overdue. Sure enough, the quarry went squit owing lots of local firms a lot of money, particularly the red truck outfit from Brinkworth. We lost £10,000 and they lost £20,000. The quarry got taken over by Cornwall Council and that seemed to be the end of the matter.

Two years on, right before Christmas, we received an order for an urgent delivery to a property in South Helford. David being very savvy, took the order. It was from the former owner of Castle Quarry who had the brass neck to order from us thinking we had forgotten about him. He rang back the morning before Christmas Eve saying that he had run out of oil… good!

David said we would do our best to get to him.

Isn't it strange, time and again how executives who collapse their companies to avoid debts rarely suffer themselves? As usual, the fancy executive house and flashy German 'executive mobile' are still there which makes them fair game for a bit of retribution.

We were actually too busy delivering to good customers to prioritise a cheapskate con man who significantly had made no offer to pay by card upfront. No real commitment had been given by us, only that we would do our best. Of course, he didn't get his oil, although we were actually delivering nearby at the very time and could easily have accommodated a genuine person.

When we returned to work the day after Boxing Day there were a series of increasingly irate and abusive calls on the answering machine from the non-customer who was obviously freezing. Strangely, every other customer had got their oil and we had been on our way home by midday Christmas Eve. Good result.

David then rang him to inform him exactly why he had not got his delivery. Naturally, "we had done our very best" he said, "but like your payments at the quarry, our best simply wasn't good enough for you." It really does work both ways.

To counter the negative drag of a bad customer, there were thousands who were brilliant and some remembered fondly for their uniqueness and friendship.

Donovan Wilkins

Donovan was another of those memorable characters and loyal customers who stand out in a crowd. He was a skilled engineer, explosives expert, gunsmith, butcher, dowser and mystic. I first encountered him when working on the Camborne bypass. He was blasting out the ditches where the bedrock was too hard to rip out with bulldozers.

A long-time friend of my father, he became a fuel customer and our friendship grew out of a shared interest in the natural world where he introduced me to the mysteries of dowsing and ley lines which had always fascinated me. A delivery to Donovan could be a lengthy affair best done at the end of the day.

His elderflower champagne may have been low in alcohol but it was always memorable when he cracked open a bottle and started to tell a few yarns.

The lake

He once told how the boggy meadow between his house and the river was pretty useless as it was so he dug out a lake. It must have been the best part of an acre with an island in the middle where the ducks were safe from foxes. The lake constantly filled with sparkling spring water that overflowed into the river. He stocked it with trout that he used to catch if he fancied one for tea.

Tregothnan Deer Park

In his spare time, Donovan oversaw the deer park at Tregothnan. He invited me to visit the 400-acre park with him to see the deer. It was a magnificent setting perched high above the confluence of Ruan Creek and the Truro River to the south and east of Tregothnan House. The deer were not easy to spot despite the fact that they were often hidden in plain sight, they were masters of camouflage.

Eventually we ended up at the highest point and then things got really interesting.

The mysterious, blue elvan pinnacle

Right at the highest point looking down over the confluence of the Fal and Truro Rivers towards Cowlands and Roundwood Quay, a massive fang of blue elvan* protruded probably ten feet skywards. It was totally incongruous in that otherwise soft landscape setting.

As I was looking up at the point of the stone, Donovan said, "do you see anything?"

Well I could see a fine piece of rock for sure, but he said, "look again." For a July evening it was really chilly, grey and overcast, then against the dark grey sky I saw it, a definite heat signature shimmering away from the topmost point.

He said, "touch the rock." I did and it felt unbelievably warm considering how chilly it really was up there in the cold breeze. Then he picked up a piece of stag antler and handing it to me he said, "hit the rock." I did but not to his liking, so he repeated, "hit it hard four or five times harder" and I hit it again as instructed. He continued, "now what do you see?" indicating the point. Looking up to my amazement, the heat signature was going wild, then he said, "touch that rock again." I did and quickly pulled my palm away before the stone burned it, the rock was too hot to touch.

Then Donovan got a dowsing stick out of the truck – his day job being a water diviner and well sinker. He showed me how to hold the forked handles of the stick and told me where to walk with the rider, "don't try to resist the rod if it moves because it could break your wrists."

Walking round the rock, the rod suddenly dipped. There was no doubt about it. Being impossible to resist, the end was pointing at the ground and quivering. Next, he produced a couple of wire rods and again told me where to walk. This time, at a certain point, the rods moved from pointing ahead through ninety degrees – one toward the rock and the other toward Roundwood across the water on the Feock shore.

This was gripping stuff and I could feel something in my hands like the mildest electric shock as the rods diverged to form the alignment described. Donovan then said, "you have just dowsed the Michael Line," explaining that it was a powerful ley line that runs from St Michael's Mount to Glastonbury Tor.

Next, he showed me a hole he had drilled through the rock that aligned with the sunrise on the longest day so that the sun cast its light through the hole and onto the ground behind it. The alignment of the ley line appeared to be the same as the bearing of the rising sun on that longest day.

Incredibly, many years later, it turns out that the Michael Line also runs diagonally through the old converted chapel I live in, in retirement near Gwennap. This was discovered

*'Elvan'… a hard intrusive igneous rock found in Cornwall, typically quartz porphyry.

accidently while dowsing for a new borehole in the garden. Water makes the rods dip, a leyline causes the rods to form an alignment with the ley line which is an as yet, unexplained manifestation of the Earth's energy.

Newdowns Quarry

St Agnes Beacon is a very prominent hill set between St Agnes and Chapel Porth and separated from the cliffs by a level coastal strip called 'Newdowns,' on its northern flank. It is a geologically interesting area and around four hundred feet above sea level.

When the sea was much higher (or the Beacon was possibly much lower), St Agnes Beacon was an island and Newdowns was the beach evidenced by the alluvial deposits of fine silica sand and brown pottery clay that are extracted from Newdowns Quarry.

The area was also rich in tin. Quarry operations had exposed an elvan dyke and the miners had worked up under it almost to the surface. This is where Donovan's, nine ton, fourteen foot, fang of elvan originated. On one side, the faint chisel marks could still be discerned where the old men had removed the tin, bearing jet black crystals of cassiterite.

The massive piece of elvan was transported to Tregothnan and erected by Donovan at the high point of the deer park where he had previously dowsed the ley line. This must have been a substantial undertaking for him.

Out with a bang

Donovan's health was deteriorating due to heart failure. In the past, he had once cast a small cannon which he mounted on a wooden carriage overlooking the lake. In his own inimitable way he had a job in mind for it.

He had left clear instructions that on his passing he was to be cremated without fuss and later his ashes were to be placed in the cannon and fired out over the lake… going out with a bang so to speak. His wish was duly carried out in the presence of many of his friends – a truly fitting tribute to a unique, multi-faceted character for sure.

Another convulsion

The next big thing to crop up on the oil front was the sale by Chris Walters of Falmouth Oil Services to Miami-based, World Fuel Services following the breakdown of the relationship with Chevron and the stalled terminal rebuild project due to the uncertainty of supply. It was another potentially serious problem for us.

The oil industry really is like the Planet Kazoo… in a state of constant flux and turmoil.

Chapter 17
Some interesting observations and turns

The tragedy of decline

The descent into mediocrity and chaos that in the end benefits no one is a temptingly easy path to follow, compared to the long climb to excellence and order that benefits everyone that sadly has been ignored.

The past 50 years in Cornwall has been an accelerating race to the bottom in the name of pointless change and unsustainable, inappropriate growth that becomes a bigger disaster with every passing year. Cornwall will never truly prosper while it remains an extractive economy where so much profit migrates elsewhere.

During my lifetime, I have borne witness to a troubling cycle of seemingly endless decline and change for the worse.

To begin with, small farms largely disappeared as places that once gave a living and reared families. Then our mining industry fell victim to international financial shenanigans and our 'white gold' (clay) fell into the hands of French industrial conglomerate, 'Imerys' – an acronym of which spelt 'misery,' when weighed against Sir Alan Dalton's glory days.

For many years, the International Tin Council kept a floor in the price of tin under a London-based cartel arrangement, controlling prices by buying up excess tin. However, when world demand for tin dropped in the 1980s and as production grew, buying up the excess production became untenable and the tin price crashed, with serious ramifications for the Cornish mining industry.

The first casualty was exploration and the tiny, recently opened, Wheal Concord at Blackwater, then Mount Wellington, Wheal Jane and Wheal Pendarves all went, leaving just Geevor and Crofty mines to stagger on. Soon, Geevor succumbed, leaving Crofty to linger on until 1997 when it too ceased on what was Cornwall's darkest day.

The true beating heart of Camborne and Redruth lay silent and flooding.

Seemingly everything else so many of us held dear and which provided so much prosperity and employment was falling into the hands of asset stripping corporations.

Camborne-based Holman Brothers were a world class manufacturer of mining equipment and compressors, employing around 2,500 skilled engineers. The company suffered death by a thousand cuts following its acquisition by Broome and Wade – a classic case in point.

Even the artisan homes in our picturesque villages have fallen victim and one by one, like dominoes, they've been acquired via the fat chequebooks of incomers, coveting them as second homes. In so many prime locations the lights were all out on winter nights. Then the schools closed, along with the shops, the post offices and finally, the pubs.

Our timeless village communities that evolved over centuries and generations to fulfil a real purpose have become sterile, gentrified ghettos occupied by a metropolitan elite who lack soul and empathy. In effect, a passive, aggressive, hostile occupying force who see the population they have displaced as a source of cheap cleaners, gardeners and maintenance men and not much else.

To add insult to injury, the second homes enjoy favourable tax status, paying no council tax if registered as small businesses. They even got a £10,000 handout to 'assist' them through the COVID-19 pandemic shambles which is astounding!

There was suddenly no one to speak for us in Westminster

This dreadful cycle of negativity really got going with the tragic loss of *'The Voice of Cornwall,'* David Penhaligon MP who died in a car crash on 22nd December 1986. David was universally respected and loved.

He was actually our village Postmaster in Chacewater and was almost certainly destined to lead the 'proper Liberal Party' as it was then, rather than the useless apology for an organisation it has become today.

Part of the decline can be traced to the loss of that Cornish Methodist Liberal tradition of decency, equality and fairness that sustained so many through brutally hard times. Dog-eat-dog politics and extreme self-interest now rule the agenda and the results are there for all to see in the low calibre chancers of every political persuasion who pretend to rule us.

David Penhaligon MP

Corporate developers set a disastrous agenda

It is very interesting that the most accurate figure of genuinely local people needing homes is almost exactly the same as the number of second homes that exist in Cornwall. There's the question of who sold the houses to become second homes in the first instance, but rightly or wrongly, as always, money talked. However, the question remains, who really benefitted?

This 'identified need' has unleashed a corporate-fuelled drive to build more homes (do large corporate political donations buy Government policy?) that will see Cornwall lumbered with 80,000 more unwanted homes (largely unaffordable to local people). This is fuelling inward migration on a scale that cannot sensibly be absorbed by existing infrastructure.

The disgraceful 'Local Planning Hearing'

In 2016, there was a hearing held at the Atlantic Hotel in Newquay to finalise the omnishambles that was the Cornwall Council Local Plan. It was presided over by Bristol-based, planning inspector Mr Simon Emerson, one of the rudest, most overtly-prejudiced, public servants it has ever been my misfortune to encounter. He was in my humble opinion, a disgrace to his office.

It was glaringly obvious from the start that he was under strict orders to deliver the developers' demands and to brush aside all reasoned objectives to the imposition of an unrealistic 30-year housing target that would only enrich the developers, while leaving Cornish Council taxpayers with the glaringly obvious ongoing cost implications.

Sadly, the objectors were humiliated by the gallery of smirking, self-assured, corporate developer executives and their posse of highly paid land agents and property barristers.

Needless to say, the developers got exactly what they wanted. Cornwall will inevitably inherit the malign consequences of that disgraceful episode where Cornwall Council was effectively the collaborator in chief by the wilful dereliction of its duty of care to the electorate it exists to serve.

I confidently wager that history will judge harshly and roundly condemn each and every individual involved or implicated in this disgraceful episode.

The final jewel in the crown teeters on the brink.

The situation in Newlyn was festering away as the 'Firm's' decline gathered pace. It was in serious danger of taking the Harbour down with it as revenues were declining following years of unprecedented boom times.

The 'Firm' had been flouting EU regulations by selling over quota, so-called 'blackfish'. Granted, they were providing a service to boat owners, but any realist could clearly see that, whatever the rights or wrongs, it was bound to end in tears given the ruthlessly vindictive nature of the detested regime charged with enforcing the draconian regulations that required the dumping of tons of good fish.

A decommissioning scheme compounded the misery as many good boats were cut up when the owners decided to take the generous cash terms offered and leave the industry while being allowed to retain whatever quota they had. This quota then acquired a considerable value by becoming a tradable commodity instead of a national asset allocated from a central pool under public ownership.

With much of the fleet scrapped, the fisheries officers pounced, raiding various fish merchants' premises and fishermen's homes to build a case against them for landing and handling blackfish. The case rumbled on for what seemed an eternity and it broke many of those involved both mentally and financially. Penalties were harsh and nobody involved on either side emerged with a lot of credit.

Deliberate and wilful disruption

For my part, I was increasingly frustrated with the state of Newlyn Harbour and its ever more shambolic, day-to-day management. We had been doing good trade fuelling visiting vessels, which did nothing to increase my popularity with the ruling hierarchy who were as obstructive as it was possible to be behind the scenes.

I had made a number of complaints to the Department for Transport about the way certain independent harbour traders were being discriminated against, citing examples.

Peppercorn rents

We had taken over the B J Ridge agency in Newlyn who had been long-established fish salesmen and oil merchants with an office and store on the North Pier. Not being interested in the fish sales side, it was the oil merchant angle and the rented premises as a base on the Harbour to operate from that interested me.

The Harbour lease was transferred at an increased rent around double what others were paying, which perversely, was still ludicrously cheap by accepted standards. It was not hard to see why the place was becoming so run down when there was no money coming in to repair and renew the infrastructure.

It all came to a head one afternoon when one of our tankers was unable to leave the pier, having completed its delivery to the Crystal Sea and on a tight schedule for another delivery. There was also an artic waiting to load the Crystal Sea's fish which was also on a tight schedule. It was unable to access the pier because one of the 'Firm's' beamers had lowered its derrick across the pier. This often happened and was obviously a deliberately disruptive delaying tactic sanctioned by Billy Stevenson.

My driver, Irwin Humphries, was a slight but fiery Ulsterman who had been a Chief Petty Officer in the Navy. He had a fearsome reputation as an absolute sod if crossed, however

Irwin Humphries -
Photo courtesy
Kernow Photography

he was courteous and waited for the task to be completed so the derrick could be raised.

It was obvious that the sneering engineer working on the derrick was labouring under the delusion that deliberately messing around and wasting other people's working time was highly amusing. It was patently clear that he didn't realise what he was dealing with!

Irwin's fuse burned down and highly amused witnesses later testified how he leapt out of his cab and in his very best CPO manner, strode up to the smirking engineer with a very clear and extremely curt ultimatum… "fella… if that derrick is not lifting by the time I count to ten I am going to rip your fucking head off and throw it in the Harbour."

As if by magic, after two words into his walkie talkie handset to the skipper up in the wheelhouse, the derrick lifted. A clear case of needs must and another obvious coward in rapid retreat.

I receive a writ from the 'Firm'

Not long after the derrick fiasco I was reading a forum on the Cornishman webpage discussing the lack of coherent management in Newlyn. Me being me, I waded in with a killer comment which I never expected to get past the censor. Even by my standards it was a humdinger and to my surprise and slight concern, it got published. All hell broke loose.

I made three clear unequivocal statements:

Firstly, as a recently convicted criminal, perhaps William Stevenson ought to consider his position as Chair of Newlyn Pier and Harbour Commission?

Secondly, as Chair, he was in a unique position to influence the rents of harbour property that his company populated in the 'Firm's' favour at peppercorn rents.

Thirdly, that he treated the Newlyn Harbour Master as his own, personal, private assistant there to do his bidding.

The next day the comments disappeared from the Cornishman page as Billy's blood-curdling threats caused them to offer a grovelling apology and undertake to accept a draconian gagging order and pay unspecified damages to a charity of Billy's choosing. Truth was the victim of the Cornishman's feeble capitulation.

I was on my own and the realisation sunk in that this was going to be serious. There was no way that I was going to retract because I knew that I was telling the truth and that truth needed to be out there.

The next thing, out of my office window, I saw a Smart Car pull up bearing the logo of Follet Stock who were the 'Firm's' solicitors. They had recently got them out of the fish scam mess with only tiny fines - the rub being that they had charged them the best part of a million quid in fees to do so.

These characters were no slouches. They had teeth and they were obviously relishing the prospect of sharpening them on me.

They slapped a writ in my hand, curtly advised me to seek legal advice and left.

I really was on my own, but I have always had great faith in my own solicitor.

I carefully read the contents of the writ and what was required of me to close the matter. Then I rang my friend, Ross Pascoe, who was the Managing Partner of Nalders Solicitors in Truro at that time. Ross listened to what I said and arranged an appointment for me to see him at 10:00 the following day.

The first thing Ross did was give me a serious bollocking in a manner only a person on friendly terms could get away with. Over a cup of tea, the next thing he said was, "it is unprofessional of me to admit this but I really do not like these characters at Follet Stock and relish the prospect of beating them."

Then we got down to the serious stuff. He said, "I hope you clearly understand that if you lose this it could easily cost you everything you have?"

No one understood that better than me!

An unassailable defence is assembled

What evidence do you have to back them up because it really does need to be absolutely watertight if I am to get you out of this mess?"

In response to the first allegation, Billy along with his skipper David Hooper, had recently been convicted of illegal fishing after Billy had ordered David Hooper to fish with his then flagship beamer, 'Daisy Christianne' in the closed, Trevose Box.

245

Skipper David Hooper R.I.P. - a true gentleman

David Hooper who was still aggrieved about the episode was prepared to testify for me about how he was convicted of a criminal offence because he obeyed Billy's orders under duress. Billy as the owner was fined £28,000 and Skipper, David Hooper £4,000. Both were criminal offences.

As the offences were still current and criminal in nature, that was my defence.

"Right" said Ross, "we need the conviction certificate from the Crown Court and if that is as you say it is, you are in the clear on that one."

On the second instance he said, "this is still a very serious allegation – first we need to define the term 'peppercorn'." Down came the Oxford English Dictionary from the shelf and 'peppercorn' was defined as 'nominal'. Ross continued, "just to be on the safe side, let's define 'nominal' as a term." 'Nominal' was defined as 'virtually nothing.' Being the consummate lawyer he was he then asked, "what other evidence do you have to back this up?"

Someone, hearing of my plight had sent me a copy of a confidential report prepared for the Harbour Commissioners by Plymouth-based, Hyder Consulting. It outlined what was wrong with Newlyn and specified what needed to be done to get the place back on a sounder footing. It made particular reference to the totally unrealistic, 'peppercorn' rents set for certain harbour property leases.

Having received the copy of the conviction certificate and had sight of the Hyder Report, (which I was not supposed to have) Ross looked up, smiled and said, "well, you are in the clear on those two and the third is just an opinion... even a headstrong bugger like you is entitled to an opinion."

He dictated a response to Follet Stock. Three short paragraphs refuting their allegations on the grounds stated, with the rider that if their client chose to pursue the matter it would be vigorously defended and an order for costs sought against him.

That was it. Nothing ever came back. They had tried their usual, bully and bluster tactics and they had not worked.

It was not long after that Follett Stock Solicitors collapsed in a spectacular manner due to an intervention by the Solicitors Regulation Authority following allegations of very serious financial irregularities.

The papers relating to this episode have been deposited in the Newlyn Archive as an historic record of the other side of a story that has largely been erased from the record by dark powerful forces akin to gangsterism.

It proves once more and reinforces yet again that bullies can only be beaten by being faced down. It must be done no matter how scary it is because the alternative is unthinkable.

A new Harbour Commission

Following many complaints and allegations regarding the goings on around Newlyn Harbour Commissioners, the Ports Division of the Department for Transport finally stepped in and disbanded the Old Harbour Commission.

When the call for new commissioners went out I applied and was very proud to be accepted as a commissioner in 2009. I am currently (2020) the only remaining, original member of the New Commission and am also proud to be the Vice Chair. Along the way, I like to think we have done some good but would the first to admit that not everything has been done right.

The Stevenson era culture still persists. Even though its teeth have been drawn, there is a culture of negativity and treachery in certain quarters causing some to refer to Newlyn as the 'Snake Pit'.

In 2019, a 70% stake in Stevensons was acquired by Edward Lakeman and his father Andrew Lakeman who trade as 'Ocean Fish'. The Lakemans are a Mevagissey family who can be traced back to 1740. They are very 'go ahead' fish traders and boat owners who, if anyone can, will take Stevensons forward in a positive manner.

The real tragedy is the way the Stevenson family suffered such a decline from the undoubted success they achieved over three generations. They did a lot of good for many years but could have done so much more and been so much more respected had they been less paranoid and more business-like in their dealings with everyone following the passing of Jacqueline Webster.

Newlyn Harbour status

As a trust port effectively owned by its stakeholders, Newlyn Harbour is akin to a parish council, with the harbourmaster as chief executive. There are exciting plans for the future of Newlyn as a 'warts and all' industrial working port.

I remain firmly of the belief that employment-wise, given the right kind of sympathetic investment, Newlyn is the only show in town in West Penwith, economically speaking.

Chapter 18
A costly business

The tuna fishing adventure

An adventure that cost me a packet!

Sometimes, like you do, I got involved in an adventure completely unrelated to oil. I returned to fishing to fulfil a forty-year ambition to fish for albacore tuna, having seen them being landed in Camaret in 1970.

Tuna had been landed in Newlyn for several years until the drift nets they were caught with were banned by the EU. A period of several years elapsed when there was renewed interest in a hook and line fishery for them. It was the same way as the Basque and Spanish boats had always caught them and in a very clean fishery with virtually no by catch other than an occasional swordfish.

The method was completely whale and dolphin-friendly, unlike the banned drift nets.

It all came about as a result of a conversation with a character called 'Quentin Knights', who was obsessed with the idea and got me interested because his enthusiasm was infectious to an old romantic like me. Most people would buy a motorbike at my age but not me and as it soon turned out, I was about to buy a bloody great fishing boat!

Anyway, as usual, bugger the expense, give the cat another goldfish so to speak. Much to the horror of Bernard Pooley, we formed a limited company called, 'Cornish Tuna.Com Ltd'.

249

Legendary sea boat 'The Ben Loyal'

I took an all-embracing debenture over everything for my own protection, given that I would be injecting a very sizeable sum into what I fully realised was a risky venture. As part of the deal, Quentin had to put £20,000 in to show good faith.

Having looked at several other boats we bought one named the 'Ben Loyal'. It was a former Scottish boat built by Herd and McKenzie in Peterhead in 1960. She was 18.2 metres long, with a lovely, ultra-reliable Gardner 8L 3B engine.

The Ben Loyal was a legendary sea boat and no stranger to the tuna job when in Newlyn previously under the ownership of John Turtle who was forced to sell her due to involvement in the notorious 'fish scam trial'. The Turtle Family were hung out to dry for landing over quota blackfish, while others just as deeply implicated got away virtually scot-free.

The Ben Loyal was laid up in Yarmouth on the Isle of Wight and the seller, who bizarrely was a Hampshire chicken farmer, had tried to catch albacore for the previous couple of years, but it was a disaster and he had pulled the plug. She was rigged with a US, West Coast trolling rig which was not in the same league as the Basque rig we were going to fit.

We went down to Bermeo in the Basque Country, which is the tuna capital of Biscay to collect the hydraulic reels, lures, fish bags and all the essential paraphernalia associated with the job. The fishermen were brilliant. A couple could speak English and a great friendship sprung up which would stand us in good stead at sea.

The deal was that the Ben Loyal had to be delivered to Toms Yard in Polruan in preparation for an extensive refit. Prior to this and subject to the completion of a satisfactory hull examination on the slip, the money would change hands.

The fun soon started when Quentin Knights showed his complete inability to compromise. He went to war with Alan Toms who was just as pig headed. The refit became a bloody warzone as the extras demanded totted up which Quentin then disputed even though he hadn't a leg to stand on.

I kept out of the line of fire as much as possible while the two arrogant pricks slugged it out and the bill mounted.

One of the extras, which I did not consider necessary, was an additional 500 gallon fuel tank fabricated down in the forepeak. Gardners are famous for their fuel economy and the engine room tanks held fuel for 14 days, which was more than enough for a projected maximum 12 day trip.

The job eventually ran its course, with neither of the pricks emerging with much credit. That said, most of the work was good but the bodge ups which came to light later detracted from that. The hefty bill was settled and off we went for Newlyn.

In Newlyn it got worse. Having just had a major refit, Quentin Knights demanded a complete, 'back to primer' paint job. That was not in the budget, the original plan being to get fishing with a boat that could do a few months to earn some money before painting because paint is not cheap and time really was money.

The boat's bottom had been worked on, the propeller balanced and rudder bearings renewed because excessive prop noise or a rudder rattling on its bearings would seriously affect fishing performance.

Anyway, 'Donkey Bollocks' got painting. The young, inexperienced crew including my son, had to do their bit unpaid but when they had finished, the old girl was gleaming. They had done a really classy job. Then the gear needed to be rigged and with 14 lines, that was not a straightforward job. To his credit, Quentin was a perfectionist but it was becoming obvious that he was a classic, narcissistic obsessive.

It was the first week in June and with the gear rigged, boxes aboard, fuel topped up and grub put away in the fish room, we took 15 tons of ice and we were ready for the off. Due to the (again in my opinion excessive) quantity of ice forrard in addition to the extra 2.5 tons of fuel, she was down by the head more than I would have liked. But it wasn't his money he was spending.

Bounders

We went away on a lovely fine night stopping outside the harbour to rig the 18 metre long trolling poles in their fishing position within their clamps on the rail aft of the wheelhouse. The old girl certainly looked the part.

Ahead of us was a better than two day, 500 mile steam SW of Land's End to the anticipated start point on some seamounts around 200 miles west of Cape Finisterre on the NW corner of Galica, Northern Spain. It's a long way from home if anything were to go wrong but the boat really was properly fitted out for the job in hand, so best foot forward.

24 hours later we were approaching the 'Shelf', the edge of the Continental Shelf where in the space of a few miles the depth increases from around a hundred fathoms (600 feet) to

11,800 feet.

Approaching the Shelf edge, we began encountering big regular swells in the region of 30 to 40 feet high and about 1,000 feet apart, which was quite normal in that area due to the rapidly shallowing water.

With the force 4 to 5 SW wind, a few green ones came over the bow due to the weight of the ice and fuel forrard of midships. But, the magnificent old boat ploughed on through the darkness making nothing of it.

In the early hours of the third day, after a 54 hour steam, we could see lots of lights ahead and there they all were, the Spanish albacore fleet. There were around 130 boats in total spread out in every direction as far as the eye could see. We were the only Cornish boat.

The seamounts were literally underwater mountains rising as much as 3 or 4,000 feet out of the abyssal plain. They caused upwellings of nutrient rich water that attracted an amazing pelagic biomass consisting of krill, anchovies, prawns, and squid which was like a food takeaway for the albacore and other fish present.

Barren indeed?

We were always told that beyond the Continental Shelf the ocean was virtually barren. Well, let me assure you that it was not. We had two echo sounders working on different frequencies which showed a heavy trace at 40 to 50 fathoms. It looked like an actual bottom trace as you would see up on the Shelf.

During the day, down there in the twilight zone was an amazing pelagic eco system, which during darkness would dissipate and rise toward the surface before dropping back down again at first light.

The 14 lines were got away as the light came in and trolling along at seven knots, the odd fish started hitting the close in stern lines right in the prop wash. The fish were right under the boat and we were catching them. It was amazing and the weather was really fine.

The Basques maintain that the albacore think a boat's hull is a whale and shelter beneath it in its shadow, darting out to feed. That is almost certainly why the short lines off the stern right in the prop wash are often the most productive, ramming home how vital a quiet prop and rudder bearing were.

The fish didn't last long and all day the fishing was slack. The Spaniards were complaining, fish could be seen everywhere, basking on the surface in the sunlight. We saw several huge fin whales, one broached right alongside and it was longer than the Ben Loyal. There were pods of dolphins everywhere and in the afternoon we saw several pods of huge black, sinister looking, sperm whales.

The night of the crabs

The basking albacore would not feed through the day. Late in the evening we had a few more. As it darkened, we were bagging up the few fish that had been kept in slush ice in the insulated tubs on deck when we noticed what looked like dimples of raindrops on the oily calm surface, but there was no rain!

Turning on the very powerful deck lights, they shone deep into the crystal clear water and it was like a snowstorm down there. There were countless millions, billions even, of creamy grey and green speckled swimming crabs going down and coming up to the surface.

They were causing the dimples on the water.

They were only a few inches across but it was the sheer numbers that stick in my mind. A few times you would see a huge slash as a swordfish fled away from the boat. This was the experience of a lifetime, real 'Blue Planet' stuff. All this life was eating or being eaten by something else in an amazing cycle of natural productivity.

Our Basque friend on the radio was convinced that tomorrow would bring big fishing as the fleet were sitting on a huge patch of albacore covering several square miles, with the Basques who were probing in all directions still finding fish.

At first light we were ready to go, Quentin had closed off the forrard fuel tank, switching over to the main engine room tanks. As soon as the lures went in the water there were fish. Just a few at first but then a complete full house and an albacore on every line. Great care had to be taken to avoid an almighty frap up.

The fish were from 8 to 10 kilos each and at £5 a kilo it did not take a mathematical genius to work out how the value would rack up if we could get four or five days like this under our belts.

But it was not to be!

Around 45 minutes after the tank changeover the engine died to a lumpy tick over, this was not good!

It was obviously fuel-related. Gardners are very simple engines and easy to bleed. There was a lot of air in the fuel system, and having bled it off, we went again only for the same thing to happen again 45 minutes later. It was not only frustrating but potentially serious if the weather turned poor.

We checked the fuel filters and they were spotless as they should be, given the tanks had been opened up and cleaned. There were three stages of primary filtration before the secondary filters on the engine itself. When bled, the engine was running like a sewing machine as it should.

Where the hell was the air coming from?

It was a case of home and try to get it sorted. What a let-down. A few fish aboard and the long steam home if not exactly with our tails between our legs, our heads hung low, demoralised and puzzled. We had to get it sorted or we were finished before we even started.

The trip home involved bleeding the engine every 45 minutes or so which was a nightmare. The spotlessly clean engine room reeked of diesel and we did as well, despite washing thoroughly each time. The engine never stopped, there was nothing wrong with it but the build-up of air was repeatedly starving it of fuel.

If truth be known, I had not been feeling too good for a while and was suffering serious pain in the left side of my neck, behind the ear. It came and went at odd times.

I put this down to the old injury sustained on the Caroline 20 years earlier. My marriage had recently broken down and I was starting to feel my age. The added stress of this was telling on me.

We spent a couple of days going through everything and having filled up with fuel, once again set off, convinced the problem was solved as the engine ran beautifully. The fish had moved north so they were the best part of a day nearer but the weather was not great, with a persistent cold northerly force 5 or 6 blowing and leaden skies.

The big blue one

We started fishing where the Spaniards were 350 miles west-south-west of Newlyn. They were not catching and blaming the unseasonal weather. On the third day, still towing roughly north-north-west, I was in considerable pain and feeling cold and miserable. My gut feeling was telling me this was not going to be a good day.

When the forrard tank was shut down that morning we ran about three hours without problem and thought the fuel gremlin had been banished. Then it happened again. The engine lost revs and there was air in the system once more. Down in the engine room I had to go back into the cabin because I suddenly had a job to breathe. This was not at all like me. I was angry with the problem, all the effort, time and money that had been wasted trying to sort it and now this. Suddenly, the shortness of breath became scary as a crushing pain like nothing I had ever felt before seemed to have my chest in a vice and I vaguely remember passing out as I slumped down on the cabin floor.

I came to in a lot of dull chest pain, but I could breathe again. The vice had been loosened. Apparently, I had been out for about two minutes. I was given two aspirin and a few sips of water to wash them down by Thomas, my son, who remembered this from the first aid course he had recently done. This probably saved my life.

Laying there helpless, I had been travelling down a tube towards a warm bright light with nothing but an utter sense of peace and serenity. All the pain had gone, when suddenly a gentle warm breeze was wafting me back. My time had not come. I know that there is nothing to fear and there is definitely something at the end of that tube or tunnel when your time does come. I find that very reassuring.

*'Juan De La Cosa' -
the ship that
saved my life!*

Medical evacuation

To say that I was in a pickle would not be putting it mildly. Quentin called Falmouth Coastguard on the shortwave radio set. They could hear us, but they were not coming through clearly. We were at least 150 miles outside the range of a Culdrose helicopter and probably an 18-hour steam to a rendezvous.

Suddenly the VHF set burst into life on channel 16 with a Spanish accent repeating our call sign, 'Gulf Bravo Papa Echo' and vessel name. It was the Spanish hospital ship, 'Juan de la Cosa' which had been monitoring the radio traffic to Falmouth Coastguard. They were 12 miles away and were on their way to assist.

This was a truly amazing little ship. It was about the size and general appearance of the Scillies' cargo ship, 'Gry Maritha'. She was equipped with a dental suite, small operating theatre, and a two-bed cardio unit. She also had a full engineering workshop, including a range of spares plus fuel and water if needed by a boat. It was paid for jointly by the Spanish government and the fishermen of the large fleet she served.

We made best speed towards them as they were heading towards us. They soon had a powerful RIB alongside and a doctor and nurse leapt aboard. They had a portable ECG machine, oxygen and morphine etc. Then a mask was fitted to me and the oxygen turned on. I felt a slight scratch as the morphine was administered and then the nurse stuck electrodes on me to run an ECG.

I don't mean to be flippant, it is just my gallows sense of humour, but when you are lying there helpless, wondering how things might pan out for you, I think this way… the ECG machine is the Crypton tuner, the Glyceryl Trinitrate spray is Easy Start and an angioplasty is the Dynorod Treatment. They were all part of my life support system for a while.

The ECG confirmed that I had suffered a heart attack and I would need to be transferred to the Juan de la Cosa for further tests. I was strapped very securely to a stretcher and ominously a flotation device was then attached onto my chest.

The RIB was standing off the Ben Loyal's port side as I was carried across the deck and balanced in what seemed like a precarious manner on the rail. There was a bit of swell, one minute the RIB was feet below and then level with or above the rail. I was thinking, if I have a flotation device they must have dropped one or two in the past, bearing in mind the 12,000 feet of water under the boat. But I was also fully aware that you can easily drown in your bath. Either way you would be no less dead. Thanks to the morphine I was resigned to my fate whatever that might be.

Then, without warning, at exactly the right moment, I landed softly on the deck of the RIB and the doctor and nurse were aboard like a pair of cats. I could almost see the keel of the Ben Loyal as she rolled away, turning for home and the last thing I saw was Thomas looking very worried as we sped away.

The recovery of the RIB was a very slick operation which must have been practised thousands of times, bearing in mind that it had to be launched first to require recovery. I learned later that they could evacuate a casualty in practically any conditions and often did.

Stabilsation

I was met by waiting medics who helped carry me off the boat deck into the hospital deck where a cabin was waiting for me. The ship's interior was bright and modern and the medical staff were amazingly kind and caring. They were consummate professionals.

I was then put on what looked like a much bigger ECG machine and a 60 inch plasma screen on the wall came to life. Unbelievably, I was being assessed via a satellite link by a cardiologist based in Madrid.

If you had to have a heart attack this, unbelievably, was probably as good a place as any given the speed and skill with which assistance was rendered and treatment commencing. They would have been hard put to be quicker, or indeed better, on dry land.

I was on the 'crypton tuner' and mildly sedated but vaguely aware of the regular 20 minute checks. It was late evening by the time I was settled for the night. The ship was obviously stabilised given the lack of movement in the swell.

Evacuation by chopper to Ireland

I actually slept albeit a bit fitfully. Given my needle phobia, I was a very good boy because I must have had more needle pricks than a pin cushion that day. The cabin blinds were drawn but it was obviously getting light outside when suddenly, the cabin door opened and in walked a chap in an orange flying suit with the broadest, Irish accent you would ever hear.

It was the Irish Coastguard and they were in a hurry. They were on their absolute maximum range and hover time was limited as I was strapped onto another stretcher to be winched up to the chopper above.

That really was a surreal experience looking at the Juan de la Cosa below and up at the spinning blades of the chopper above. As I was being dragged through the door the chopper was already moving. I was told that we would be flying into Shannon where I would be transferred to the Western District General Hospital in Limerick for further treatment.

It transpired that the Juan de la Cosa had steamed overnight to the rendezvous point with the chopper and regrettably in the rush I had not had the opportunity to thank my rescuers. It truly was humbling to think of the resources that were deployed without any reservation to save me that day.

Sadly, in 2017 the helicopter that rescued me was lost in a tragic accident. This is the report In the early hours of 14th March 2017… '*A Sikorsky S-92 helicopter operated by CHC Helicopter under contract to the Irish Coast Guard (call sign 'Rescue 116') crashed into the sea while supporting a rescue operation off County Mayo, on Ireland's west coast.*'

Like the loss of our own Solomon Brown, this highlights the dedication to the saving of life these amazing people show without hesitation. Whenever they answer a shout, it could cost them their own life.

To the Western General Hospital in Limerick

An ambulance was waiting on the apron at Shannon and I was transferred, having properly thanked the chopper crew for their service. Irish roads are not the smoothest and the one we travelled made the trip excruciating. I felt every last bump even though I was utterly fatigued.

On arrival, the hospital could have been Treliske apart from one thing, casualty was rammed with patients, but everything was at a standstill. Armed Gardai (Irish police officers) were stationed at the entrance, while domestics with mops and buckets were busy cleaning up what was obviously a lot of blood.

The ambulancemen, who stayed with me until I was handed over to the hospital staff, said that there had been yet another drugs-related shooting in Limerick previously. There were two, critically injured casualties ahead of us under armed guard. Apparently, the Limerick drug dealers' weapon of choice and status symbols were Uzzi sub machine guns, so the victims were likely peppered, sure enough.

It was Saturday late morning and there I was, waiting in a hospital corridor in a foreign country looking at grim-faced, automatic weapon-toting, Gards while waiting for treatment. Eventually, I was seen by a junior doctor who told me that I would be seen later on his rounds by Professor Thomas Kiernan, their top man. Just to be on the safe side, I got another jab in the stomach that stung like hell.

I was then despatched to a ward in the old part of the building rammed with very sick people that actually made me look and feel quite well by comparison. The beds were very close together so there was no privacy and precious little peace. Most of the patients looked terminal to me. I was just hoping against hope that I wasn't going to be one of them!

I suddenly realised that I had nothing to eat and precious little to drink for over 24 hours. At 17:00 tea was served. I was given a cup of tea that tasted as good as Mother's milk and a ham sandwich with a fruit yoghurt. I then had a second cup of tea but no more to eat. Then the Professor arrived, a great character with a posse of students in tow hanging on his every word.

He looked intently at the last ECG and listened to my chest for what seemed like an age. His bedside manner was reassuring, saying that I probably needed a couple of stents fitting, whereafter I would be as good as new again. He put me on his list for Tuesday.

There wasn't a lot of sleep that night. The poor nurses were run off of their feet and in the small hours it was obvious that some poor, unfortunate near the door had passed on. I was comforted by the fact that the sickest ones were near the door while I was way up at the far end.

On Sunday morning, breakfast was a choice of scrambled eggs and leathery-looking, burnt toast or porridge. The porridge was delicious. Later in the day the Bishop came round. They always remind me of crows and it seemed obvious that he was only interested in certain patients who looked to be the ones with money. Fortunately, he didn't give me a second glance.

I had got talking to a couple of young men, with the oldest being around 30. Both were suffering from liver failure and both admitted that they were alcoholics who were unlikely to get transplants. They had resigned themselves to a bleak future.

I received a visit from the local Fishermen's Mission man but, apart from a pleasant yarn and a couple of magazines, there was not a lot he could do. First thing Monday I called Consols Oils and spoke to Paul. His eldest son Mark, a chartered civil engineer, was living and working in Limerick and Paul kindly arranged for him to visit and bring me some cash and a pair of shoes.

When I was evacuated from the Ben Loyal they sent my sea bag with me. It contained a few changes of underwear, a couple of shirts and a spare pair of trousers. In the rush, my toiletries were left in the washroom and my shoes also were forgotten. The only footwear I had was my Wellington boots which I had been wearing when evacuated.

The visit from Mark Tonkin was welcome. I was able to get some fresh fruit, a bar of soap and a tube of toothpaste from the shop in the hospital foyer. Then, back on the ward, I had a shower and shave and felt a lot more presentable and ready for the following day.

On the Tuesday morning I was prepped for the angioplasty and told that I would go down after dinner. However, it was not to be, as a couple of emergencies came in and that was that. The Professor promised that I would be at the top of his next list in a week but I was not inclined to spend that long in that depressing ward.

I did a runner

I was feeling better so I got Paul to check out potential flights home, preferably to Newquay. My reasoning for this was that I was occupying a bed that someone else needed and I wanted to be home. There was a flight on Thursday afternoon from Cork to Newquay and I was booked on it.

On Thursday morning I discharged myself, admittedly against advice, and caught a bus that went direct to Cork Airport. I have never been so glad in my life than when that plane swooped down over Watergate Bay and touched down on the St Mawgan runway. As much as I love all things Irish, I was so thankful to be back in God's Country, still alive and kicking, against considerable odds.

Back home, I went straight from the airport to my own doctor's and gave him a letter from the Professor in Ireland. He examined me (including another ECG) and said that arrangements would be made for the angioplasty to take place.

Fella do you want to live?

A couple of days later the appointment came through for six weeks hence but a fortnight later I had another event and was admitted as an emergency case. I was under the care of Dr Robin Vanlingen, a bluff South African consultant cardiololgist who did not mince his words. "Fella do you want to live?" "Of course doctor," I replied… "then stop bloody smoking!"

I had never been a heavy or indeed, addictive smoker but I did enjoy a pipe of roll tobacco or a decent cigar and consumption rose in stressful situations. Luckily, not being addicted, that was it. In over ten years I have not smoked at all and do not miss it. It really is a mug's game.

The angioplasty was amazing. There was no pain but there was a definite feeling of something 'going on in there' and I could see the procedure taking place on the large screen above my head. They injected dye to delineate the arteries which was weird and there was a 'whoosh' of heat from head to toe as it went in.

As they were finishing, I felt a now familiar crushing pain in my chest and the tension was palpable in the team. I felt something cold in my arm and the pain went. Apparently, they had lost a large clot which was recovered and the cold was a dose of anticoagulant just in case.

As I was being wheeled back to the ward, I could feel the relief of a fully restored circulation once more. The 'Dyno Rod' treatment had worked.

Heart problems had been a feature of my father's family, several of whom had succumbed to what I had. His twin brother Glenlee had dropped a few years previously before the ability to treat heart problems the way they do now. I would have been a gonner as well, so there really is a lot to be thankful for due to the amazing skills of the likes of Dr Vanlingen and our NHS.

The Ben Loyal did eventually catch a trip of five and a half tons of albacore taken in three days west of Ireland. There is a great video by Larry Hartwell on YouTube under, 'Ben Loyal Albacore Trip', which is all I really have to show for my investment. Even so, I survived and it was a real adventure for sure.

The Ben Loyal was sold very cheaply and I lost a packet. Off she went, whelk fishing in the North Sea until 2019 when she was sold again to be converted into a houseboat. Her fishing days finally over marked the end of an era, but I'd like to think that I saved her from the breakers.

Chapter 19
Exit strategies and take overs

The deal of a lifetime

After a brief period of convalescence, I was soon back at the day job feeling like a new one, the only real difference being the need to take five tablets a day, which is a small price to pay for getting your life back.

The World Fuel Services takeover of Falmouth was getting into its stride and they appreciated the fact that we were their biggest customer in Falmouth. A meeting was called to outline their plans for the facility going forward.

At the meeting we met Alex Garcia, the Miami based Vice President of Land Sales Europe and Craig Roberts, a former US Military Officer in charge of the London Office.

They went to great lengths to explain that they saw Falmouth as a key strategic location. The company's main emphasis was, at that time, marine-based but they saw the potential for inland sales and, as the biggest volume customers, we were seen as a key part of that strategy.

It was obvious that this pair were serious players, men with a plan. I was aware of the fact that the Brinkworth outfit with red trucks and our hostile neighbours out on the A30 were not happy that we were making such good use of Falmouth, which they were refusing to use and, as a result, cutting off noses to spite faces. This achieved nothing for them but plenty for us.

As we were talking I dropped a casual remark into the conversation that the Brinkworth outfit had been trying to buy us, which was not a lie, but I did add as a kite flying exercise, that given my recent health problems, I was in the process of considering the offer.

The response from Craig Roberts was exactly what I wanted to hear, but never in my wildest dreams expected to. These guys were deadly serious, he said, "don't do anything hasty, we don't want to buy you, but give us a few days while we consider an offer to persuade you to stay."

World Fuel Services were not an oil company in the conventional sense, they were traders with their roots deep in the marine bunkering trade, hence their purchase of Falmouth as predominantly a marine terminal. They were, on their own frank admission, 'asset light,' so in this sense their recent purchase of Falmouth was a bit of a departure for them. However, they so obviously had serious money available to invest.

An unbelievable offer

True to his word, a week later Craig Roberts was back and what he had to say was like a birthday, Christmas and Easter rolled into one. He was frank and said that they were thinking long-term and that they were looking for a ten year 'exclusive supply' agreement. In return, they would guarantee 100% product availability which was all I was really expecting at best.

It got even more interesting when he started talking about structured finance, whereby our credit limit would be set at 85% of monies owed on 30 days rolling credit, meaning no more grovelling to the bank for an inadequate overdraft facility. Effectively, our overdraft facility would expand and contract according to need, regulated by a contract that was clear, fair and unequivocal.

If the facility was needed, all that had to be done was to withhold an invoice or invoices back for up to 90 days with the interest payable at the standard rate previously charged by our bank. Given that we only ever used the facility occasionally for a few days at a time, we really were quids in over time and suddenly aware of exactly how much the bank had been creaming off us previously.

Unbelievably, as a final gesture, they would pay us £500,000 upfront to invest in the business to be written off (not repaid) at £50,000 a year over the ten years, interest free.

Obviously given that they were effectively becoming our bankers they would require a fixed and floating charge over the business in case of default and an option of first refusal in the event of any future sale of the business conditional on World Fuel Services matching any other offer on the table.

To say that our flabbers were ghasted would not be to understate our sense of disbelief. Contacting Bernard Pooley, who as ever the accountant, he wanted to see full details of what was outlined before passing formal judgement, but I could hear him practically falling off his seat in surprise at this remarkable development.

Due diligence got underway as a formal contract was threshed out between our solicitor and accountant and the WFS team who conceded that they were dealing, unexpectedly, with a formidable negotiating team on our side. As a final outcome, everyone got what they wanted.

Financial freedom

With the £500,000 in the bank, I horrified David and Tom by saying that I was going to invest the cash in a complete fleet renewal programme over five years, but it really began to pay dividends as the vehicles came on stream. By putting down 50% deposits and taking full advantage of capital allowances, we really were reaping the rewards of previous thrift as trucks were paid off in half the time without strain.

The freedom from the straitjacket of an overdraft was liberating and it was easier to concentrate on the stuff that actually made money. The new trucks coming on stream did wonders for our image and there is no doubt that after personal recommendation, the livery on the side of a smartly presented vehicle is the next best thing.

From that day on, we never looked back.

We had tragedies as well

Over the years, we lost some remarkable people from our tight-knit team. Roger Stones' health was never good but he cheerfully worked away until kidney failure caught up with him and he passed away at an age where he should have enjoyed another forty years.

David Eustice had five fantastic years with us after being written off by doctors. He courageously fought his way out of his wheelchair and always said that his job with us gave him back his dignity. It was a two-way street though because he gave so much more in return. Similarly, David ought to have had many more years than he did but unlike poor Roger, David's end was sudden after a massive heart attack.

Then we lost David Pearce, he was a former farmer and fisherman who could and did turn his hand to anything. He was predominantly our main artic driver, fetching the loads of fuel into our depot from Falmouth.

On the day he passed, he'd left work as usual at around 15:00. David lived in Gunwalloe on the Lizard and was busy restoring a vintage car in his garage at home. When he didn't come in for his tea as usual, his son went to call him and found him. He'd passed away, a fit, healthy, forty year old who was loved by everyone he met. He left a wife and three young boys.

The following morning at 07:00, the sight of eleven grown men arriving at work, having heard the terrible news and collapsing in floods of tears was heartbreaking. We closed the yard and went home out of respect. I had the difficult job of seeing his dear wife to offer our condolences and it really was hard to find the words to say anything.

David's funeral was massive. Again, out of respect, the yard was closed for the day. I think the entire Lizard closed down judging by who was there at the tiny church at Gunwalloe Church Cove. It seated just 87 people but it was estimated that around 700 stood for nearly two hours in beastly cold, hard rain. Everyone was soaked but that was inconsequential, the cortege left the church to the song 'Always Look on the Bright Side of Life' but that was not easy on that terrible day.

Symbolically at the graveside, the rain ceased and a watery, golden sunlight illuminated the sky in an ethereal glow. I am sure that it was a sign from David to his devastated family. It was another of those tough days that we all have to weather together. It was a proper Cornish funeral in the best tradition of paying our last respects to an exceptional Cornish man.

There were also numerous funerals of respected customers that we were morally obliged to attend due to the friendships that grew over the years. It says a lot about a person when so many turn out to pay their respects. It is so sad when only a few turn out.

Cornish funerals in my circle tend to be big affairs because of the still strong family ties and community spirit that sadly seems to be vanishing in some places.

That is the circle of life and death. The birth of my own son was life changing and I felt blessed with such a precious gift. It was always good to share in the births and marriages of those around us, especially when our lovely Judith married Ron Jones, who was a Consols Oils tank fitter.

The couple enjoyed some wonderful years together but Ron succumbed to the curse of cancer which ran its inevitable course in a short time.

Fred bows out

Fred Davies decided to retire early. There had been friction with Roger Stone previously and he was always worried about risks, seeming unable to grasp the simple, inescapable fact that rewards did involve them. It wasn't all about just profit, because investment must take priority and in the final analysis, it was my house that was always on the line. Consequently, the biggest risk was always mine.

Fred was a very good salesman and ambassador for our firm which he brought a lot to. He also took rather a lot in the form of his share when he left in haste, which was at a time that I could have well done without after I refused to sell the business to Watson Petroleum. Ironically, after he left, a couple of the windfalls mentioned earlier put us on a very firm footing, which he really did miss out on and my house finally ceased to be on the line.

In retirement Fred continues to work for an undertaker but our original, warm friendship withered away as our paths diverged. Quite frankly, I felt he had let me and the firm down by being greedy and selfish but it was never worth a major fall out over. He got some of what he wanted and I shed a potentially much worse problem further down the line.

One of the best things Fred did was to facilitate the recruitment of David Nichols AKA 'Gweek Boy', who came to us at 19 after working in a bank and hating it. David was 'off the farm' and it was obvious from the start that he was an exceptional find. Twenty one years on, having taken over the reins from me over several years, he now runs Consols Oils for its new owners.

An awayday at the races and a winning bet

A letter containing an invitation landed on my desk one morning. It was from Ross Pascoe kindly inviting me to a Nalders Corporate day at Newton Abbot Races which I gladly accepted given my deep regard for Ross.

We assembled at Nalders' HQ in Truro to board the coach. I had a lift into town knowing full well I was unlikely to be in any fit state to drive back on our return. Nalders' staff looked after our needs well with an excellent lunch on arrival in the corporate hospitality area. This got everyone in the mood for a flutter.

I have never been a betting man in the bookmaker sense, although I do enjoy the spectacle of an occasional day at the races. I have a rigid rule that a fiver is the maximum stake however, this day, the fiver on the first race returned three to one odds so the stake money was placed on the next race at two to one.

Following the penultimate race, in the bar relating my success at having won on every race to the others, one of them, a youngish executive who had rather a lot to say for himself, chipped up saying, "I bet you can't do that again!"

The gauntlet having been thrown down I responded, "I will have fifty quid with you that I can." Thinking he was on to a sure fire winner, he snapped my hand off and we were on.

I had won well over a £100 that afternoon and could easily have lost £50 but I wanted to teach the kitten not to mess with the old tom cat. A brainwave solved my dilemma, I put a fiver to win on all five horses in the race and the winner came in at ten to one… happy days.

After the race the pace of drinking was picking up as, having shown him the winning betting slip, I collected on my wager with him while he scratched his head as to how I had picked every winner that afternoon. The bet was only that I would pick the winner in the final race and not, how I would do it. I didn't have the heart to tell him what I'd actually done.

But as always, five out of six wins were pure luck because I know virtually nothing about racehorse form. The chance of that luck holding out for the sixth time was remote, so feral cunning was necessary in response to a cheeky challenge.

Getting back to Truro well over £200 up on the day, I was very glad that I had a lift waiting. Predictably, I was in no fit state to drive. What a fantastic, fun-filled day it was. When I rang Ross to thank him the following day I told him what I had done. I was afraid he was either going to have a seizure, wet himself, fall off his chair or all three judging by the laughter which went on at the other end of the line.

A change of heart

I always said that I would never sell Consols Oils and for many years ploughed onwards and upwards because the job was not only about making money. We could actually have made a lot more if we were greedier but I detest greed. I'd much rather be respected, knowing full well that respect must be earned and it is so easy to lose. All that aside, I was still enjoying myself.

David, Tom and myself shared the same philosophy. We had to be profitable but it is wrong to take advantage of people as some do. We have to live amongst our customers who rely on us to deliver a first class service at a fair price. Living in the same community, it is necessary to put something back in the form of donations and sponsorships. We rarely refused a request for help.

This was where the true value of the business lay and both competitors and suitors understood this, realising that our community-orientated approach to business was where both our profitability and resilience came from.

World Fuel acquires Watson Petroleum

The deal with World Fuel Services worked exceptionally well for us for around six years. As always with big corporate outfits, personnel move on and things change. The asset-light philosophy went out of the window as WFS went on the acquisition trail. They bought Henty Oils in Liverpool - a marine bunkering operation, then London-based, Linton Petroleum - our former premium paraffin supplier.

The next move meant that the writing was on the wall for us. Watson Petroleum, the outfit that operated red trucks out of Brinkworth (which had been our sworn enemy for years) was on the market. World Fuels snapped them up, allegedly paying way over the odds for a dinosaur that was rumoured to be heading for trouble along with several other mid-market distributors at the time.

Watson Petroleum ran around 300 tankers, with less than a third of those operated by the mega distributor DCC who had bought O J Williams earlier. The oil distribution sector was rapidly moving into a 'dick waving' phase as everyone scrambled to be bigger rather than better. They eyed up the next acquisition and distressed outfits fell like dominoes as they coalesced into the mega camps.

Tying the diverse cultures of the acquisitions into a coherent business unit with unified IT systems must have given the suits involved a few headaches and sleepless nights while it was all going on.

Who took over whom?

In a bizarre twist the takeover of Watson Petroleum by World Fuels conveyed the distinct impression that they had, in reality, been taken over by Watson Petroleum rather than vice versa.

Watson's former MD was on a retainer as part of the deal and from where I was standing his power base was, if anything, stronger. As Watson Petroleum got more involved in managing World Fuels' UK inland business, at the end of the retainer, he left to play golf and there then appeared to be a power vacuum at the heart of the operation.

We were keeping our heads down as the dinosaur's tail lashed around but things did not bode well given that our long-standing enemy now had access to our volume and pricing data. A replacement for the golf-playing Watson fugitive who having trousered the considerable loot and exited stage left was recruited (poached) from DCC who, I wager, were not best pleased.

The contempt was obviously mutual

Oil company executives are prostitutes! Guns for hire to the highest bidder! Temporary loyalty has a price and that price is what the highest bidder is prepared to pay. They hawk their knowledge gained at their previous post around and the worst the previous employer can do is enforce whatever furlough clause they wrote into the contract of employment and grind their teeth.

Another even more bizarre coincidence was the fact that Watson Petroleum's second in command was the brother-in-law of the new chief beef. Suddenly for us, this was becoming incestuous which made it a highly toxic place to be as we waited for the almost inevitable shit storm to break on our heads.

Our contract with World Fuels was broken out and intimately re-examined. Fortunately, it offered us a fair degree of protection thanks to Bernard Pooley's original negotiating skills. As we had to buy our fuel from them and they had to supply us subject to our credit rating which Experian rated at the highest level, the contract had around two years to run by this time, but then what would happen?

As usual something turned up!

Two things in fact. Out of context, the first was like a bolt from the blue!

A chance encounter with a clumsy puppy

Around the time all of this takeover business was happening, I was walking my dog on Porthtowan Beach one July evening in 2017. I was minding my own business when suddenly this crazy young Labradoodle dog came bounding over only to career straight into that delicate part of the male anatomy that resides between one's legs.

I went down on my knees in agony while the mutt tried his damnedest to lick me to death and his distraught owner (who happened to be blond and very attractive) came running over, full of apologies. Being a gentleman I was very diplomatic, while resisting the instinctive urge to murder the bloody dog.

The lady offered to buy me a drink in the Blue Bar to make amends. Well it really would have been rude not to accept her kind offer. Helping me up from my knees she said, "I am Louise, what's your name?" and we got chatting as if we had known each other for years.

Emboldened, I suggested a date for a meal and it just went on from there. I was smitten. She was an 'Aggie Maid' which was a plus and to cut a long story short, we fell in love and got married on 2nd November 2019 at Gwennap Church, having just bought the beautifully restored chapel at Geor on the road to Stithians from Burncoose, right on the Gwennap Parish border.

The 'Get out of jail FREE' card

The second thing in quick succession was to shape the future financially for me in a very positive way subject to some carefully contrived turbulence along the way from the very pissy, World Fuel Services' minion who ran the Watson Petroleum Division.

NWF, a Cheshire-based, former agricultural cooperative had become a PLC and its fuel division was on the expansion trail. I was aware of them through my time as a director with the Federation of Petroleum Suppliers and I regarded them as a decent, straight company. They were expanding and we were in their sights. They signed a non-disclosure agreement and talks got under way.

I was comfortable that at 69 years of age it was time to bow out if the terms were right. The first offer was derisory. A nice try but we were not distressed and did not have to sell. They went away and then came back with a better offer. It was still not good enough. We only had this one opportunity so we sent them away again.

They wanted to be in Cornwall and they knew full well that a well-regarded, going concern was a far cheaper proposition than a cold start. Even at a considerable premium, they came back the third time with an exceptionally good offer and heads of terms were agreed.

'Right of first refusal' dirty tricks

That was when the shit really hit the fan!

The terms of our contract with World Fuels stated that in the event of a potential sale to a third party, World Fuels must be given first refusal at the best offer price. When they learned what the offer was they went ape, but like it or not, they had ninety days to decide whether to match the offer. It was then that the dirty tricks started as the Watson chief beef did his utmost to wreck the deal.

I had one thing over the unpleasant Mr Paul Vian who seemed to have a very high opinion of himself and his senior executive status. I had built my little company from nothing over 33 years and happened to own 80% of it, with David and Thomas owning 10% each of the balance. Vian was, in reality, but a minion with less clout than he gave himself credit for given that he actually owned nothing of his company.

World Fuel Services were not prepared to pay anything like the price on the table from NWF but still insisted on invoking the 60-day option to purchase clause. They were, via Mr Vian, extremely bad losers but they were basically stuffed if they did not match the other offer. At one point a classy, charming, female Russian executive took it upon herself to descend from World Fuel Services London HQ with the expressed intention of finding out what "made me tick"… her words not mine.

Well she had no chance finding that out because most of the time, even I had no idea what was going on in my head to make me tick – other than the need to earn a crust for everyone. I never realised how important we were to warrant this degree of attention but she returned back to HQ empty handed.

About five weeks into the 60-day option period the Russian decided that the notice had not been served in accordance with the contract which was obviously a delaying tactic. So, we had to start over again. Having commissioned our solicitor to redraft a notice that really was watertight, off we went again.

It was glaringly obvious that Vian was trying to force us into a corner as he showed his hand in various ways. He was hell bent on distressing us but try as he might, we were far too tough, resourceful and resilient for him, which made him even more nasty.

The very unpleasant Watson chief beef then breached the non-disclosure agreement by talking to an NWF depot manager at a corporate golf day who happened to be the son of the NWF MD. Not content with this, he then tried to stop our credit, even though we were within terms and so it went on until the second notice period stuttered over the line and they had shot their bolt.

I wanted to sue him for the serious matter of his breach of the non-disclosure agreement but the sensible advice was to focus on getting the NWF deal over the line.

How much easier it would have been if the idiot had been pragmatic and accepted the abrogation of the contract over to NWF for its duration, given that we were quite prepared to return the balance sum from the original consideration as per the contract.

All that really came out of his ill will and petulance was to make a serious enemy of me and to come very close to the loss of business going forward from NWF who, having to negotiate a new contract, came very close to walking away from Falmouth due to Vian's highly obstructive attitude.

A month before the sale completed we paid our fuel bill right up to date which stopped any nonsense about creditworthiness. We then waited for the days to tick down until a very considerable sum of money landed with our solicitor.

Every cloud has a silver lining. The upside of Vian's shenanigans being that within the five month delay he caused in the sale, we delivered our most profitable year ever. This effectively enhanced the already excellent sale price. Perhaps I ought to have sent him a drink in gratitude? Perhaps I will send him a signed copy of this book instead? Who knows, he might even learn something.

They said it would be hard, but they never said it would be this hard.

Chapter 20
Stand firm, stand true and stand alone if necessary

Gifford Pound

Gifford Pound was one of those characters that on first encounter you take an immediate dislike to only to be proven completely wrong and then becoming warm friends. He was a fearless and accomplished amateur scuba diver and wreck hunter and also ran Tallack Windscreens in Penryn which we always used for our replacement windscreens.

The wreck hunter

I first met Gifford back in the Caroline days when he asked for any information we might have about wrecks, particularly in the Trevose to west of Lundy area. He was particularly interested in evidence of any wooden wrecks.

This was very interesting insofar as this was the track the wooden sailing schooners would take when plying their trade between Cornwall and South Wales in the mining heyday around the mid 1800s.

Given that on one terrible stormy night alone it was said that sixty vessels were lost, we often got a pull on the warps while towing which would be recorded as an obstruction on the plotter roll. On hauling, there would often be evidence of a wooden ship in the form of worm- eaten timber or some coal from a long lost cargo.

Over the years these wrecks had deteriorated and were often hit by heavy trawl gear until very little remained other than the odd rib appearing and disappearing in the shifting sandy seabed which caused those odd pulls on the warps.

I never thought much more about it for many years until in the run up to my retirement, Gifford called in at work to see me. Sadly, he was dying from cancer and a shadow of his former, ebullient self. Obviously in serious discomfort, what transpired was deeply touching and worth recording as one hell of a tale of derring-do and borderline piracy.

He checked out the locations I had given him one by one and found not a lot in the process. One day, a way to the north of the Heads, a blackened, battered, oak rib obviously from a wooden ship was seen poking out of the shelly sand. Checking it out by brushing some sand away by hand, there was a treasure trove.

The ship was loaded with tin ingots bearing the phoenix stamp of the Carvedras Blowing House in Truro. Over time, the ingots were salvaged and handed to the receiver of wrecks as prescribed in such cases. However, Gifford being Gifford, he kept a couple of ingots for himself as momentoes.

But the plot thickened further in the most unlikely way.

The tin strip mould

Tremough Convent in Penryn was latterly a school which was sold to become part of the new Tremough University Campus. An auction sale was held to dispose of the contents of the building and one of the items was a striking, white, Italian marble hip bath that the nuns had formerly used. It was latterly used as a flower planter outside the main door, which Gifford intended to buy for his wife.

Unfortunately, someone else outbid Gifford and got the bath, which Gifford saw being emptied of soil for removal after the sale. In the bottom was a rusty metal box measuring about 18 x 6 inches. When it was opened, it was found to contain a stone mould the significance of which was only clear to Gifford, who, as a second prize decided to buy the box and contents from the purchaser of the bath.

Gifford knew what he had. It was the old Carvedras tin strip mould bearing the distinctive phoenix emblem, the same emblem as that on the salvaged tin ingots and bore the name, 'Lewis Chas Daubuz, Truro.' Tin strips were individual to each blowing house and cast to accompany consignments of refined black tin ore to certify the provenance of the ore.

When he was taken ill, Gifford decided to take one of the Carvedras tin ingots he had and cast a strictly limited series of a dozen tin strips to give to his friends as thanks for a past favour. I was both humbled and thrilled to accept the one he had brought me and it is now one of my most prized possessions of great sentimental value.

To show their origin as recent castings, each of the tin strips Gifford cast has a small, deliberate flaw in the casting. Mine has a small indent above the 'A,' as if there had been a bubble in the molten metal.

Retirement and no regrets

After 55 years of toil, including 33 in the fuel distribution game, I had made it over the finish line. I was a little better off than I had started out as a boy on the farm and it had been quite a ride with lots of luck and even more 'neck', occasionally tempered with fun and laughter, tragedy and triumph, all in equal measure. What a ride!

On 30th March 2019, I walked out of the yard for the last time. There was no looking back and no regrets. Just many fond memories.

In the interim, I have resisted every temptation to go back because as always, forwards has been the only way that has ever worked for me. I have retained ownership of the yard, with NWF on a ten-year lease and the rent generated is, in effect, my pension, while the land is hopefully there for my son to inherit – given that no more land is being made, it will hopefully be worth something to him.

None of this could have been achieved without the loyalty and goodwill of those colleagues who worked with me and who, in the final analysis, were and continue to be the firm's greatest asset.

Not ever having had any formal business training, I quickly grasped the need to employ the best advisors and admin staff possible. I am a 'big picture' man and fully appreciate that the minutiae of the business was best left to those more capable than me. It really is true that delegation and real teamwork is the art of successful management.

I love business where everyone benefits. What is the point otherwise because everyone needs to live?

Marf

In my orbit of our Cornish culture, nobody is anybody without a nickname. 'Washballs', 'Squirts', 'Sarge', 'Nutty Noah', 'Benny' and my own, 'Stankers', spring to mind.

No one seems to know how Stephen Long came to acquire the nickname 'Marf', but there are some who will not know his proper name. He is a legend in his own lifetime, my wingman, partner in crime and trusted best man at my marriage to Louise.

You often hear 'Marf' long before you see him. His deep, bass, Cornish accent belies his slight wiry stature. You half expect a giant to appear. His most striking feature is his awesome set of whiskers (he reminds me of 'Animal' from the Muppet Show) and the good-humoured twinkle in his eyes. He was a very successful scallop fisherman aboard the boat he worked so hard to build, the 'Marel Margh' (Black Horse). Like me, 'Marf' is 'sort of retired', but is still kept occupied as ship's husband for the boat, now worked by his son, Austin. Marf is brutally straight talking and exactly the way I like real friends to be. He seldom takes prisoners, while his whole life revolves around his family, especially the grandchildren.

We've enjoyed a couple of past road trips to Ireland to the Fisheries Exhibition in Galway.

My wing man Stephen 'MARF' Long (right)… a legend in his own lifetime pictured above with his son Austin

The first time, we took the scenic route back to Rosslare via the Great Atlantic Way. We travelled through Clare, Kerry and Cork visiting Mountain Mine at Alihies, which had a beam engine built by Harveys in Hayle who had it shipped it over the Celtic Sea to Castletownbere, thence over the mountains to Alihies. This must have been one hell of a job given that true to its name, Mountain Mine sits near the top of a wind-blasted mountain looking out over the wild Atlantic.

On our final night in Kinsale, we fetched up in Daltons Bar where a 'mighty sesh' developed. We presented them with the last of the supply of Baner Sen Piran's we had taken as gifts for our friends over the water. Away back to Rosslare the following day for the night ferry and back to Pembroke, we managed a flyby of Waterford's 'Copper Coast'. There is another scene of historic Cornish activity in the copper mines there.

The following year saw us fly to Dublin. Picking up a hire car, we again went across to Galway and again went the long way back to Dublin, this time via Donegal. We met our friends, Frank Galagher and Eamonn Rodgers in the Burtonport area of the Rosses before making Malin Head and back via Derry and Belfast for another memorable trip. Times like these are precious for sure.

Epilogue

As it was, is now and ever shall be

There was mining, fishing and farming and each in their own unique ways were the spiritual and fiscal backbones that underwrote the Cornish way of life that some of us have been so fortunate to have been born into and to have lived to the fullest extent possible, while benefitting greatly from so doing.

This created an informal mix and match, needs-based approach to life. As my own experience clearly demonstrates, an ability to adapt to changing circumstances, a desire for betterment, an aptitude for enterprise and an innate curiosity combined with a boyish sense of fun and adventure has shaped some of our lives.

Time to push back

My view is that a clear line in the sand must be drawn, which means a determined push back against excessive development needs to occur. A perfect place for this to play out is at the former Penhale Camp that was quietly sold to a developer with the tacit approval of the National Trust and Cornwall Council who then went on to grant outline approval for 134 holiday units in this priceless location.

With protesters outside 'Kremlin Kernow' in 2019… Never be afraid to stand up for your beliefs!

Ravaged by time - The Penhale site formerly scarred by silver and lead mine workings. The engine houses were demolished by the US Army during WWII and used as target practice

The beautiful Penhale site on the north coast of Cornwall remains spoiled to this day

275

This is another cause I'm prepared to fight for. I hope others will join with me.

The project to buy back Penhale as a National COVID-19, Pandemic Memorial

The North Coast of Cornwall from Pendeen Watch to Trevose constitutes some of the finest seascapes to be found anywhere in the UK. There are wild majestic cliffs, various offshore islets, surf-pounded strands and extensive dune systems that support highly vulnerable flora and fauna, all of which are under serious threat due to mass tourism and seemingly endless housing developments.

The clear and present danger is that without sympathetic stewardship, the vast numbers of tourists and the seemingly insatiable demand for coastal accommodation they generate threatens to destroy the very beauty they seek in this very special, very fragile place.

In order to ensure the majesty of this coast remains unsullied for future generations, those who love the place as deeply as I do need to be vigilant.

Mass development has reached the point where there is a need to push back against the developers and, given the significance of Penhale, this seems the ideal location to do it.

There is an unassailable case for a managed return back to nature of a classic brownfield site originally taken over by the MOD as an exigency in WW2. The development currently proposed is simply not right adjacent to a spiritual peninsula of big windy skies that recently returned choughs have chosen to repopulate.

The idea is to launch a national 'Crowdfunder' appeal to raise the considerable funds that will be necessary to buy Penhale back from the developer at a fair market price, where the developer would not be out of pocket.

The objective would be to re-wild the entire headland as a National Memorial to all victims of the 2020 COVID19 pandemic and the frontline workers involved in its control. A wild place where those who wish to could visit, reflect and heal.

This would give added weight and relevance to the appeal for the tens of thousands of victims, their families and all the frontline staff who have done so much to fight the pandemic. It is only right that this should be remembered and celebrated in the meaningful manner that could be achieved by securing the future of Penhale for future generations.

Were the developer amenable to this proposal as well as a fair profit for not incurring the significant costs of development, they would gain the potentially massive kudos that would come from facilitating such a unique project on behalf of our nation. If a successful appeal gifted Penhale to the nation as a COVID-19 Pandemic Memorial in perpetuity.

Soundings have been taken locally, Perranzabuloe Parish Council appear to be favourable and within minutes of mooting the possibility of an appeal, £11,000 was pledged locally should it proceed.

I have always felt that deep sense of belonging, an unbreakable bond that has always reinforced a desire never to leave this land, blessed and truly nurtured by the legacy of St Piran.

The official Penhale story so far from Rob Norrington...

In 2019 we were informed that, as part of a periodic Governance Review process by Cornwall Council, a request had been received to re-locate the ancient Parish boundary at Penhale Point. The reason given was a hard-won planning consent, granted by Secretary of State Sajid Javid in 2018, for a 132 house development on the 40 acre site of a former army camp, now derelict and home to all manner of wildlife, to which there were many strong objections four years ago from such as The National Trust, English Heritage, The Wildlife Trust, Natural England and a number of local residents.

Thus our neighbouring Parish Council felt that a substantial part of the Section 106 money (a fee paid by developers to the local authority to support new infrastructure provision) should be given to them, as the only viable access to the new development would be through their locale and that the well-established natural boundary should be redrawn to place the new development within their aegis so that they could also benefit in perpetuity from the precept of Council Tax which would be paid by residents.

Perranzabuloe Parish Council, over the past year, have fought a strong, and largely successful campaign to defer any decision on the matter so that, for the time being at least, we will retain the 1,000 year old boundary exactly where it is. At the same time we learned that the original developer, Comparo Ltd of Cheltenham, has been attempting, for two years, to sell the development on. This invites the possibility that the largely unwanted holiday home estate, where most properties would be far too expensive to meet local housing needs, could be halted and the environment saved from further despoiling.

So the next phase of our campaign will be to try and buy back the site itself into public ownership, to set up Penhale Conservation Trust tomanage it and to institute a programme of conservation and preservation of this precious and historic coastal environment which is surrounded on the coastal side by a designated Site of Special Scientific Interest and on the landward side by a Special Conservation Area which is currently managed by Cornwall Wildlife Trust. We estimate that the purchase price will now be in the region of £1-1.5 million so that gives us an initial fundraising target. We are attempting to crowdfund the project at the ,memnt but are also looking for a large injection of cash from local businesses, wellwishers, the Heritage Lottery Fund and from the local authority.

The latest evidence we have regarding the derelict and vandalised state of the remaining buildings on the site shows that, since being abandoned by the MOD some ten years ago, Penhale Camp has provided a home to many native species of wildlife including a colony of bats who have now taken up residence in the old shower block. Naturally we would like these species, some of which are recent arrivals and some of which are on the 'endangered' list, to remain there and, given the funds and a viable conservation plan, we would be able to provide a protected environment for the benefit and education of future generations.

To this end we are currently speaking to The National Trust, English Heritage, Cornwall Wildlife Trust, the MOD and inviting the interest of anyone who feels they can support the conservation of this vitally important natural habitat. Last week we received a letter from The Secretary of State for Housing, Robert Jenrick (attached) which suggests that the Government is going to encourage a 'greener' attitude towards the future development of open spaces. Also we have arranged a meeting with our local MP, Cherilyn Mackrory in early December.

We have heard this week that the Langholm Moor Appeal, in Scotland, to buy back into public ownership a large grouse moor at a cost of £3.8 million, has hit its target which is tremendously encouraging for our campaign to re-wild Penhale at a similar cost over the next two years. Also the news today that the Secretary of State has backed local objections to a new housing estate at Mullion proposed by The Church of England.

There is now much cause for hope that we can succeed in returning Penhale Army Camp to the natural state it was in before the War Department took it over in 1939, protect the wildlife there and the unique, historic coastal habitat as well as honouring the 22 service men who died when a German plane dropped a bomb on the camp in 1940.

Please feel free to address any questions or suggestions to myself here, or to the 'Hands Off Perranzabuloe' Facebook page, or to Perranzabuloe Parish Clerk – and please keep watching this space. Thanks.

Rob Norrington 24/11/20;
algernonbear_34@outlook.com
07713 013846

Donate
Please make a donation to the Penhale Conservation Fund:
https://www.facebook.com/donate/757214138219056/212797070321607/

Or by post to:
The Parish Clerk, Perranzabuloe Parish Council, Chyanhale, Ponsmere Valley, Perranporth, TR6 0DB.

to the future... my son and grandchildren

"I am the past, living in the present, our children are the future,"
as the Rev. Julyan Drew R.I.P. said.
"It is better to build strong children than mend broken adults."

To try your very best against all odds without success is not failure!

Failure is to wallow in apathy and defeatism without having the courage
or conviction to even try at all to progress.

To dare to dream and to be brave is to live well and be true to yourself.

Hope is all we have...
''SO MOTE IT BE''